1996

The Politics of Health Legislation

An Economic Perspective

SECOND EDITION

00 99 98 97 96   5 4 3 2 1

Library of Congress Cataloging-in-Publication Data

Feldstein, Paul J.
    The politics of health legislation : an economic perspective / Paul J. Feldstein. — 2nd ed.
      p.   cm.
    Includes index.
    ISBN 1-56793-045-X
    1. Medical economics—United States.   2. Medical policy—United States. 3. Medical laws and legislation—United States.   I. Title.
    RA410.53.F46   1996
    338.4'33621'0973—dc20   96-11238
                                             CIP

The paper used in this publication meets the minimum requirements of American National Standard for Information Sciences—Permanence of Paper for Printed Library Materials, ANSI Z39.48-1984. ∞ ™

Health Administration Press
A division of the Foundation of the
   American College of Healthcare Executives
One North Franklin Street
Chicago, IL 60606
312/424-2800

The Politics of Health Legislation

An Economic Perspective

SECOND EDITION

Paul J. Feldstein

Health Administration Press
Chicago, Illinois 1996

To two special people,
Rita and Joseph Shore

PREFACE

MY INTEREST in health politics was first stimulated by economists who extended economic analysis into nontraditional areas, such as regulation and legislation. My 1979 book, *Health Associations and the Demand for Legislation,* focused on one aspect of the economic approach toward viewing health legislation, namely producer regulation. This book continues that analysis.

Producer regulation is only one activity of government. Here I also consider legislation directed toward controlling externalities, such as pollution and medical research, and toward making explicit redistributions among population groups, as occurred with Social Security and Medicare.

To be useful, an analytical framework for viewing legislative outcomes should be generalizable over a wide range of government activity. That is what I have attempted to do. My purpose, which may seem quite ambitious, has been to use the taxonomy of economics to explain legislative outcomes in the health field. An analytical framework should be explicit in its assumptions as to what motivates the various decision makers. Self-interest, among individuals, groups, and legislators, is assumed to be the underlying motive generating legislative change, thereby giving rise to the hypothesis referred to as the Self-Interest Paradigm.

Economics is exciting because it is a way of thinking. One can use economic analysis to explain various types of events, whether they be historical, current, or political. To the extent that the Self-Interest Paradigm illustrates an economic approach for explaining legislative outcomes and provides insight into previous health legislation, this book will have served its purpose. It is hoped that those interested in health policy find the discussions and analyses useful. To make this book suitable for a diverse audience, no prior knowledge of economics is assumed.

An author is always indebted to others for assistance, critiques, and comments. For the first edition, I particularly want to thank Jack Tobias,

Reference Librarian at the School of Public Health, University of Michigan, for his aid in locating various source materials. Jeremiah German, Stephen Crane, and Kathe Fox made detailed comments on the manuscript for which I am grateful. I was also fortunate to have received extensive and useful comments from an anonymous reviewer. Needless to say, not all of those who provided me with comments necessarily agreed with all the analyses presented here.

This second edition updates the material and references and also adds two new sections, a discussion of the changes to Medicare and Medicaid being proposed by the 1995 Republican Congress (Chapter 9) and a new chapter (Chapter 10) on healthcare reform, which discusses the failure of President Clinton's health reform proposal. These two redistributive proposals provide new material to test the validity of alternative legislative theories.

Paul J. Feldstein
Irvine, California

CONTENTS

1

INTRODUCTION

Which Theory of Legislation?
Types of Legislation Examined
  Producer Regulation
  Externalities
  Redistributive Legislation

I n 1966, the first year of Medicare and Medicaid, total personal expenditures on medical care in the United States were approximately $40 billion. Almost 30 years later, personal medical expenditures had risen more than twentyfold, to almost a trillion dollars.[1] The rise in medical expenditures has exceeded the rate of inflation over that same period and has risen faster than any other sector of the economy. In 1966, 5.2 percent of our gross national product (GNP) went to medical care; almost 30 years later more than 14 percent of GNP was being spent on medical care.

The rapid rise in medical expenditures and its increasing share of this country's resources represent a massive redistribution of wealth. The flow of money has gone from the working population, who have had to pay for these increased expenditures, to healthcare providers. The burden on the working population of this shift of wealth has been both direct and indirect. When employees and their families have to pay higher prices for medical services and a larger premium contribution each month for their health insurance their awareness of their role in financing medical care becomes more obvious. However, the purchase of health insurance, by employers (with before-tax dollars) makes many employees believe that such insurance is "free," when, in actuality, the employee ends up paying for it through lower wages. The working population also finances the federal and state governments' medical expenditures, which now represent about 44 percent of total medical expenditures, through higher taxes. These indirect methods of financing medical expenditures, through employer-paid health insurance and higher taxes, has, until recently, tended to make the financing burden less noticeable by the working population.

The rapid increase in medical expenditures was caused by several factors: the inflation that occurred in all sectors of the economy; the growth in the population of approximately 1 percent per year; the aging of the population; and, importantly, the medical innovations and improved treatment techniques that enable people to live longer, in less pain, and with fewer debilitating illnesses.

Despite this vast increase in medical expenditures, there are still many who are uninsured. Estimates are that 15 percent of the population, or 35 million people, are uninsured. Many others who are eligible for government programs serving the poor (Medicaid) receive inadequate access to medical care. And, there is concern that the huge increases in medical expenditures have not been well spent. Many believe that there has been inappropriate use of services and excessive inefficiency in the delivery of medical services. Physician incomes have been higher than necessary to attract new people to the health field; there has been unnecessary duplication of costly facilities and equipment; and there has been "too much use" of medical care, since the cost to patients has been greatly reduced by private insurance and government programs.

The federal government's role in healthcare increased dramatically in 1966. Federal expenditures under Medicare (healthcare for the elderly) and Medicaid (a federal-state matching program for payment of medical services to the poor) rose from $5.3 billion in 1966 to more than $290 billion in 1996. Initial expectations of the cost of these programs were greatly exceeded and a number of changes have been instituted to reduce expenditure growth. In the mid-1980s, hospital prices for serving Medicare patients were controlled as well as how fast they are permitted to increase each year. And yet, the Medicare Trust Fund is still estimated to go broke by 2002.

As states have seen their Medicaid expenditures rise from approximately $5 billion to about $60 billion a year (the federal government matches that amount), many have cut back on the eligibility definitions of those who are poor and receiving their medical benefits. And perhaps worst of all, after hundreds of billions of dollars have been spent on Medicare and Medicaid, it is widely acknowledged that Medicare does not meet the health needs of many elderly and that large segments of the poor do not have adequate access to needed medical care. Many elderly who depend on Medicare have to fall back on the state as Medicaid recipients.

Medicare and Medicaid are the two major healthcare redistributive programs. Neither of them have lived up to expectations. They have never been as efficient nor as equitable as they might be. The performance of these government programs, however, is the rule rather than the exception. Few if any federal (or, for that matter, state) programs are as efficient or as equitable as they might be.

It might be said that the extraordinary growth in medical expenditures could not have been anticipated; that the resultant inefficiencies in this sector and its poor economic performance are the result of rapid growth. If only the policymakers had known, payment systems would have been designed differently. If we were to do it all over again, a more "rational" system could be put into place.

These explanations are based on an assumption of ignorance on the part of well-meaning policymakers and legislators. The history of the health field since the late 1940s, however, should not be so easily dismissed or misinterpreted. Health legislation is a continuing process. Those who believe that future policies are likely to be more "rational" because well-meaning legislators and policymakers are now better informed are likely to be disappointed once again.

Health legislation and regulation are generally not based on ignorance. Instead, the type of legislation that is enacted (as well as not enacted) is the result of a very rational process. The resulting legislation and regulations are, for the most part, what was intended. If the legislation was "poorly designed," that is, the costs are greater than the presumed benefits or even greater than necessary for achieving its stated purpose, then why not assume that was the real intent of the legislation? This view does not mean to imply that all participants in the policy process have perfect information on the consequences of their actions, rather that the process is sufficiently rational to serve as the basis for understanding legislative outcomes.

Our purpose is to demonstrate that legislative and regulatory outcomes in healthcare are consistent with the hypothesis that individuals, groups, and legislators act to serve their own particular self-interest, *which in the case of legislators is to be reelected.* A basic assumption underlying this approach is that the legislation that was passed, and the design of that legislation, was as intended by the legislature.

An economic approach to politics is not new. Concerns about the use of government for selfish interest have existed as long as the idea of government itself. Moreover, they have been amply recorded: James Madison and Adam Smith wrote on the subject. More recent formalizations have been provided by such economists as Anthony Downs, James Buchanan, Gordon Tullock, Mancur Olson, George Stigler, Richard Posner, and Sam

Peltzman.[2] No new theoretical contributions are provided here. Instead, the economic approach for viewing legislative outcomes is applied to healthcare and used to provide an understanding of the type of health legislation this country has or has not had.

The approach used in this book to explain legislative outcomes—the "Self-Interest Paradigm"—assumes that individuals act according to self-interest, not necessarily in the public interest. Individuals, as legislators or voters, are assumed to act no differently when it comes to politics than they act in private economic markets; they pursue their self-interest. For example, legislators (and regulators) are assumed to act so as to maximize the political support they receive. Legislators require political support to be elected, which the late Sen. Everett Dirksen claimed is the first rule of politics; the second rule is to be reelected. Organized groups that are able to provide greater political support are expected to have greater political influence than groups or voters who are not organized. Organized groups seek to achieve through legislation what they cannot achieve through the marketplace. Such legislative benefits provide producers with greater incomes and organized, politically powerful, population groups with economic gains such as net subsidies or legislation mandating their social preferences.

The massive redistribution of wealth that has occurred in the medical care field has particularly benefited two groups: First the aged, who, as beneficiaries of the federal Medicare program, have received medical services whose value greatly exceeds what the aged have paid. The second group of beneficiaries are those employed in the medical sector, health-care suppliers, and health providers, such as hospitals and physicians, whose revenues have risen more than would otherwise have occurred. These two beneficiary groups have provided legislators with the necessary political support for receiving legislative benefits.

Which Theory of Legislation?

Alternative theories of legislative outcomes exist. At different ends of the spectrum are the "public interest" and the "economic" theories. The basic assumption underlying the public interest theory is that legislation is enacted because well-meaning legislators act according to what they believe is in the public interest. The outcome may not always be as satisfactory as desired because of ignorance or unexpected occurrences. The underlying motivations of the participants and legislators differ in each of these theories as do the theories' predictions and conclusions. While our emphasis is on applying the Self-Interest Paradigm, which is similar to economic theories, to the health sector, at times this approach is contrasted with the public interest theory. The underlying hypotheses and predictions of the Self-Interest Paradigm are clarified when its explanations and predictions are contrasted with an opposing approach.

The public interest theory assumes that there are two basic objectives of government, to *improve efficiency* and, second, to *redistribute income in a more equitable manner.*

The reasons for market inefficiency, justifying government intervention according to the public interest theory, are twofold: *monopolization of a market,* such as a utility company being the sole supplier of electricity services for a region, and the *existence of externalities,* which may occur when, as a by-product of producing its product, a firm produces air or water pollution that harms members of the community. In both of these instances, the government can improve market efficiency if the costs (marginal) of producing the service are more closely aligned to the benefits (marginal) received from that service. In the case of the monopoly utility, the price of electricity may be regulated to bring it closer to the cost of producing electricity. When water or air pollution occurs, the government should assess the cost of such pollution and add it (via a tax) to the costs of the product sold by the firm, so that the purchasers of the product bear the full costs of the goods they buy.

The second objective of government, redistribution, is based on the values of society, namely, how equitable should be the distribution of resources? Should society decide that medical services should be more equitably distributed, then those with lower incomes would be expected to receive net benefits (their benefits exceed their costs or taxes) and those with higher incomes should incur net costs (their taxes exceed their benefits) from the legislation. Crucial to the evaluation of redistributive legislation is which population groups are eligible for the benefits and the types of taxes imposed to finance those benefits. When eligibility is by income and income taxes are used to finance the program's benefits, it is likely that redistribution occurs from high-income to low-income groups.

The government has three policy instruments it can use to achieve its two objectives: expenditures on a program, tax policy, and the use of regulations.[3] Further, each of these policy instruments can be directed to the demand (purchaser) or supply (provider) side of the market. For example, the government has subsidized (expenditure policy) medical schools to increase the number of physicians (supply side) and has also subsidized the purchase of medical services by the aged (demand side). Tax policy has benefited employees by excluding employer-paid health insurance from taxable income (demand side) and enabled not-for-profit hospitals to pay lower interest costs by issuing tax-exempt bonds (supply side). State government regulations specify which medical services and practitioners must be included in health insurance sold in that state (demand side) and some states require government approval for building a hospital facility (supply side).

In contrast to the public interest theory, there is only one government objective to be achieved under the Self-Interest Paradigm, namely redistribution. However, redistribution is not meant to result in a more equitable redistribution of medical services. Instead, the power of the government is used to redistribute *wealth* to those able to offer political support, while financing that redistribution by imposing costs on those unable to offer political support. Those who are able to offer political support are typically middle-income and high-income groups, not those with low incomes. The same three policy instruments are used to achieve the wealth redistribution objective.

Thus these two theories have opposite predictions. In one case the policy instruments of government are meant to improve market efficiency and to achieve a more equitable distribution of medical services. According to the "economic" theory, the only objective is to use the policy instruments of government to increase one's wealth. To test which theory is more accurate, it is necessary to examine the objective to be achieved when one of the different policy instruments is used by government. Is it the efficiency and redistribution objective of the public interest theory or is it the redistribution of wealth of the Self-Interest Paradigm? If government policies result in greater market inefficiencies and the middle-income and high-income groups receive net benefits, while those with low incomes bear net costs, then the Self-Interest Paradigm is a more accurate description of the political process.

To be useful, a theory should be able to predict better than alternative theories. A theory does not have to be 100 percent correct to provide a useful framework for understanding health legislation. A theory that explains 70 percent of legislative outcomes in healthcare is preferable to one that can explain only 40 percent. Until a more accurate theory comes along, one that predicts better than random guesses is more useful than no theory at all. Although not 100 percent correct, such a theory still provides useful insights.

Another criterion to be used for determining which is a more useful theory is a theory's generalizability. Constructing a separate theory for each legislative outcome is not as useful as one theory that applies to a wide range of legislation. Unique legislative theories are not theories of legislation. Requiring a separate theory for each piece of legislation is admitting that there are no generalizable principles. If there are generalizable principles, a theory should be applicable for different types of legislation; such a theory and its assumptions should provide greater understanding of the legislative process.

Economists have often been criticized because of their simplified assumptions and their disregard for the richness of detail and the complex interactions of personalities, aspects that others believe are necessary for understanding legislation. Many policy analysts emphasize the idiosyncrasies of individual legislators in determining the outcome of legislation. The case study approach often emphasizes the participants involved. The result is usually a chronological review of what occurred and why as the legislation moved through the various sub-committees and committees, and how it was amended as it made its way to final passage or defeat.

While case studies can make a valuable contribution to understanding a particular piece of legislation, they do not enable us to generalize across different types of legislation. Case studies may suggest some hypotheses, which can later be tested, but, by their emphasis on detail, generalizable principles are often neglected or downgraded. Further, without some generalizable principles of legislative outcomes to guide the investigator, case studies may neglect appropriate data. When the detail surrounding each piece of legislation achieves overriding importance, then it becomes difficult to develop generalizable principles. Unless one knows what to look for, the underlying motivations of the participants and the organizations they represent might never be questioned.

To construct a generalizable theory, it becomes necessary to simplify the determinants of legislation. Information regarding legislators' personalities and institutional settings may at times have great importance. However, if generalizable principles are to be developed it becomes necessary to cut through much of the detail.

Once generalizable hypotheses have been developed, incorporating institutional detail into the theory may improve its explanatory power. However, the main test of a theory is its ability to predict and to be able to do so, generalizable principles are necessary. Detail may serve to further illuminate what happened. But without a theory, detail merely provides interesting background information.

In constructing a theory of legislative outcome, certain simplifying assumptions regarding human behavior are necessary. For example, legislators are assumed to act *"as if"* they were solely interested in maximizing their chances for reelection. Knowledgeable students of the legislative process could immediately provide examples of legislators who were more interested in the public interest than in their own prospects for reelection. There are (and undoubtedly have been) legislators who "would rather be right than President." And some legislators are ignorant of the issues. However, if we are interested in predicting the legislature's response to interest group pressures, it is necessary to have some assumptions regarding legislators' objectives.

If one were to ask legislators what it is that they desire, we could expect impassioned responses dealing with the public interest, this great country of ours, and a place in history. A few legislators might eventually mention "fair trade" for the textile factory in their district or tax breaks for a large employer. Testing our assumption of legislator motivation according to what legislators say, or making our assumption sufficiently complex to include multiple motivations is not useful. For predictive purposes, how would multiple, opposing motivations be resolved? Instead, the simple assumption that legislators act *"as if"* they seek to maximize their reelection chances enables us to predict legislators' responses to differing levels of political support.

The usefulness of these assumptions is not how realistic they are but how well the theory, upon which it is based, predicts. "The relevant question to ask about the 'assumptions' of a theory is not whether they are descriptively 'realistic,' for they never are, but whether they are sufficiently good approximations for the purpose at hand. And this question can be answered only by seeing whether it yields sufficiently accurate predictions."[4]

The public interest theory offers a set of assumptions regarding the motivations of legislative participants and a set of testable predictions. The Self-Interest Paradigm offers contrasting assumptions and legislative predictions. The purpose of this book, however, is to describe how individuals and groups—acting according to their self-interests, with legislators seeking to maximize their political support—explain legislative outcomes in the health field. While the process of legislation is complex and the participants are many, the criterion by which this approach should be judged is whether it predicts better than an alternative theory. The richness of detail from any individual legislative outcome could be used to supplement the generalizable principles proposed.

Types of Legislation Examined

The roles of the federal and state governments in health legislation have changed dramatically. Initially, states were more involved in healthcare than was the federal government. The states were responsible for public health through, for example, the control of communicable diseases and environmental sanitation. Regulation of the health professions through licensing and state practice acts was, and continues to be, a state function. The states also provided for the medically indigent and the mentally ill, generally through institutionalization programs.

Except for the care of disabled and ill seamen and Native Americans on reservations, the federal health role was relatively small until the early 1900s, when the Pure Food and Drug Act was enacted. Federal legislation was again limited throughout the 1920s and 1930s until a tragedy occurred in the manufacture and sale of drugs, at which time further drug legislation was passed. It was not until after World War II that federal health legislation became more prominent.

Federal construction subsidies for hospitals were enacted in the late 1940s (Hill-Burton Act). Federal support for medical research grew rapidly during the 1950s and early 1960s. Health manpower legislation, which consisted of subsidies for educational institutions and their students, was enacted in 1964. Federal assistance for the medically indigent (Kerr-Mills) was legislated in the early 1960s. Two large financing programs, Medicare (for the aged) and Medicaid (for the medically indigent), were passed in 1965. With federal financing of Medicare and federal matching funds to the states for Medicaid, federal expenditures began to exceed state spending in financing medical services.

The quantity of federal health legislation continued to increase throughout the 1970s and 1980s. The 1960s were characterized by legislation that required increased federal expenditures. However, as federal expenditures under Medicare and Medicaid began to exceed budgetary projections, the 1970s and 1980s were characterized by regulatory measures in an attempt to control the rapidly increasing costs of these governmental programs. Examples of such legislation were: the continuation on the medical sector, until April 1974, of wage and price controls (the Economic Stabilization Program was put in place in 1971 to control economy-wide prices and wages; it was removed in 1972); Medicare utilization review; health planning controls on hospitals' capital investment; a Medicare fee index for physicians; changes in Medicare cost reimbursement for hospitals; and a new health program that did not require a great deal of money, the Health Maintenance Organization (HMO) Act.

In the mid-1980s a new Medicare hospital payment system was initiated in which hospitals were paid according to fixed prices (diagnosis-related groups, or DRGs) rather than receiving cost-based reimbursement. Finally, in 1989 a new Medicare physician payment system, which relied on a national fee schedule and limits on total Medicare physician payments, was enacted. By controlling what the federal government spent on hospitals and physicians for Medicare patients, the federal government attempted to limit the annual increase in Medicare expenditures.

At the same time these attempts were being made to reduce the rise in federal expenditures, the tax-exempt status of employer-paid health insurance premiums resulted in large annual losses in federal, state, and Social Security tax revenues. It is estimated that these lost tax revenues were in excess of $80 billion in 1994.[5] And the ability of not-for-profit hospitals to finance their capital expenditures through tax-exempt bonds resulted in further lost federal and state taxes.

State Medicaid expenditures also expanded rapidly during this period. Unable to use deficit financing and reluctant to raise taxes or reduce state expenditures on politically popular programs, the states reduced Medicaid eligibility and limited payments to hospitals and physicians for serving Medicaid patients. As a result, provider participation in Medicaid programs declined. Several states, such as Maryland, New Jersey, and New York, instituted hospital rate review programs for all purchasers in an attempt to control rising hospital expenditures. At the same time states were reducing their commitment to the Medicaid population, they increased the subsidies provided to public medical schools.

Health policy in this country has been criticized for not being "rational." There is no consistent overall strategy for increasing the health of the population. Specific objectives and programs for achieving those objectives have not been formulated nor adopted by Congress or the president. There is limited, if any, coordination of health programs within the government. And health policies have not only been contradictory, they have often been designed to foster inefficiency and result in greater inequity.

A theory of legislation, as previously stated, should be applicable to all types of legislation, otherwise it is incomplete and its generalizability limited. To reduce the large number and different varieties of legislation so that their outcomes can be meaningfully analyzed requires classification. Three legislative typologies have been selected.[6] The basis for these three typologies is the subject addressed by the legislation.

The analytical approach used in this book, namely, the Self-Interest Paradigm, is applied to three types of legislation: *producer regulation*, legislation dealing with *externalities*, and *redistributive legislation*. The most common legislation is regulation that benefits producers.

Producer Regulation

According to the public interest theory, industries are regulated to prevent monopoly abuses. This theory would predict that those industries most likely to be regulated would be those subject to large economies of scale; a firm would have to be quite large to be efficient, thereby having few, if any, competitors. The public interest theory would also predict that regulation would lead to lower prices and profits than in unregulated markets.

The original dissatisfaction with the public interest theory arose over these predictions. If prices and profits were expected to be lower in regulated markets, then why were firms always trying to enter regulated markets? The regulatory agency, such as the Civil Aeronautics Board (CAB) or the Interstate Commerce Commission (ICC), maintained entry barriers. Further, why was there such extensive regulation of typically competitive industries (taxicabs, trucking, and TV repairmen) rather than monopolistic industries? Lastly, why were prices always *higher* in regulated industries? For example, airline prices for intrastate air travel (within California or within Texas), which was not subject to CAB regulation, were lower, for equivalent distances, than in interstate markets.

These dissatisfactions with the public interest theory led to the development of the economic theory of regulation.[7] According to the economic theory, regulation was either proposed by the industry itself or the regulatory agency was "captured" by those meant to be regulated. The result was that the regulation benefited those who were regulated. It was for this reason that prices in regulated industries were higher than in nonregulated (similar) industries; that competitive industries sought regulation, since it was the only way they could earn more than competitive profits; and that entry barriers were necessary because firms always tried to enter the higher-priced regulated markets.

Under the economic theory of regulation, legislation (or regulation) is proposed by trade associations so as to receive legislative benefits for their members. For example, the automobile industry (and the United Auto Workers [UAW]) lobbied for domestic content legislation. Such legislation, had it been passed, would have raised the cost of imported cars, thereby increasing the demand for domestic cars. Previously, "voluntary" quotas on Japanese cars reduced their availability in this country, with the result that prices and production of U.S. cars increased.

A current example of producer benefits in the health field can be found in the efforts of the auto companies and the UAW to have the federal government (as part of the Clinton administration's proposed health plan) pay 80 percent of the medical costs of early retirees. Currently, the medical costs of early retirees are paid by the companies and represent an enormous unfunded liability for those companies. (General Motors' unfunded liability for retiree medical costs is estimated to be $19 billion.)[8] If these costs were shifted to the federal government, the company's liability would be reduced and their union employees could receive part of these savings in the form of higher wages.

According to the public interest theory, the reasons most often given for producer legislation in medical care are concerns for quality, efficiency, and cost containment; that is, to prevent medical prices from rising so rapidly. The validity of these reasons must be examined alongside the effects of policies that purport to achieve these goals.

The demands by health associations for producer regulation are discussed in Chapter 4. The oft-stated rationales for such legislation (quality, efficiency, and cost containment) are compared to the effects producer regulation would have in order to determine their actual versus their stated intent. Chapter 4 examines the different types of health legislation demanded by health associations representing providers, such as physicians, dentists, nurses, hospitals, and health insurance companies.

Since the late 1970s and early 1980s, numerous industries have been deregulated—airlines, railroads, trucking companies, savings and loan associations (S&Ls), stock brokerage firms, telephone service providers, and the medical industry. Presumably the major losers from deregulation have been the regulated industries and their unions who had previously received producer-type regulation. Deregulation has led to a revival of the public interest theory. How else could deregulation of protected industries be analyzed? Therefore an opposing theory of legislation—like the Self-Interest Paradigm—should not only be able to explain the regulation of an industry but also why it is deregulated. Chapter 5 discusses the reasons for deregulation of nonhealth-related industries. The deregulation of the medical care industry is discussed in Chapter 6.

Externalities

The second type of legislation relates to market failure, or more specifically, to externalities.[9] There are several situations when markets may not perform efficiently and government intervention may be justified. Even if a market is competitive, the firms in that market may, in the process of producing their product, impose costs on persons outside that market. Air and water pollution are two such examples. Legislation directed at water and air pollution has been passed by Congress.

A public interest theory of legislation would predict that to protect society, Congress would anticipate or respond to the public's demand for protection and achieve this objective in an efficient manner. Since medical research provides benefits to all, the public interest theory would suggest that Congress provide an appropriate level of funding for medical research. Indeed during the 1950s and 1960s, medical research programs were generously funded by Congress.

It is a task of the self-interest approach, which includes the maximization of political support by legislators, to reconcile the existence of government programs whose ostensible goal is to intervene in situations where externalities exist. This issue is addressed in Chapter 7.

Redistributive Legislation

The purpose of the third type of legislation is redistribution. While all legislation is redistributive in that costs are imposed on some groups and net benefits are received by others, redistributive legislation is meant to be explicit in its effects. Redistributive programs are provided to consumer or population groups, as contrasted to producer legislation, which provides benefits to a specific industry. Redistributive legislation confers net benefits on some population groups while financing these benefits by imposing net costs on other population groups. Those burdened with net costs pay taxes that exceed the program benefits they receive.

Redistributive legislation is also politically "visible." That is, the public, particularly the population groups benefiting from the program, must be made aware of the net benefits they are to receive. The political support for redistributive programs is expected to come from the votes of the affected population groups. Examples of redistributive programs are Social Security and, in the health field, Medicare, Medicaid, and the Clinton administration's proposal for healthcare reform. Chapter 8 develops the reasons for redistributive legislation, illustrated by numerous examples. Chapter 9 applies these principles to the largest redistributive program in medical care—Medicare. And Chapter 10 analyzes the Clinton administration's proposal for healthcare reform, together with the positions taken by various lobby groups.

The stated reason for redistributive legislation is to redistribute income, either in cash or in kind (in the form of services), to those in financial need or to those unable to purchase a service society deems important. The criteria most often used to establish eligibility for these programs are income levels (e.g., Aid to Families with Dependent Children [AFDC] and Medicaid) and age levels (e.g., Social Security and Medicare), or they are universal programs, such as state support of public colleges. Under universal programs, everyone is eligible to benefit.

The presumed basis for redistributive programs, at least under the public interest theory of legislation, is society's charitable desire to help its less fortunate members. And, unless everyone was compelled to contribute (through government taxes) to charity, some higher-income individuals could receive a "free ride"—they benefit by knowing that the less fortunate are cared for through the private donations of others. Charity can therefore be considered a "collective" good. Government taxation to provide for charity would, according to this argument, eliminate the "free rider" problem. A self-interest theory of legislation has to explain why redistributive legislation is enacted when the theory's basic assumption is that individuals and groups are expected to act only according to their self-interest. Is the reason for redistributive legislation similar to producer legislation, namely, to provide politically powerful population groups with an economic benefit?

There are thus three traditional roles for government: to eliminate or control monopoly behavior, to intervene in situations of externalities, and to help those who are less fortunate. Extensive legislation exists on each of these types at the federal, state, and local levels of government. One could readily conceive of a role for government in each area according to the public interest theory. In the remainder of this book, however, each type of legislation, with applications to the field of medical care, will be examined from the perspective of the self-interest explanation of legislative outcome.

Study Questions for Chapter 1

1. What motivations are assumed to underlie the "public interest" and the "economic" theory of legislation (Self-Interest Paradigm)?
2. Must a theory be accurate 100 percent or even 80 percent of the time to be judged useful for understanding legislative outcomes?
3. How do the three types of legislation described in this chapter differ from one another?
4. What are the "public interest" explanations for each of these three types of legislation?
5. What are some healthcare examples of each of these three types of legislation?

Notes

1. Prospective Payment Commission Report to the Congress. 1995. *Medicare and the American Health Care System* (Washington, D.C.), Table 1–1, 16.
2. Anthony Downs. 1967. *An Economic Theory of Democracy*. New York: Harper & Row; James Buchanan and Gordon Tullock. *The Calculus of Consent*. Ann Arbor: University of Michigan Press; Mancur Olson, Jr. 1966. *The Logic of Collective Action*. Cambridge: Harvard University Press; George J. Stigler. 1971. "The Economic Theory of Regulation," *The Bell Journal of Economics* (Spring) 3–21. Richard A. Posner. 1974; "Theories of Economic Regulation," *The Bell Journal of Economics and Management Science* (2) 335–58; Sam Peltzman. 1976. "Toward a More General Theory of Regulation," *The Journal of Law and Economics* 19, 211–40.
3. In his review article, Barr uses a different classification of government interventions, regulation, which can apply to quality, quantity, or price of a product or service; a price subsidy, which can be direct or through the tax system; public production, such as when the government is the supplier of the service; and income transfers, which can be tied to specific products, such as food stamps or general, as with Social Security. Nicholas Barr. 1992. "Economic Theory and the Welfare State: A Survey and Interpretation," *Journal of Economic Literature* 30 (June) 741–803.

4. Milton Friedman. 1953. *Essays in Positive Economics*. Chicago: The University of Chicago Press. 15. Friedman provides the following illustrative example. "Consider the problem of predicting the shots made by an expert billiard player. It seems not at all unreasonable that excellent predictions would be yielded by the hypothesis that the billiard player made his shots 'as if' he knew the complicated mathematical formulas that would give the optimum directions of travel, could estimate accurately by eye the angles, etc., describing the location of the balls, could make lightning calculations from the formulas, and could then make the balls travel in the direction indicated by the formulas. Our confidence in this hypothesis is not based on the belief that billiard players, even expert ones, can or do go through the process described; it derives rather from the belief that, unless in some way or other they were capable of reaching essentially the same result, they would not in fact be "expert" billiard players." (p. 21)

5. Congressional Budget Office. 1994. *The Tax Treatment of Employment-Based Health Insurance*. Washington, D.C. 48.

6. For examples of legislative typologies used by political scientists, see Theodore Lowi. 1964. "American Business, Public Policy, Case Studies and Political Theory," *World Politics* 16, and Michael Hayes. 1978. "The Semi-Sovereign Pressure Groups: A Critique of Current Theory and an Alternative Typology," *Journal of Politics* 40.

7. Stigler, "The Economic Theory of Regulation."

8. David A. Vise. 1993. "GM Says Pension Shortfall Has Increased to $19 Billion," *The Washington Post*, May 14, D2.

9. Externalities also occur when individuals contribute to charity, as will be discussed with respect to redistributive programs. Since redistributive legislation is considered separately, this type of externality is excluded from this section. National defense is another example of externalities. Everyone benefits if the country is able to defend itself. Even if citizens do not contribute to the national defense, they cannot be excluded from its benefits; they receive the same protection as those that do contribute. An important political issue, however, is the appropriate size and composition of defense expenditures. National defense is not discussed in this section, although the principles can be applied to this subject as well.

AN ECONOMIC VERSION OF THE INTEREST GROUP THEORY OF LEGISLATION

L egislation redistributes wealth. Groups who are successful in the legislative arena will receive an increase in their wealth. This redistribution must be financed by imposing a tax, either direct or indirect, on another portion of the population. This chapter presents an economic version of the interest group theory of legislation. The demanders of legislative benefits, namely, certain population groups and organized interest groups, are first discussed. An important issue discussed in the following chapter is why some groups are more successful than others in being able to achieve their demands.

Second, this chapter examines the suppliers of legislative benefits, generally considered to be the legislature, the executive branch, regulatory agencies, and the judiciary. Each of these entities helps to establish the rules of the game under which business firms compete and population groups receive benefits. The main supplier of legislation is the legislature; their output is legislation. The executive branch proposes legislation, but it is up to the legislature to enact it. The legislature can also override executive vetoes. The legislature appropriates funds for regulatory agencies and passes new legislation if it disagrees with judicial rulings. It is important to understand the motivation and the response of these suppliers of legislation to the demanders of legislation.

The price of legislation is political support. Political support—votes, campaign contributions, or volunteer time—is the equilibrating mechanism between the demanders and suppliers of legislative benefits. The amount of political support determines the allocation of benefits among the various demanders.

The Demanders of Legislative Benefits

Voting Behavior

One might initially expect that for legislation to be enacted it would have to be favored by a majority of the population or by a majority of their elected legislators. This is not correct. There are a number of reasons why groups representing a minority of voters or legislators are able to secure favorable legislation.

Political markets, where benefits and costs to particular groups are distributed by government, differ significantly from economic markets. In economic markets, consumers express their desires by spending their own money on the goods and services they prefer. They bear the costs of their choices. In political markets, the linkage between the voter and legislation is not obvious; neither is the link between who receives the program's benefits and who bears its costs. As a result of these imperfections, it is possible for organized minorities to gain benefits while imposing the costs on the majority.

The following discussion examines the imperfections that occur in political markets.

First, not all eligible voters vote. There is a cost to voting; the voter must take the time to become informed on the issues and take the time to actually vote. It clearly does not pay for voters to invest time on issues that may have a small impact on their well-being. It also doesn't pay to invest time when their efforts will have little impact, if any, on the outcome.[1] The benefits of voting to the voter is the belief in the importance of the election's outcome and the likelihood that their vote will make a difference in that outcome. On a cost-benefit basis, therefore, many people do not believe it pays to vote.[2]

Second, because it is costly to become fully informed on all issues and candidates, voters look for shortcuts to collecting such information. One method of gathering information is to pay more attention to the personalities of the candidates. Another is to distinguish between candidates by relying on ideologies and political parties, which may be similar to brand names. Alternatively, the voter can rely on political advertising used by a party, such as slogans that summarize an issue. Too heavy a reliance on these shortcuts, however, may produce voters who are not well-informed.[3]

The role of political parties in this regard is of interest. Political parties can be viewed as competing firms, each selling a package of products, a set of government policies, for votes. Firms respond to consumer demands to make a profit. Parties respond so that legislators in their party can be reelected. Party identification is a means of providing, at a low cost, information about a candidate to a voter. However, the two-party system in this country may not offer some voters a sufficient diversity of choices. Each political party strives to capture a majority of the voting population by designing their package of policies to appeal to voters in the middle of the issue spectrum. As each party reaches toward the middle, voters further from the middle believe they have too little choice.

Political parties in the United States do not have as much control over their members as do parties in other countries. Presumably, if a legislator deviates from the party position on important issues, this would affect the party-information role to voters. The party would be expected to protect its "brand name" by making it costly for legislators to deviate. In the United States, however, the brand name of a party connotes different information according to region. More importantly, a legislator is generally not beholden to the party for his or her election. By raising campaign contributions from nonparty sources and by providing services to their constituents, legislators are able to establish independence from party policies.

Legislators may wish to establish their independence from their party so as not to lose any constituent votes on controversial party issues. Instead, the legislator will attempt to achieve the loyalty of his or her constituents on issues that are noncontroversial. One such approach is to engage in vote trading that will benefit the district's constituents, e.g., "pork barrel legislation." Another approach is to offer services to constituents.[4] As the size of government has expanded, together with a myriad of government agencies, constituents often need assistance in resolving problems they have with one or more agencies, e.g., eligibility for Veteran's Administration benefits. Thus we find Congress votes for increases in its staff and resources, not to be better able to handle complex national and foreign policies, but to be better able to provide services to their constituents. Legislators are able to earn the gratitude, and votes, of their constituents by this assistance. This activity loosens legislators' needs for strong party ties. As evidence of this, voters do not rely as much on party identification in electing their representatives as they once did.

Another imperfection in the political market is that some legislators face the voters only after a considerable period of time (up to six years in the case of senators); this makes it difficult for voters to register their immediate displeasure on a particular issue. At election time, in addition to remembering the various issues over the past several years, the voter is faced with making a choice between different sets of issue packages when choosing between senators.

One final distinction between economic and political markets is that legislators do not take into account all the costs of their decisions. Individual legislators are rarely held accountable for the costs of a program or for costs that exceed expectations. Further, the time horizon for members of the House of Representatives is particularly short—it is the next election. These short election periods mean that members of Congress place greater weight on the immediate benefits of a program and much lower weight on the long-term costs of that program. Similarly, with regard to the method of financing, legislators prefer borrowing (increasing the deficit) to taxing, a preference that pushes the cost into the future.

These imperfections in the political market suggest that voters are likely to be unorganized and uninformed on legislative issues. As a result, they are unable to make their voices heard, and unable to provide sufficient support in terms of votes or dollars to have an impact on specific legislation that concerns them. For a group to be effective in the legislative process it is necessary for them to overcome these obstacles.

Since the cost of political participation by individuals is high, compared to expected benefits, their voting participation is likely to be low. Further, since most legislative issues are noncontroversial and not very visible to the public, individuals have a low demand for legislation. Instead, legislation is demanded by those who are organized, act in their own interest, and are willing to provide political support to receive legislative benefits.

Organized Interest Groups

In competitive markets, there are no persistent or long-term excess profits. Firms make a normal rate of return, sufficient to allow them to stay in business. However, all firms would like to make higher profits. If the market in which a firm competes expands and the firm finds itself making excess profits, additional firms will be attracted to that industry by the higher than normal profits. As entry by new firms occurs and production expands, the excess profits once enjoyed by the firm decline until they are back to normal. The only way firms in a competitive industry can earn excess, or above normal, profits is to prevent other firms from entering their industry. Since there is no legal way to do this, the current firms in that industry are likely to try and change the legal requirements governing that industry.[5]

Similarly, a particular population group organized for some common purpose might be the demanders of legislation. The motivation is the same. This population group might be categorized by age, sex, income, or race. If such a group can receive particular legislative benefits, e.g., a subsidy or a tax advantage, then that group will be better off than it would have been otherwise.[6]

For a group to be successful in the legislative arena, it is necessary that their costs of organizing, of representing their interests, and of providing political support be less than the value of their expected legislative benefits. Groups that most often meet these criteria are organizations of producers. Producers are said to have a "concentrated" interest in regulation. Any legislation affecting their industry can have a major impact on each firm's profits. The unions in those industries also have a concentrated interest through the regulation's effect on the number of employees and their wages. Often the interests of the employees and the firms in an industry coincide, as in the case of legislation affecting import quotas or the regulation of trucking.

Groups with a concentrated interest have an incentive to organize and represent their interests before the legislature. The revenue effects of protective legislation are potentially so large as to make it worth their while to organize, raise funds to hire lobbyists, become informed on regulations affecting their interests, and actively promote their interests.[7] The members of such groups are also likely to be more informed as to the positions taken by their legislators (or those to whom they provide political support) at election time. It is for these reasons that economist Anthony Downs concluded, "Democratic governments tend to favor producers more than consumers in their actions."[8]

The gains that producer groups receive from legislation impose costs on a broad population base. Thus the impact of legislation favoring any producer group on an individual is relatively small. And individuals are, for the most part, unaware of the impact. For example, legislation providing an additional $250 million in benefits to firms (and employees) in an industry, for example, by restricting lower cost imports thereby leading to price increases of domestic equivalents, may mean an average cost of $1 per person. Consumers purchase many goods and services. If the price of one service is increased because of restrictive legislation, the effect on the consumer's income is relatively small—too small for consumers to organize themselves, to be informed on all such legislation, and to represent their interests before the legislature. The cost of being involved greatly exceeds the savings from preventing the legislation. It clearly does not pay for consumers to incur the costs to forestall such a small burden. Consumers are therefore said to have a "diffuse" interest in the enactment of restrictive legislation; the increased prices they have to pay have a small effect on their overall budget.

Industries that seek regulation are typically unable to monopolize their industry. When there are few firms in an industry, it is easier (less costly) for these firms to collude on prices and marketing arrangements and to detect which firms are cheating on the agreement. When there are a large number of firms in an industry, such as the number of physicians, it is difficult (costly) to reach an agreement among all producers. It is similarly difficult to detect cheaters. For industries with a large number of producers, legislation is a less costly method of monopolizing the industry than attempting to do so without the use of government.[9]

Those who participate in the legislative process and in regulatory hearings do so based on a rational calculation of the costs and benefits to themselves. It does not pay for consumers to participate. Thus the process is dominated by those who have a lot to gain (or to lose). Those with a concentrated interest find it both worthwhile and necessary to participate. Those with diffuse interests—consumers—are unlikely to participate.

This does not mean to imply that concentrated interests always get the legislation they desire. It does suggest that concentrated interests always have an incentive to represent their interests and provide political support to legislators when the gains are significant compared to their costs. Over time, if the regulatory costs imposed turn out to be particularly high to some groups or if there is a change in technology causing a change in the industry's cost for producing the service, other groups may develop that also have a concentrated interest in that industry's regulations.[10] *When the costs to a group change from diffuse to concentrated, then the group will find it in its interest, in terms of its benefits and costs, to represent those interests and to provide political support.* When there are opposing groups, each with a concentrated interest, then the cost to a group of achieving its objective is increased.

The Suppliers of Legislative Benefits

The Legislature

People, in general, are interested in the welfare of others, they are concerned about what is good for the country, and they are also concerned for themselves. For the most part, given the time that they spend on their jobs they are predominantly concerned with their own affairs; they are attempting to further their own careers or self-interests. The motivations of those employed in the public sector are the same as those employed in the private sector. While they are concerned with what is good for the country, they also act in their own self-interest. While acting according to their own self-interest they may also be acting in the public interest. If they are, however, it is incidental. For example, businesses introducing a higher quality product or firms introducing technology that reduces costs do so because they expect to profit from these actions (through increased market share), not because the actions will benefit the public. The same is true for legislators and bureaucrats. Their actions are undertaken to benefit themselves; only as a by-product may their actions also benefit the public.

Acting according to one's own self-interest is the basic assumption underlying an economic approach explaining legislative outcomes. One should expect this to be the case regardless of whether the individuals are in the public or private sectors. This does not mean that every individual always acts in this way, but it is a useful assumption for predicting outcomes in both economic and political markets.

As mentioned earlier, it is assumed that legislators are primarily interested in maximizing their chances for reelection. Regardless of what a legislator's motivations may be, unless he or she is reelected they would not be able to achieve them. As the late Illinois Sen. Everett Dirksen is reputed to have said, "The first law of politics is to get elected. The second is to be reelected." And to be reelected requires political support.[11]

In deciding which legislation to support and which to oppose, legislators base their decisions on which legislative positions provide the greatest amount of political support.[12] Like other rational participants in the political process, legislators also make implicit benefit-cost calculations. The benefits to legislators from providing legislation to an organized group is the political support received from that group; the cost to the legislators of providing those legislative benefits is not the dollar cost of the legislation, since they do not bear it, but instead it is the loss in potential political support from their actions. As long as legislators receive net positive benefits from providing legislation, they are expected to do so.

The earlier discussion of interest groups described why the demand for legislation is often made by organized groups representing minority interests. The method by which Congress (and other, i.e., state, legislatures) is structured also makes it possible for minority interests to prevail in the legislative arena while imposing the financing burden on the majority.

Since the legislature as a whole cannot deal with all the issues that come before it, it delegates part of the legislative functions to committees. To improve the efficiency of the legislative process, committees were established with jurisdiction over different policy areas. The committee structure enables the legislature to divide up work, develop expertise in complex areas, and provide for a more efficient size for group discussion. However, this organizational efficiency is not without cost. The legislature provides each of the relevant committees with near monopoly power over their area of jurisdiction. Approval by the relevant subcommittee and consequently the parent committee is necessary for legislation to be initiated and funds appropriated.

The committee system also provides the link between the interest groups seeking benefits and the provision of benefits by the legislature. Membership on committees is generally based on self-selection. Legislators with strong special interest constituencies have an equally strong incentive to be a member of those committees that deal with that special interest legislation. For example, legislators whose constituents are farmers seek membership on the agricultural committees and legislators from urban areas select committees whose jurisdiction deals with urban affairs. Interest groups desiring legislative benefits seek out legislators on the relevant committees and subcommittees dealing with their problems. In this manner, legislators are able to provide legislative benefits in return for political support.

An important method by which minority interests are successful in receiving legislative benefits is through the process of vote trading.[13] Vote trading occurs when legislators offer to exchange their vote on an issue of lesser importance (to their constituents) in order to receive votes from legislators on issues of greater importance (to their constituents). For example, assume that there are only three legislators. Only legislator A favors a subsidy to construct a hospital in Illinois. And only legislator B favors a subsidy for constructing a hospital in Pennsylvania. By agreeing to vote for each other's subsidy, both legislators A and B receive their subsidies, each of which is opposed by a majority of the legislators. If it were not for vote trading, it would be difficult for legislators with narrow constituent interests to get sufficient votes from other legislators to achieve a majority vote for their special interests.

As the workload of the legislature increases, legislators find it necessary to delegate some of their rule-making authority. The mechanism by which this is done is to create administrative agencies. These regulatory agencies are also able to provide political benefits. Each regulatory agency reports to a particular legislative subcommittee. The interest groups affected by the regulatory agency are the same groups that provide political support to the legislators having oversight responsibility for the regulatory agency. The regulatory agency therefore has to act in a manner consistent with the legislator's desires, otherwise the legislator would not receive political support from the groups affected by the agency's decisions. It is for this reason that regulatory agencies will not act independently of their oversight committee.

Given the limited time available to the legislator and the need to allocate that time so as to maximize the chances of reelection, it is not in the legislator's interest to be overly concerned with the oversight function. Only if there are complaints from constituents or from those providing political support does the legislator verify that the agency is acting according to the legislator's wishes. There is little need for the legislator to be concerned with the agency's performance if there are no complaints.

Legislators attempt to maximize political support, given the structure of the legislature and its rules, in the following manner.

One interest group.   The simplest case occurs when only one organized interest group has a concentrated interest in a particular piece of legislation and the costs are diffuse. The legislator will favor that legislation if the political support provided by that group exceeds the cost, in terms of loss in political support, of producing that legislation.

The cost of producing legislation is the legislator's time. The legislator's limited time has to be apportioned among a great many bills introduced during each session of the legislature. For each bill considered, members of legislative committees must hold hearings, draft bills, negotiate among themselves, and vote.[14] The time spent on any one bill means that there is less time to spend on others. That is the real cost of legislation. Legislators could receive political support by enacting other legislation, or they could provide constituent services, also a source of political support. The method by which the legislature is organized also affects the time and ease of passing (or changing) legislation. The committee structure of the legislature, whether there are one or two houses, the rules under which each house operates, whether filibusters are permitted, the type of voting procedures in each house, and so on, all affect the time, hence cost, of producing legislation.

Competing interest groups.   A different situation occurs when there are competing interest groups, each willing to provide political support to have their way on regulation. If the legislator accepts political support from one group, he or she foregoes receiving political support from the other group. (The excluded groups may even decide to back a challenger to the legislator.) The legislator is likely to receive a greater total amount

157,480

of political support in this situation if he or she can provide some benefits to each group. A compromise is likely to be reached, providing some benefits to each opposing interest. An example of this type of compromise was airline regulation.

The airlines were important beneficiaries of regulation, as were the airline unions, whose members received above-market wages because of the entry restrictions in the airline industry. As other organized interest groups, such as representatives of small communities, began to participate in the regulatory process, the profitability of the airlines declined. Small communities (represented by their legislators) were subsidized by requiring airlines to serve these communities. The airlines were in part rewarded by being awarded routes in more profitable markets. The regulators also established a method of pricing, typical of regulated industries, that set price proportional to distance rather than to cost. Since the actual costs of travel per mile were lower for long distances, setting prices proportional to distance subsidized short trips. The more profitable markets, those with prices high compared to costs, subsidized small communities as well as those making shorter trips. Such systems of cross-subsidies are typical of situations where there are opposing interest groups in the regulatory process.

Visible legislation. Producer-type regulation, such as import quotas, tariffs, and entry restrictions, tends to be anticompetitive and is generally not a visible issue to the public. The segments of the population who bear the costs of these producer benefits have a diffuse interest in the outcome of this type of regulation.

However, there are some types of special interest legislation that are more visible in their effects. Legislative benefits to particular population groups, such as Social Security, Medicare, subsidized tuition at public universities, clean air programs, and other environmental legislation, have more obvious beneficiaries. In these cases, legislators seek political support from the benefited population groups. Similar to producer regulation, the cost of these benefits is spread over a majority of the population.

When there is no organized opposition to a visible type of legislation, then legislators go overboard in their support. They do not face budgetary constraints. They gain the political support of members of groups backing the legislation and lose no support, since there is no organized opposition. Program expenditures are greater than even the beneficiaries expected. An example of this legislation was medical research throughout the 1940s and 1950s. Expenditures for medical research, as approved by

Congress, provided more money than the research agencies requested and more than could be usefully spent.

Opposing interest groups. A difficult situation for legislators arises when legislation benefiting specific population groups is opposed by other organized population groups. The legislator, when confronted with these opposing groups, will lose political support from one group if forced to choose. The best strategy to follow in a situation of controversial, visible legislation if no compromise is possible, is to not vote on the issue. This can occur when the political leadership forms a bipartisan commission to resolve the issue. Another way to avoid a loss of political support is to enact symbolic legislation. Under this method, legislation is enacted, thereby satisfying one group; however, the legislation contains limited, if any, enforcement mechanisms, thereby ensuring that the legislation will not achieve its stated goals. Early environmental legislation has often been symbolic. Symbolic legislation relies on the public's lack of knowledge of the specifics of visible legislation. Fortunately for Congress, most legislation is not of the visible, controversial variety.

Producer groups. More typical of legislation that benefits a particular population group is when a producer group, in its own interest, supports legislation favoring a consumer group, such as the food stamp program, nutrition programs, environmental programs, or Medicare. In some such cases, the legislation to aid a population group actually originated from a producer group. For example, as a means of increasing the consumption of farm products, agricultural committees promoted school lunch and milk programs.

When legislation arises from an organized population group, the congressional response is to design the program in such a way as to also produce benefits to the industry suppliers. Medicare provided care to the elderly but was also structured to satisfy the medical and hospital providers. In the case of environmental legislation, many firms actually favored the regulations that would have imposed costs on new entrants to that industry. By granting grandfather clauses, these firms received a competitive cost advantage over new firms. Even though legislation may impose costs on an industry, it does not impose those costs evenly.

Legislators require political support to be reelected. At times the political support is provided by a single organized group. At other times legislators refrain from making any choices for fear of losing political support from one of several opposing groups. However, whenever there is a possibility for legislators to extract political support from more than one group, such as from a population group and a producer group, they will find a way to do so.[15]

The Executive Branch

The executive branch (the administration) is both a demander and a supplier of political benefits. It proposes policies to Congress, and Congress decides whether to enact them. To receive congressional support for its policies, the executive branch, acting as a supplier of political benefits, can provide political support to legislators by judicial and governmental appointments, by locating projects in their districts, and by providing the support of a popular president at election time. The executive branch also appoints agency managers and judges (with the consent of Congress) and has an important influence on the shape of the overall government budget and on departmental expenditures.

The motivation of the executive branch is assumed to be similar to that of the legislative branch, namely, re-election. However, there is an important distinction between the two. The executive branch, because of its stated functions, faces certain constraints on its efforts to maximize political support that are not found in the legislative branch. For example, the executive branch is held responsible for this country's foreign affairs. This constrains its support for politically popular legislation to restrict foreign imports, e.g., textiles. Another important constraint on the executive branch is its concern over the size of the government budget. The president is held responsible for the performance of the economy. A prosperous economy with rising incomes, low inflation, and low unemployment is believed to provide electoral benefits to the party in control of the executive branch. Neither large deficits nor the taxes to erase those deficits are politically popular. Further, both may have an adverse effect on the economy. The executive branch therefore has a concentrated interest in constraining expenditures. (Individual legislators are not usually held accountable by their constituents for increases in government expenditures.)

The executive branch's concern over spending and its distribution has had important consequences for health policy, at times bringing it into conflict with Congress. An example of this conflict occurred when President Ford vetoed a renewal of the Nurse Training Act. Health programs have always been politically popular and Congress, more mindful of the immediate political benefits than the subsequent budgetary costs of the Nurse Training Act, easily overrode President Ford's veto.

One method used by various administrations to circumvent their concern over the budgetary impacts of politically popular legislation is to shift the costs of such programs to others. Presidents Nixon, Carter, and Clinton proposed national health insurance programs. In each case, the administration sought to receive political support for proposing a new, highly visible benefit to the voting (working) population. Business would have been required to provide the government-mandated benefits to their employees. The cost of financing an employer-mandated program is no different from one financed by the government. However, by requiring business to provide the benefits the government did not have to ask for an explicit tax. Requiring business to provide the benefits would make it appear that business firms were financing the program. However, in reality, these costs would eventually have been shifted to their employees, who would have ended up paying for the mandated benefits through reduced wages.

Had these national health insurance proposals been presented in the above manner, their political appeal would have been greatly diminished. Those receiving the benefits of the mandated program would have had to pay the full costs. Unless they were receiving some net subsidy, why would the employees have favored such a program?

Another advantage of shifting the financing cost to business and off the government budget would occur if expenditures under such a program exceeded expectations, as has occurred under Medicare; the additional financing burden would fall on business and their employees rather than on the government.

As government expenditures under the Medicare program began to exceed budget projections, successive administrations have been faced with politically difficult choices. *One approach* is to fund rising Medicare expenditures through another increase in the Medicare portion of the Social Security tax. *An alternative approach* is to ask the aged beneficiaries to pay a greater portion of the program's cost. (The hospital deductible for which the aged are responsible has been slowly increased.) *A third alternative* is to pay physicians and hospitals less. There are no political benefits to an administration from any of these actions. However, the political burden of finding a solution to this dilemma has typically fallen more heavily on the executive branch than on the individual members of Congress because the executive branch is held more responsible for budgetary consequences.

The behavior of the executive branch with regard to the health field can be explained by its desire to maximize political support while being constrained by the budgetary implications of its actions. Successive administrations have continued to propose politically popular health programs, for example, funding for medical research and health professional education. Such legislation is both highly visible and valued by the public, according to public opinion polls. At the same time, successive administrations have tried to reduce the rise in expenditures of existing health programs, e.g., Medicare, thereby forestalling the need to either call for tax increases to fund those programs or to impose costs on politically powerful beneficiaries, such as the aged.

Agency Bureaucracies

The performance of a regulatory agency depends upon the goals and objectives of those in charge of the organization. Their motivations are assumed to be job security and higher salaries, both of which result from being the managers of a growing agency. Promotions and job prestige are more likely to occur when an agency's budget is expanding.[16]

To achieve these goals, agency managers engage in several types of behavior that maximize the agency's political support. In fact, if the agency loses the support of its legislative sponsors, the job security of its managers and the very existence of the agency itself may be threatened.[17]

A regulatory agency, therefore, is dependent upon the policies and desires of its legislative sponsors. A regulatory agency is unlikely to enforce legislation in a manner that is considered consistent with that of the public interest *unless* the agency's oversight committee so intends. In initiating legislation, a legislative committee has a certain purpose or set of purposes and would want the agency to behave in a fashion consistent with its intentions. Congressional oversight, which includes authorization, appropriation, and review of the agency, exists to ensure that the agency is behaving as the legislators intended, rather than what others may perceive to be the public interest. Lack of congressional oversight does not mean that Congress is neglecting its duties. Instead it is more indicative that the congressional committee is satisfied with the agency's performance.

Agency behavior can best be understood by examining legislative behavior. Both the agency and legislators attempt to maximize their political support. The groups that provide political support to the agency are the same as those that provide political support to those legislators serving on the committee having jurisdiction over the agency. The only difference is that the agency also tries to provide the members of the legislative committee with political support. The agency provides services to constituents in the legislator's district and attempts to generate support by stimulating the demand for its services.[18]

There are a number of examples in the health field where regulation has not achieved its stated objectives. One can only infer from this that the *stated* objectives were different from the *intended* objectives. For example, there has been concern for years with the quality of care provided by nursing homes. State regulatory agencies have long had at their disposal various mechanisms to ensure that nursing homes provide a certain standard of care. The state agency is permitted to make unannounced visits and deny reimbursement to the home. Additional legal remedies are often not needed to ensure quality. However, state regulatory agencies rarely use their power to make unannounced visits or remove patients. State nursing home associations are the major group with a concentrated interest in how existing regulations are applied. Neither the state regulatory agency nor the legislators having oversight responsibility are likely to change their behavior as long as the major source of their political support comes from the association whose members are regulated.

When Medicare was enacted, health providers were paid according to their existing payment mechanisms. Payment was based on a fee-for-service basis; that is, a fee was charged each time the patient received service from a provider. However, alternative delivery systems, such as prepaid organizations (HMOs), charge an annual fee per patient regardless of the number of times a patient sees a physician or enters the hospital. Such prepaid organizations have a different incentive than fee-for-service providers. Their incentive is to provide less service while the existing system of fee-for-service has an incentive to provide more services. Fee-for-service providers are in competition with prepaid organizations. At the time Medicare was passed, the American Medical Association (AMA) and the American Hospital Association (AHA) were the two most important health associations. At that time, these organizations, particularly the AMA, were the source of a great deal of political support to Congress. It is no surprise therefore that the Social Security Administration, the agency administering the Medicare system, did not permit prepaid organizations to be paid according to an annual capitation fee; they were paid the same as fee-for-service providers. This policy, in effect, eliminated any financial incentive for prepaid organizations to recruit Medicare patients. (This policy was finally changed in 1985.)

An agency must avoid adverse publicity in order to retain political support. Criticism of the agency makes it appear that the legislative sponsors of the agency have not been performing their oversight function. An agency therefore will attempt to prevent "service" failures in the industry it regulates. One such example is the treatment of the drug industry by the Food and Drug Administration (FDA). If a new drug causes medical problems or death to a small number of those taking it, the regulatory agency, the FDA, would receive adverse publicity for approving the drug. Unfortunately, it is not possible to anticipate all the side effects of new drugs, particularly when they are taken in conjunction with other drugs.

It is only after a drug has been introduced that these problems come to light. To minimize the possibilities of adverse publicity, however, the FDA has raised the testing requirements for approval. The result of this strategy is that increased testing requirements increase the costs of new drugs, reduces their potential profitability, and, consequently, makes fewer drugs available. As a result of FDA policy, many people have been denied the benefits of new drugs while the drugs await approval. It has been estimated that the "cost" of fewer new drugs and the drug lag, in terms of foregone benefits to consumers, has been far greater than the cost of permitting new drugs to enter the market early.[19]

Thus there is a trade-off between possible deaths due to too rapid introduction of a new drug and deaths that could have been prevented had that drug been on the market sooner. The first type of death is "visible"; they are actual people with families and their pictures may appear in the papers. The second type is "statistical"; deaths that could have been prevented. For an agency concerned about adverse publicity, it is more important to prevent visible deaths. By placing too great an emphasis on preventing visible deaths, however, the agency gives too little emphasis to statistical deaths, which are many times greater. This agency's weighting scheme may be quite different from those who would prefer to purchase the drug.

The FDA's policy of reducing the rate of innovation of new drugs, however, does not necessarily harm all firms in the drug industry. Firms are able to charge higher prices for their existing drugs and these drugs are able to retain their market share for a longer period of time because the entry of new drugs has been limited.

In addition to maximizing its political support, the regulatory agency attempts to achieve and maintain a monopoly position over the provision of its services.[20] If Congress were to establish a competitor agency, the managerial goals of the initial agency would be threatened. The agency may see part of its appropriations go to its competitor and the performance of the agencies could then be compared.[21] Thus any attempt to decrease the monopoly power of an agency is likely to bring forth strong defensive actions. The following two examples show bureaucratic response when the monopoly position of a health agency was threatened.

After World War II, Congress wanted to increase funds for medical research. A representative of the U.S. Public Health Service, the federal agency responsible for medical research, testified that the agency could not profitably spend the additional funds. This spokesman was quickly retired by the agency. His replacement welcomed all the additional funds Congress decided the agency needed. The Public Health Service was fearful that if they did not go along with congressional interests, Congress would set up another government agency to carry out its desires. Rather than have these funds go to a competitive agency, the existing agency accommodated congressional interests. (The role of Congress in medical research is discussed in more detail in Chapter 7.)

In the 1970s, conquering cancer was perceived as having large public support. To demonstrate their concern, several legislators favored establishing a separate, highly visible cancer center that would be independent from the National Institutes of Health (NIH), which at that time was the main government agency for medical research. The threat of a competitive agency that would draw funds away led to a vigorous defense by NIH of their research efforts and a downgrading of the idea of a separate cancer establishment. For their defense, NIH was able to generate support from medical schools and other medical research institutes they supported. (These constituencies were afraid that they might receive less funding from a competitive agency.)

To achieve their goals, the managers of an agency require increased budget appropriations. The managers of an expanding agency are able to justify increased staff, increased responsibilities for themselves, and, consequently, higher salaries.

Whenever there is a situation of a "bilateral monopoly," that is, two monopolists dealing with one another, the agency as the sole seller of a service and the legislature as the sole purchaser of that service, the outcome depends upon the relative bargaining power of the two groups. When this situation occurs in the private market, such as between a union selling the services of its members to the only coal mine in a town, the result is a compromise depending on relative strength in the bargaining process. When the bargaining is between an agency and the legislature, two not-for-profit organizations, the outcome usually favors the agency. There are several reasons why this is true.

The bureaucratic agency in bargaining with the legislature has more information available on the cost of providing its services. Since there are no competitors, the legislature cannot simply compare the agency's cost of providing the service with that of another organization. Further, the agency has more at stake over its budget than does the legislature. Thus the agency will devote more time and effort toward justifying its need for a larger budget. The legislative subcommittee with jurisdiction over the agency, however, has limited time to devote to the agency's budget. Legislators are involved in many other activities and whether or not the agency's budget is somewhat larger than necessary will have no adverse effect on their chances for reelection.

The agency is also fairly well-informed as to the value the legislature places on its services, that is, the legislature's demand for the agency's output. The agency is responsive to the organized interests affected by the agency. These same interest groups lobby the legislature for the benefits provided by the regulatory agency and the legislature will seek to accommodate them. The agency will try to benefit legislators by, for example, locating agency facilities in the legislators' districts.

The agency also tries to generate demand for its services. Regulatory agencies concerned with more visible issues, such as the environment, will try to stimulate interest in the issue through the use of public relations. The agency becomes a focal point for bringing the issue to the attention of the public. It is in the agency's interest to continue to focus attention on the problems that concern the agency. An agency successful in maintaining public interest in the issue strengthens its hand in bargaining over its budget.

Government agencies were an important source of financial support to groups that had a similar political sympathy, according to one study of interest group financial support.[22] By providing funds to groups for training, staff assistance, or other purposes, the agency also builds support from these groups to lobby Congress to continue and expand these programs. This symbiotic relationship enables the agency to increase its demand by organizing constituents that would have had a difficult time organizing themselves.

Because of the agency's control over information and its ability to marshall constituency support, it has a strong position with the legislative subcommittee in negotiating its appropriation.[23]

Agency growth, however, has not been particularly noticeable in the health field despite the fact that health expenditures, both public and private, have been increasing rapidly. An important reason for this is that when Medicare was enacted, hospital and physician organizations insisted upon being paid by nongovernment agencies. In most cases, these "intermediaries" between the Medicare patient and the health provider were hospital-controlled Blue Cross associations and physician-controlled Blue Shield plans.

In summary, the hypothesized goals of agency managers are job security and higher salaries, both of which result from promotions and the increased prestige of being managers of an agency with a large budget. To achieve these goals the agency must first have the confidence and political support of those legislators having oversight responsibilities for their agency. To do so means that the agency attempts to minimize any adverse publicity, to provide services for those legislators, and to generate favorable support from groups having an interest in the agency's functions. To ensure that increases for their agency's functions go to their agency and not to competitors, managers are expected to oppose new agencies with similar functions and to favor eliminating competition ("duplication") among agencies.

One implication of an agency's necessity for political support is that the agency ends up protecting an industry that they are ostensibly meant to regulate in the public interest. However, in doing so they are merely following the legislators' desires, since the regulated industry also provides political support to those regulators.

The Judicial System

According to the economic or self-interest version of the interest group theory of government, the legislature supplies legislation in return for political support. An independent judiciary, however, can nullify special interest legislation. If a judicial system is able to invalidate the legislature's actions, interest groups would not be willing to pay as high a price for the legislation. What role, therefore, does an independent judiciary play in an interest group theory of legislation?

The federal judicial system was designed to be protected from current political pressures. It was the intent of the authors of the Constitution that there be three branches of government and that the judicial system be independent. Federal judges, under Article III of the U.S. Constitution, are appointed rather than elected, their appointments are for life, and Congress is forbidden to reduce their salaries.

There are some methods by which the other two political branches of government can influence court decisions. The executive branch exerts its influence through its appointment of judges; however, this process may take many years before its effect on desired legislation occurs. The executive branch can also fail to enforce decisions that it opposes. Congress can fail to appropriate sufficient funds for salary increases and for judicial staff, create additional federal jurisdictions that vitiate existing courts, and pass new laws, with the concurrence of the administration. Except for the latter, these approaches, however, must be viewed as long-term attempts to control the decisions of federal judges.

Rather than being an obstacle to the provision of special interest legislation, an independent judiciary is viewed as an important part of the interest group theory of government.[24]

If one Congress "sells" special interest legislation, it cannot ensure that a future Congress will not overturn it. A new Congress with a different composition and other interest groups will not have to abide by the decisions of a previous Congress. Thus if a subsequent Congress amends or nullifies that special interest legislation, the value of that legislation will be worth less than if the legislation had some long-term stability. A special interest group would not be willing to "pay" as much for legislation that lasted only a short period, or if there was uncertainty as to how long the legislation would last. Since legislators would like to receive as high a price (political support) as possible for their services, it is in their self-interest to increase the durability of special interest legislation.

The procedural rules of a legislature add some stability to enacted legislation. There is the time that legislators must spend in committee hearings, drafting the legislation, and voting on the legislation. The time spent on one piece of legislation could be spent on other legislation. Legislation must be approved by a majority in two legislative bodies and not be vetoed by the executive branch. These procedures reduce the amount of legislation produced and, consequently, raise the cost to subsequent Congresses of overturning previously enacted special interest legislation.

Also providing stability to contracts entered into by a particular Congress is an independent judiciary that is willing to interpret the law according to congressional intent. A legislature is able to extend the life of its legislation, thereby increasing its value, as long as the judiciary accepts congressional deals as given. If the courts interpret the law according to the discussions by Congress and the intent of the act at that time, then a Congress is able to provide a special interest group with a long-term contract.

If a judiciary were more susceptible to the intent of a current Congress (i.e., not independent), then court decisions would rely more heavily on current political pressures than previous congressional intent. It is thus in the economic interest of Congress to have an independent judiciary so as to interpret the law as the enacting Congress intended.

Examples of "dependent" judiciaries were the regulatory agencies established by Congress, such as the Interstate Commerce Commission (ICC) and the Civil Aeronautics Board (CAB). The current Congress determined the budget of these agencies and the members of the regulatory agencies served specific terms. Since regulatory agencies are more dependent upon the current Congress, an interest group would not be willing to pay as much for legislation establishing a regulatory agency as it would for more secure legislation. Regulatory agencies, however, may be more suitable for legislative benefits that depend on local variations in services and rate setting. In this way the special interest group can bypass dealing with separate state legislatures. Federal regulatory agencies may also be a way of having Congress bypass the independent judiciary if previous legislation would be in conflict with the new special interest legislation. An example of this latter case was the regulation of prices and entry used in the railroad and airline industries, which conflicted with the Sherman antitrust laws. The fact-finding function of enforcement proceedings is assigned to the regulatory agency rather than the courts.

This view of the judicial system as a mechanism for enforcing long-term stability to contracts provided to politically powerful interest groups by Congress has several implications. The perception that the courts are above politics enhances the value of previous political contracts. Rather than being a constraint on special interest legislation, " . . . they enforce the 'deals' made by effective interest groups with earlier legislatures."[25]

The self-interest view of the federal court system (and its interpretation of the Constitution) does not imply that all legislation and judicial decisions are necessarily against the public interest. Its view is merely that the independent judiciary and the Constitution are viewed as a means of providing durable protection to politically powerful special interests. The First Amendment rights are viewed "as a form of protective legislation extracted by an interest group consisting of publishers, journalists, pamphleteers, and others who derive pecuniary and nonpecuniary income from publication and advocacy of various sorts."[26,27]

The independent judiciary has been important in understanding change in the regulatory environment of the medical sector. The antitrust laws provide protection to both consumers and potential producers from monopoly power. Some protectionist legislation, enacted at the behest of powerful health interest groups at a state level, has had the effect of providing these health interest groups with monopoly power; restrictions were placed on price competition and on the formation of alternative delivery systems for providing medical services. The independent federal judiciary has been called upon to resolve conflicts between federal law (the Sherman Act) and state protectionist legislation. These decisions by the judiciary, particularly by the Supreme Court in 1982 (discussed in Chapter 6), have had a profound effect on the structure of the medical care system in this country.

Concluding Comments

Economic markets reflect the desires of those willing to purchase specific products. Producers respond to purchasers' demands. There is a close matching of costs and benefits in economic markets; those receiving the benefits of their purchases pay the full costs of the goods and services received. In political markets, however, the legislative benefits provided to a group exceed their associated financial costs. Those groups receiving legislative benefits are able to achieve them by imposing part or all of the cost on others.

The ability of certain groups to successfully use the legislative process to redistribute wealth away from others to themselves results from imperfections in the political marketplace. Voters are generally uninformed on specific legislative issues. Many voters do not even vote, and when they do, they vote on sets of packages rather than express their preferences on each issue of importance to themselves.

These differences between political and economic markets enable organized groups to be more successful in political than in economic markets. Groups with a concentrated interest, generally producers, are more likely than consumers to be successful in the legislative arena. The costs of organizing themselves, representing their interests, and providing political support to legislators are lower to those groups with a concentrated interest than the value of their expected legislative benefits. The costs of providing legislative benefits are imposed on those with a diffuse interest. It is less costly for consumers to pay slightly higher prices for particular goods or services than to incur the burden of what are generally "invisible" costs to finance producer benefits.

The motivation of the suppliers of legislative benefits makes it possible for organized groups to receive benefits at the expense of politically unorganized groups. Those who run for political office, as well as those who work for the government, are no different from anyone else. They are concerned with what is in their self-interest. To maximize their chances for reelection, legislators require political support. As such, legislators are more likely to respond to the demands of those offering political support.

The approach used by legislatures to organize themselves also enhances the ability of organized groups to secure favorable legislative benefits. Congress relies on committees and subcommittees to sort out the various demands for legislation. Legislators on subcommittees having jurisdiction over particular special interest groups therefore have an undue influence over legislation affecting those groups. Thus legislators receiving political support from particular organized constituencies are often the same legislators proposing legislative benefits to those same groups. Vote trading also enables legislators representing minority interests to enact legislation on behalf of their constituents' interests.

In addition to legislators, the other participants affecting legislation and regulation are the executive branch, regulatory agencies, and the federal judiciary. The executive branch also seeks to maximize its chances for reelection; unlike legislators, however, it faces certain constraints in its attempt to maximize political support. The executive branch is held responsible for the budgetary implications of its actions and the conduct of foreign policy. Regulatory agencies are not viewed as independent organizations. The managers of such agencies require the backing of their legislative sponsors if the agency is to receive annual increases in its appropriations. Thus the actions of regulatory agencies are expected to reflect the desires of those legislators having jurisdiction over their agency rather than the manager's perceptions of the public interest. Lastly, the federal judiciary is viewed, according to the economic version of an interest group theory of government, as providing durability to legislation enacted by Congress.

To be generalizable, a theory has to be stripped of much detail. The hypotheses must be abstractions from reality. The resulting theory may then appear to be too simplistic. However, the true test of a theory is how well it predicts, not whether it includes all the appropriate institutional detail of the legislative process. Further, to be useful for understanding legislative outcomes and for predicting likely changes in the future, a theory does not have to be 100 percent accurate; a theory merely has to predict better than an alternative theory. When the Self-Interest Paradigm is evaluated, this criterion for judging the usefulness of a theory should be kept in mind.

In subsequent chapters, the self-interest approach to legislation will be used to explain why specific health legislation was enacted and why the public interest was not the *intent* of the legislation, although it is often the *stated* goal. First, however, it becomes necessary to explain why certain health associations were more successful than others in achieving their legislative goals.

Study Questions for Chapter 2

1. What is the presumed purpose of all legislation according to the "economic theory" of legislation?
2. How do the concepts of "concentrated" and "diffuse" interests determine whether a group represents its interests before legislators?
3. Why are producer groups more likely than consumer groups to be successful in all the legislative marketplace?
4. Once enacted, why may legislative benefits received by a group eventually diminish?
5. What objectives are legislators presumed to have and what types of cost/benefit calculations are they presumed to undertake, according to the economic theory of legislation?
6. Explain how "vote trading" enables legislators representing minority economic interests to receive legislative benefits for those interest groups.
7. When is the "visibility" of legislation considered desirable by its proponents and when is it considered undesirable?

8. Why are regulatory agencies more likely to represent the interests of those whom they regulate rather than the public's interest?

9. Contrast the public interest view of government to the economic theory of legislation in terms of the likely effect of government policy on economic efficiency and the equity of redistribution policies.

Notes

1. Much has been written on voting behavior. A classic book on this subject is Anthony Downs. 1957. *An Economic Theory of Democracy*. New York: Harper & Row.

2. It was found that voter turnout was proportionately smaller the larger the population in an area (indicating that a voter in a more populous area has less likelihood of affecting the vote outcome) and the more one-sided the election. When presidential and senatorial elections were held at the same time as local elections (greater importance of the election), the voter turnout was greater. Yoram Barzel and Elliott Silberberg. 1973. "Is the Act of Voting Rational?" *Public Choice* 16 (Fall).

3. Given the limited time voters have to become informed on issues and candidates, a voter may concentrate on only those issues of overriding importance. This phenomenon helps to explain the rise in political power of single-issue groups. Such groups collect and disseminate relevant information to their members, focusing on their special concerns, thereby economizing on the cost of the voter being informed. By controlling the information flow and summarizing the implications for their members, single-issue groups have greater influence on the voting behavior of their group.

4. Morris P. Fiorina. 1977. *Congress: Keystone of the Washington Establishment*. New Haven, CT: Yale University Press.

5. There are many other methods besides limits on entry whereby legislation can affect the firm's profits. For example, each firm in the industry can be granted a subsidy (e.g., farmers). Again, the motivation underlying each type of legislation is the same: firms desire to become more profitable than if left to the outcome of a competitive market.

6. The group may also benefit by imposing its preferences on the rest of the population, for example, eliminate abortion, permit prayer in the schools, or ban nuclear weapons.

7. There are several factors that affect the demand for legislation by a group:

(a) In any economic market as the price of a good increases, the quantity demanded of that good drops. The same is true in political markets. The higher the political support required (the price), the lower the quantity demanded of legislation. It is assumed that the demanders are aware of the value of legislative benefits. They would therefore be willing to pay, in terms of political support, a price that does not exceed the value of their legislative benefits.

(b) The value of legislation to a group and what they are willing to pay for those benefits is affected by the durability of the legislation. The more permanent the legislation, the greater its value.

(c) When the demand for the producer's product increases, the value of legislation, hence the producer's demand, also increases. That is, the value of legislation to a group is greater the larger the market in which that legislation is applicable. For example, as the amount of dollars spent on health services by consumers has grown, so has the value of legislation that limits the number of health professionals that can practice in that market.

(d) When there are opponents who are also willing to provide political support, then the group demanding legislative benefits will have to pay a higher price in terms of political support. Thus whether or not there is opposition to a group's demand for legislation will affect the price a group has to pay for legislative benefits, as well as the amount of legislation they receive.

8. Downs, *An Economic Theory of Democracy*, 297.

9. When there are a large number of firms and their employees, such as the textile industry, they are more likely to rely on the voting pressure they are able to exert directly on legislators to achieve protective legislation. Fewer, larger firms, such as in the auto and steel industries, cannot exert similar voting pressure. Instead their strategy is to rely more on public relations campaigns to exert political pressure, such as by claiming "fairness" in reducing imports that compete with their products. In this manner they hope to sway legislators not dependent on their votes. Robert Baldwin. 1989. "The Political Economy of Trade Policy," *Journal of Economic Perspectives* 3 (4) 119–135.

   Regulation and monopolization of an industry become more profitable when the overall demand for the industry service is "inelastic." That is, when supply is restricted an increase in the price of the product would result in an increase in total industry revenues.

10. When imperfect information exists, there is opportunity for "political entrepreneurism." A political entrepreneur, who is usually a politician, helps to improve the performance of the political marketplace, particularly with respect to "visible" redistribution. For example, in the special Fall 1991 Senate race for an open seat in Pennsylvania, a relative unknown, Harris Wofford, ran against the Republican nominee, Richard Thornburg, who had been the U.S. Attorney General and was strongly favored to win the election. The main issue Wofford ran on was healthcare reform, which Thornburg ignored. Wofford was successful in making healthcare reform a salient issue in the minds of the voters, thus he changed the outcome of the election. By demonstrating healthcare reform as a winning issue in a state race, he captured the attention of the Democrats, who then made it one of their campaign issues in the 1992 Presidential election. For a discussion of political entrepreneurship, see Roger Noll. 1989. "Economic Perspectives on the Politics of Regulation," *Handbook of Industrial Organization*, vol. II, R. Schmalensee and R.D. Willig (eds.) New York: Elsevier Science Publishers. 1253–1282.

11. The discussion that legislators are primarily interested in maximizing their chances for reelection assumes legislators are not monopolists, that is, they face competition in their bids for reelection, not only in the general election but also with a possible challenge in the primary. It is this concern over challengers that causes the legislator to respond to political support. Some legislators, however, are either unopposed or win by such large margins that they do not have to respond to the political support offered by an interest group. When the interest group has no alternative but to deal with the particular legislator, the legislator has greater flexibility to act on issues.

12. While political support is often thought of as being votes, volunteer time, or money, political support may also be the ability of a group to disrupt legislative

programs. For example, during the negotiations leading to the passage of Medicare, legislators were concerned that if physicians and hospitals were not paid according to their payment preferences, they would not participate. Legislating benefits for the elderly but not being able to ensure that they would be delivered would have had the effect of nullifying the program. Congress could then have lost the political support they thought they were going to receive by passing the program in the first place.

13. Some persons draw a distinction between logrolling and vote trading. Logrolling is used when the groups involved consist of a majority; in vote trading, the participants are a minority.

14. Isaac Ehrlich and Richard A. Posner. 1974. "An Economic Analysis of Legal Rulemaking," *Journal of Legal Studies*, 3 (1) 257–86. *See also*, Mark Crain. 1979. "Cost and Output in the Legislative Firm," *Journal of Legal Studies* 8 (3) 607–21.

15. Milton Friedman explains the 1986 tax reform legislation that eliminates many of the loopholes providing advantages to special interest groups in the following way: "From Congress's point of view, tax legislation has an . . . important function: It is a way to raise campaign funds. . . . That is why members of Congress put such a high value on being assigned to the Ways and Means or Finance committees. . . . The Senate Finance Committee discovered that this process had come to a dead end. . . . the tax space was overcrowded with loopholes. There was no room to add anymore without destroying the tax base altogether. . . . Senator Packwood's approach was an ingenious solution to the potential collapse of tax reform as a source of campaign funds. . . . It . . . wipes the slate clean, thereby providing space for the tax reform cycle to start over again. . . . If my interpretation is correct, the improvement will turn out to be temporary. . . . As members of Congress try to raise campaign funds, old loopholes will be reintroduced and new ones invented. . . . The process will be strictly bipartisan—as it always has been. The only partisan element will be the rhetoric used to defend the changes."

   In a letter to the editor on this subject, Ralph Nader said that his recent experiences convinced him that Friedman was completely correct in his analysis of Congress's interest in tax reform. Milton Friedman. 1986. "Tax Reform Lets Politicians Look For New Donors," *The Wall Street Journal*, July 7, 10.

16. The following references concern the behavior of regulatory agencies: Aaron Wildavsky. 1964. *The Politics of the Budgetary Process*. Boston: Little, Brown; Gordon Tullock. 1965. *The Politics of Bureaucracy*. Washington, D.C.: Public Affairs Press; Anthony Downs. 1967. *Inside Bureaucracy*. Boston: Little, Brown; William A. Niskanen. 1971. *Bureaucracy and Representative Government*. Chicago: Aldine Atherton Publishing Company; William A. Niskanen. 1975. "Bureaucrats and Politicians," *The Journal of Law and Economics* 18 (3) 617–44; Albert Breton and Ronald Wintrobe. 1975. "The Equilibrium Size of a Budget-Maximizing Bureau," *Journal of Political Economy* 83 (1) 195–207; M.D. McCubbins, R.G. Noll, and B. Weingast. 1987. "Administrative Procedures as Instruments of Political Control," *Journal of Law, Economics and Organization* 3 (2) 243–77.

17. An example of what happens when an agency's policies (the Federal Trade Commission) diverge from those of its sponsors (the Congress) is discussed in Barry R. Weingast and Mark J. Moran. 1983. "Bureaucratic Discretion or Congressional Control? Regulatory Policymaking by the Federal Trade Commission," *Journal of Political Economy* 91 (5) 765–800.

18. In their work on the economic theory of regulation, Stigler and Peltzman do not distinguish between agency and legislative behavior. This is presumably because they expect the actions of both groups to be similar, that is, the agency is a creation of and controlled by the legislature. Their concern, therefore, is just with the legislature.

19. Drug legislation is also covered in more detail, together with appropriate references, in Chapter 7.

20. Bureaucracies are generally monopolist suppliers. The U.S. Postal Service, the Department of Defense, municipal garbage collectors, the local health department are all monopolist sellers of their services. In fact, various government study groups (commissions) often recommend that duplication of government agencies should be eliminated. Thus if there are overlapping jurisdictions, reorganizations eliminate them, thereby ensuring that the agency has a monopoly.

    In economic markets, a monopolist charges a higher price than if competition existed. The result of monopoly behavior is that prices are higher, profits are greater, and output of that service is reduced. Bureaucracies, however, are not organized for profit. The agency cannot keep the difference between their total revenues and their total costs. Therefore they receive no benefit from increasing the profits of their agency. Further, bureaucratic agencies do not sell their services on a per unit basis as does a private firm. Instead, an agency generally receives an appropriation from the legislature to cover the costs of their activities. Thus the agency does not face many purchasers of its product but instead only one, the legislature.

21. From the perspective of economic efficiency it would be worthwhile to decrease the monopoly power of an agency. One way this has been achieved is by contracting out the agency's function to the lowest bidder. An example of this approach is in municipal services, (e.g., garbage collection). The cost savings have been dramatic. Another method has been to ask existing government agencies to bid against one another on performing a government function. This approach was used during the Vietnam War when the Coast Guard received a contract over the Navy for performing certain naval combat functions.

    Permitting agencies to offer bids on functions performed by other agencies would force those other agencies to hold down their costs. It would be embarrassing to an agency manager if at appropriation hearings another agency offered to perform certain functions at one-half the appropriation.

    Lastly, agency efficiency would increase if agencies with a national jurisdiction were subdivided into separate regional entities. In this way, cost and productivity comparisons could be made between the various regional agencies.

    The above suggestions, which have been made many times by others, assume that legislators are concerned with agency efficiency. If instead the legislators are more concerned with maximizing political support and the existing agency structure helps them to achieve this goal, then it is unlikely that legislators would favor such radical changes.

22. Jack L. Walker. 1983. "The Origins and Maintenance of Interest Groups in America," *The American Political Science Review* 77 (2) 390–406.

23. Perhaps the most well-known observations on agency size are attributed to C. Northcote Parkinson. Parkinson's two axioms were, "An official wants to multiply subordinates, not rivals," and "Officials make work for each other." Parkinson finds empirical support for his "laws," the most notable being the British Navy from 1914 through 1928. Though the number of ships decreased by 67 percent

and the number of officers and men actually on ships decreased by 31 percent, the number of admiralty officials increased by 78 percent. This led one observer to comment that Britain had " . . . a magnificent navy on land." Bureaucratic expansion occurs regardless of whether the work load decreases. Similarly, as the number of British colonies declared their independence, the British Colonial Office continued to expand. As the number of farmers in the United States declined, the Department of Agriculture's budget and personnel increased. C. Northcote Parkinson. 1975. *Parkinson's Law*. Boston: Houghton Mifflin Co. 35.

24. The discussion in this section is based on the article by William M. Landes and Richard A. Posner. 1975. "The Independent Judiciary in an Interest-Group Perspective," *The Journal of Law and Economics* 18 (3) 875–901.

25. Ibid., 894.

26. Ibid., 893.

27. Controversy occurs when the independent judiciary acts in a truly independent fashion. When the courts provide the politically powerless, namely criminals, with rights not provided to them explicitly by the Constitution, as was done by the "Warren Court," there is debate whether the courts have gone too far. An interest group view of government that interprets legislation and even the Constitution as protection for the powerful would not expect that the framers of the Constitution wanted to confer such rights on powerless, unrepresented groups. Whether (and how) the poor and powerless should be protected by society is a value judgment and is separate from the analytic issue of what the framers of the Constitution had as their intent.

THE RELATIVE SUCCESS OF HEALTH ASSOCIATIONS

S ome health associations, such as the American Medical Association (AMA), have been much more successful in the legislative arena than others, e.g., the American Nurses Association (ANA). The most direct measure of this success is the relative incomes of their members. Throughout the post-World War II period, physicians have earned "excess" rates of return; these rates of return were greater than what would have been necessary to produce the same supply of physicians. Nurses, on the other hand, have either earned lower or similar rates of return to those earned in professions with comparable training; they have not earned excess rates of return.[1] While the success of an association is affected by a number of factors, such as whether other concentrated groups oppose their legislative proposals, there are several characteristics of an association and of its members that affect its ability to achieve favorable legislation. These attributes are useful predictors for judging the success of an association. The following is a brief discussion of the determinants of an association's success in the legislative marketplace.

Similarity of Members' Interests

When the members of a group have similar interests, the costs of organizing the group are less than if the members disagree on what it is they want. When members' interests differ, negotiation among those with divergent views must occur before they can arrive at a mutually agreeable position. Large differences in members' positions or in their perceived interests may cause defections from the group. These defecting members may then claim that they speak for the industry or profession. Legislators will not be certain who speaks for the members' interests when there are multiple spokespersons and each subgroup provides political support and presents different proposals. Differences in interests among group members will also lessen the likelihood that members will contribute to a group whose legislative proposals differ from their own.

Consumers have different interests. They have different occupations, live in different regions, and have different values. Thus it is very difficult, i.e., costly, to organize consumers around one particular economic issue. Further, the effect of any economic policy may have a relatively small effect on their incomes. (The effect of such a policy on consumers is said to be "diffuse.") Consumers may not purchase particular products very frequently and when they do, the effect of a given policy on the prices they pay may be relatively small. When consumers favor a specific visible issue, it is easier to organize and represent that specific issue. For example, opposition to gun control and abortion are two issues a number of people feel strongly about. It is therefore much easier to organize consumers on these issues than on others. However, given the heterogeneity of consumers and their interests, it is generally difficult to organize consumers into political groups.

Producers in a particular industry, on the other hand, generally have homogeneous interests; they want to increase their incomes. The revenues of firms in an industry come from similar sources, and producers are aware of the effects on their incomes of policies that either affect their costs or the demands for their product or service. Because producers' interests are similar, it is less costly for them to organize and represent their interests. It is for this reason that we observe so many more organizations representing producers than consumers.

A potential problem for producer associations occurs when certain subgroups seek to receive a competitive advantage over other producers in that association. When this occurs, the producer association must continue to represent the common interests of all producers—otherwise the association will fractionate into separate groups, each group seeking to gain advantage. Should this occur, no one group will then be interested in representing the common interests of all producers.

Dental Associations

Dental associations have a relatively homogeneous membership. Dentists are predominantly in fee-for-service practice, most often as solo practitioners. Most dentists are also general dentists, as compared to being members of different specialty groups. General dentists represent the vast majority of all dentists. Dentists who become specialists are required to limit their practice to their specialty. Specialists in dentistry, therefore, are limited to a smaller portion of the total market for dental care and cannot compete with general dentists. Dentistry has handled the specialty "problem" by not permitting specialists and general dentists to become competitors. General dentists were able to impose these conditions on specialists, and the dental associations were then able to continue to represent the common interests of all.

American Nurses Association

Nurses have not had similar interests. Approximately two-thirds of registered nurses work in the hospital while the remainder work in other settings, such as in public health agencies, physicians' offices, and schools. Even those nurses employed in hospitals may be specialized, such as nurse anesthetists and critical care nurses. In the nonhospital setting, nurses' roles also vary, from being a general nurse in a physician's office to being a privately employed nurse-midwife. Nurses, therefore, have specialty nursing associations that more closely represent their professional roles. There is greater similarity of interests among nurses within these associations than within the ANA.

The number of nurses within a specialty is sufficiently large, in the tens of thousands, to support a national specialty association at a reasonable cost. Nurses in specialty roles and general duty nurses are not in competition with each other. There are no barriers in the path of general duty nurses who desire to take additional training and move into specialty roles.

In addition to a lack of similar economic and professional interests, many nurses have not looked upon nursing as a long-term career. Many nurses viewed nursing as an occupation until they became married. After marriage, many nurses left the profession to raise a family. Once their children had grown, some returned to nursing, others did not. In addition, many nurses did not view themselves as the primary wage earner in the family. Instead, they viewed their income as supplementing their spouse's income. The economic benefits of joining a national nursing association were, therefore, questionable.

The political effectiveness of the ANA has been further weakened by the types of legislative issues they favored. Rather than representing the common economic interests of nurses, the nursing associations, have lobbied for broader (nonnursing) social issues. It is unlikely that nurses desire to provide financial support to the ANA for achieving broad societal changes. Instead of concentrating their political support on issues that affect their members' economic interests, nursing associations backed legislation on the nuclear freeze and women's rights, in addition to those that affected their members' economic interests.

American Medical Association

The AMA, considered to be the most successful of the health associations, has, until recently, been able to deal with a membership whose interests are not always homogeneous. As early as 1883, the AMA was concerned by the growth of specialization and the formation of separate societies to represent those physicians.[2] As the number of specialties began to rise, it became more and more difficult for the AMA to represent physicians whose field of practice and method of practice were changing.

The growth of physician specialty societies threatened the role of the AMA as the representative of organized medicine. Specialists wanted to restrict certain tasks to those physicians who were specially trained to perform them. At the same time, specialists, if they are not busy, wish to be able to perform generalist tasks.[3] From a generalist perspective, if specialists are successful in limiting the services they are permitted to perform, there would then be less demand, hence income, for generalists. The conflict between specialists and generalists becomes a problem when there is insufficient demand facing each practitioner and when specialty services begin to cover a significant portion of all physician services. To prevent themselves from being limited to a smaller market, generalists wanted to be able to continue performing all tasks.

Board certification was a compromise between specialists and generalists. Generalists were still permitted to perform all medical services, but board certification helped to distinguish between physicians who were specially qualified, in terms of education, training, and examination, to perform the same tasks.[4]

The AMA was able to overcome the potentially divisive issue of specialty societies by understanding and representing the common economic interests of all physicians; namely, the maintenance of fee-for-service practice without government interference. They were also able, until the late 1960s, to maintain tight control over the supply of physicians. By being able to understand the common economic interests of all physicians they have historically been able to mobilize all physicians, as in their legislative defeat of President Truman's proposal for national health insurance.

But the characteristics of physicians have changed in the last 15 years. There are a greater number of female physicians; more physicians belong to medical groups, which are becoming larger; and more physicians receive a significant portion of their income from large healthcare organizations, such as health maintenance organizations (HMOs), preferred provider organizations (PPOs), and vertically integrated hospitals.

Along with changes in the characteristics of physicians, there are corresponding changes in physicians' attitudes and economic interests. According to surveys of physicians, their attitudes toward economic issues depend on where they work, whether they are salaried, their age, their geographic location, and their specialty. For example, family practitioners were more likely (28.1 percent) than surgeons (14.6 percent) to agree with the statement that "California law should be changed to allow employment of physicians by hospitals, corporations, and similar entities".[5] Further, physicians working in prepaid group practices do not believe that quality of care will be as adversely affected as a result of competition and employment of physicians as do physicians working in a fee-for-service setting.[6] And older physicians are more opposed to advertising than are younger physicians.[7] Another survey that examined physicians' attitudes on issues of peer review, prepayment, and delegation of tasks found a similar diversity of opinion depending on the physician's characteristics. Physicians who were younger, salaried, and in specialties such as psychiatry are more favorably inclined toward these issues than are surgeons, older physicians, and those in fee-for-service practice.[8]

As its membership has declined (from over 70 percent of all physicians in 1962 to about 45 percent currently), the AMA has had to search for common interests among the increasingly diverse physician population. To attract younger physicians, the AMA has been more vocal on such issues as tobacco subsidies, boxing, and seat belts. These broader issues have helped create a new image for the AMA, but the organization has not neglected the economic interests of all physicians. For example, the AMA opposes reductions in the Medicare program, a program it once strenuously opposed, since Medicare is a major source of income for many physicians.

The growth in the number of physicians and actions by the federal government to reduce Medicare expenditures have placed great strains on the AMA. The supply of physicians has risen from 141/100,000 population in the early 1960s to about 250/100,000 today. To maintain their incomes, the different physician specialties are engaged in competition over a more limited patient market. Specialists would like to restrict the tasks that nonspecialists can perform, while family practitioners would like to be able to continue to perform a broad range of services. Each organization is supported by large numbers of physicians.

In 1992 the federal government initiated a new physician payment system for Medicare patients. The Resource Based Relative Value Scale (RBRVS) has several parts, but the aspect that has caused each specialty to come into conflict with every other specialty concerns the rearrangement of the physician fee structure under Medicare. Fees for cognitive services were increased while fees for performing procedures were decreased. This rearrangement of physician fees was intended to be "budget neutral," that is, the total amount spent by the government on physician Medicare services was supposed to be unchanged. Thus the only way in which one physician specialty could receive higher fees was to cause a decrease in fees for other specialties. Changes in a specialty's fees had a direct effect on the incomes of physicians in that specialty.

To protect their members' interests, each physician specialty had to engage in the political process. As the separate specialty societies competed among themselves to ensure that their members received a "fair" share of government expenditures, the AMA found it difficult to take sides lest it antagonize one or more of the physician specialty societies. The main role of the AMA was to ask for "more" and try to represent the common interests of all physicians.

"Budget neutrality" has brought to the forefront the divergent economic interests of different physician specialties and in doing so has strengthened the role of the specialty societies. The specialty societies now have an important lobbying function, to represent their members' interests regarding changes in Medicare physician fees. The rise in each specialty's political power has made it more difficult for the AMA to speak for all physicians on all issues. Moreover, the AMA will have to negotiate with the separate physician specialty societies that maintain their own Washington lobbyists.

Given the increasing divergence of economic interests among physicians, the AMA will find it more difficult to find a common set of economic goals for which it can claim to be the physicians' representative. The viability of the AMA will, however, depend on its ability to find a common set of economic interests. Some such issues are higher federal payments for physician visits, limits on increases in the number of physicians (particularly those trained overseas), and excluding payments to nonphysicians under public programs.

American Hospital Association

The American Hospital Association (AHA) has been the major trade association for hospitals. Its constituency, however, has been very diverse. Its membership consists of large and small hospitals, hospitals located in urban and rural areas, hospitals that are major teaching institutions, and not-for-profit as well as for-profit hospitals. Each state also has its own state hospital association. In the past, particularly from the late 1940s through the 1970s, the AHA was generally able to represent the common interests of all hospitals. The AHA was successful in having legislation enacted that increased revenues and decreased costs to all hospitals. For example, the AHA successfully lobbied for hospital construction subsidies (the Hill-Burton Act in 1948), for federal subsidies to increase the supply of nurses (the Nurse Training Act in 1964), and for generous federal payment to hospitals under Medicare. It was relatively easy to represent the common interests of all hospitals at a time of expanding federal budgets. There was no need for either the government or the AHA to choose which hospitals would benefit.

The success of the AHA's lobbying efforts under Medicare resulted in rapidly rising hospital expenditures, duplication of expensive services, and inefficiency in the provision of hospital services.

Successive administrations, both Republican and Democratic, attempted to reduce Medicare hospital expenditures and, as a result, developed an adversarial relationship toward hospitals. As hospitals had to compete, legislatively, for a more limited share of federal expenditures, it became more difficult for the AHA to represent its members' common interests. If small and rural hospitals were to receive increased funding, it would be at the expense of urban hospitals. Under a system of "budget neutrality," where the total amount of money spent by Medicare on hospitals was fixed, increased funding for one type of hospitals had to come from funding for another group of hospitals. As federal efforts to reduce hospital expenditures intensified, each group formed its own association to protect its own interests while trying to shift the burden to other hospitals.

Faced with limited Medicare funding, a diverse membership, and additional trade associations, the AHA found it difficult to take a proactive role in formulating legislative policies. The AHA could not favor one membership group over another. It was less disruptive to its membership interests for the AHA to oppose administration proposals or simply ask for more for everyone. The AHA became less influential in the legislative arena since it could not speak as the representative of all hospitals. One example of the conflict within its membership was the issue of for-profit hospitals receiving a return on equity as part of its Medicare payment. The opposition by not-for-profit hospitals to the economic interests of for-profit hospitals led to for-profit hospitals leaving the AHA.

To prevent further defections from its organization, the AHA attempted to incorporate these divergent interests into its association and to give each separate interest a voice in policy issues.

Constituency Sections within the AHA allow specific types of hospitals that share common interests, functions and concerns to directly participate in AHA policy development and to participate in educational and informational programming suited to their interests.

There are eight constituency sections that serve the diversity of AHA members and their special interests. There are three general constituency sections for general hospitals that are either small or rural hospitals, metropolitan hospitals, or federal hospitals. There is one section for hospitals that are healthcare systems, and four special constituency sections (psychiatric, rehabilitation, maternal and child health, and aging and long-term care) that serve specialty hospitals and general hospitals with related specialty services.

Through membership in the AHA constituency sections, members have the opportunity to voice their special interests to the industry, the association, and its policymaking process. Each section is allotted delegates to the AHA House of Delegates, the highest AHA authority for making policy, which gives each section a vehicle for being heard in AHA policy decisions.[9]

The "Free Rider" Problem

Until the mid-1960s, it was generally believed that the common interests of individuals or firms would lead necessarily to an organization to represent those interests. This reasoning was, however, faulty; it neglected an important aspect of organizational development, the problem of "free riders."[10]

When individuals with a common interest organize to achieve favorable economic legislation for themselves, all individuals with that common interest gain, whether or not they participate in the organization. For example, when some dairy farmers form an organization and contribute to have representation for increasing milk price supports, then, if the legislation is enacted, all dairy producers benefit—even those who have not contributed to the association. High milk price supports is a "collective" good—no dairy producer can be excluded from benefiting from the policy. Since a producer cannot be excluded from the resulting legislation, there is no incentive for the individual producer to contribute to the group's efforts. The individual producer who does not contribute can get a free ride, thereby obtaining the legislative benefits without sharing in the costs of producing those benefits.

Unless a group can overcome this free rider problem, they may be unable to raise sufficient funds to lobby for their desired policy from those likely to benefit. Overcoming this free rider problem is an important determinant of the legislative success of a group.

Labor organizations are a prominent example of organizations overcoming the free rider problem. A labor union negotiates wages for all employees in a plant. It would clearly be in the economic interest of each employee not to join the union and thereby save themselves the union dues. However, if each employee acted according to individual interests, it is unlikely an effective union to serve their common interests would be formed. It is for this reason that unions seek a "closed shop." Once a union has been certified in a plant, all employees are required to join. If not, some employees would receive a free ride on the union's collective bargaining activities. The union would be unable to raise sufficient dues to undertake their collective bargaining activities. Congress and the states have granted unions special exemptions from the antitrust laws to overcome the free rider problem.

Producers in an industry, however, cannot coerce one another to contribute to the industry's trade association. Instead, trade associations attempt to overcome the free rider problem in one of several ways. One method is to tie membership in the national trade association to membership in a local association in which the firm or individual is economically motivated to join. (This method is used by the American Dental Association and is discussed later.) The local association then remits part of the firm's dues to the national organization. Another approach is for the association to require any person desiring certification to become a member of the association; assuming certification leads to a higher income, the individual then has an economic incentive to join. This approach, however, was declared illegal by the Supreme Court in 1978 in the case of the National Society of Professional Engineers.

The most common approach for overcoming the free rider problem is for the trade association to sell "private" services to its member firms and withhold these services from nonmembers (or sell them at a much higher price). The "profits" from the sale of these private services are then used to support the lobbying activities of the industry. The lobbying efforts of an association are a by-product of the services that the organization sells to its membership.[11] If the association has a monopoly position over the sale of those private services, it is more likely that the individual will purchase the services from the association and that the association will be able to charge a high price. Unless the association can find unique services to sell, competitive sellers of such services will be able to provide them at a price lower than that offered by the association.

American Medical Association

In the past, a physician desiring hospital privileges was required to be a member of the county medical society. Unless a physician had hospital privileges, he or she could not provide complete medical treatment to the patient. If a patient had to be hospitalized, a physician without hospital privileges had to refer the patient to a physician with such privileges. This would place the referring physician at a competitive disadvantage. Membership in the county medical society was particularly important for specialists, such as surgeons, whose place of practice was the hospital. Membership in the county society also offered physicians greater protection against medical malpractice. Not only was it easier for a physician to purchase such coverage but other member physicians would be more likely to testify on their behalf. Thus the county medical society was in a powerful position. If the county society chose to deny membership to a physician, the physician would not be able to practice in the community.[12]

The AMA used to be a federation of state and county medical societies. Thus if physicians joined the county medical society, they were automatically members of the national organization, the AMA. Part of each physician's dues was then remitted to the AMA. The AMA was thus able to overcome the free rider problem through this agreement with their constituent societies. This system of membership prevailed until 1949. In 1950 the AMA, presumably in an attempt to increase its revenues, created a separate dues-paying membership. (This was the period of intense AMA opposition to national health insurance proposals.) Physicians could join just the county and state medical societies and not have to join (and thus not remit part of their dues) to the AMA. Many state medical societies, however, continued to include the AMA's dues as part of their own dues structure. (These state societies were referred to as being "unified.")

AMA dues were relatively low during this time (in 1958 annual dues were $25), and physicians perceived that the benefits of AMA membership exceeded the relatively small cost. Since AMA membership was quite large, representing approximately 74 percent of all physicians, the free rider problem was not extensive.

As the dues increased, however, the number of unified medical societies declined. Currently, only five state medical societies are unified. Since the benefits offered physicians by the county medical society are more limited, state and county medical societies are fearful of losing members if they continue to be unified and include the AMA's annual dues with their own. As the cost of the annual AMA membership rose (over $400 a year) compared to perceived benefits, AMA membership declined to 45 percent of all physicians. Many physicians decided to take a free ride on the AMA's legislative efforts.

To raise sufficient funds to continue their lobbying efforts, the AMA has tried to sell private services to physicians, thereby making it worthwhile for them to join. Savings on participation in retirement plans, e.g., Keogh investment plans; educational programs; and journals are important inducements for membership. In addition, the AMA is providing incentives to their state medical societies, for example, offering the state additional delegates in the AMA's House of Delegates, if they become unified state medical societies.

American Dental Association

The ADA has perhaps the most effective system for overcoming the free rider problem. Membership in the ADA is tied to membership in the local dental society.[13] Part of the dues is remitted to the national organization. A dentist, however, does not need a hospital to practice. Thus other inducements are necessary to have dentists join their local society. Malpractice insurance, which is sold by the state dental association, is the main benefit. Another service provided by some state dental associations is the use of credit cards in patient payment and collection. The ADA also provides some private services in return for part of the dentist's dues: they offer life and disability insurance, retirement plans, and access to educational programs. Currently, approximately 75 percent of dentists are members of the ADA and their local societies.

The dues that can be charged for "private" services to induce dentists to join their local societies are less than if membership were required to earn a living, as was previously the case for physicians. For example, a drive by the Florida dental society to increase its membership found that nonmembers cited the high annual dues as the main reason for not joining.[14]

American Nurses Association

The ANA is a federation of state nursing associations. A registered nurse who is a member of a state nursing association is automatically a member of the national nursing association. This organizational structure was adopted in 1982. Previously, nurses could join the ANA directly or join the state association without becoming a member of the national organization. Currently, membership dues vary based on whether the member is also covered by collective bargaining (Category 1 membership). Category 1 members pay $515 to the state association, $85 to the national association, plus $25–$50 to the local association, for a total of $625–$650 in annual dues. Other members pay less, between $310–$318 annually.

As of 1993, less than 10 percent of all registered nurses were members of the ANA. This low membership percentage has been fairly constant over time.

There are a number of reasons why membership in nursing associations is such a small portion of all trained nurses. Previously, the number of employed nurses as a percentage of the total number of nurses (the participation rate) was approximately 50 percent. Starting in the late 1960s, the participation rate increased, in part because of increased nurses' wages, to where it is now—approximately 80 percent. Those nurses not working are generally not seeking employment. Further, employed nurses are not all working full time. Nurse employment, as mentioned previously, varies according to the life cycle of the nurse. After graduation, the nurse participation rate is high. After marriage and the birth of children the participation rate falls, and then increases again as the children become older. Nurses also have generally not been the primary wage earner in a family. Thus many nurses have not viewed membership in nursing associations as important to either their careers or to their ability to find a job. Nurses sought jobs in those areas where their spouse was employed. To many nurses the costs of ANA membership exceeded any of its economic advantages.

In addition to all of the above, it has been very difficult for the ANA to overcome the free rider problem. To increase membership, the ANA and state nursing associations are involved in several activities. They are attempting to become the collective bargaining unit for representing hospital-employed nurses. Once a hospital signs a collective bargaining contract with a nursing association, all registered nurses in that hospital, as well as future employed nurses, become members of the state and, consequently, national association. This is the strategy used successfully by unions.

State nursing associations are also offering various "private" services, such as insurance coverages, loans, retirement plans, and discounts on purchases of automobiles, to induce nurses to join. As indicated by their low membership statistics, the ANA has a long way to go before they can state before any legislative body that they represent all nurses. (Before the ANA can represent the interests of nurses, they must first determine what those common interests are, i.e., whether they are related to nuclear testing, women's concerns, or economic issues.)

American Hospital Association

There are about 6,700 hospitals in the United States. Of these, 4,800, or approximately 72 percent, belong to the AHA. The membership dues vary according to the size of the hospital. Hospitals can also join their state associations without having to join the AHA. When hospitals were reimbursed according to their costs, the size of their membership dues was not a concern. As hospital occupancies fell and as the hospital market became more competitive, hospitals have been attempting to reduce their costs. It is likely that in the years ahead more hospitals will attempt to receive a free ride from the AHA's legislative activities. Similar to the other associations, the AHA offers a number of private services, such as educational programs and data reporting services, to make it economically beneficial for hospitals to remain as members.

Costs of Organizing a Group

The greater the costs of organizing a group, the less likely that the group will be formed. Conversely greater similarity of interests among its potential members and ease in overcoming the free rider problem, as in the case of unions, lower the costs of organizing a group and increase the likelihood that an association will be formed. Another important organizational cost relates to the size of the group. The larger the group, the more difficult it will be to organize its members. Although unions are very large today, the first unions to organize were small craft unions, such as printers, workers in the building trades, and shoemakers. Employees in large factories, such as automobile production with their greater organization costs, organized later.[15] These union locals are then joined together in a national organization, which in turn provides collective benefits to each local.

This pattern of growth was very similar for the AMA. Physicians were more likely to join the county society for the benefits the local society could provide. The AMA was then a federation of local societies, as were unions.

In addition, the fewer the number of members in a group, the easier it is for the group to monitor the performance of its members. Peer pressure can be placed on each firm or professional to contribute to the group. Each firm will perceive that it has a large stake in the outcome because the benefits will be distributed over a smaller number of firms.

Size of the Potential Benefits

As the potential benefits from legislation increase, the rewards to the firms from organizing are greater. If the potential benefits are relatively small, then each firm is unlikely to contribute (invest) a great deal of money. However, as the potential benefits increase, so should the firm's willingness to invest.

One major reason changes in the payment and delivery of medical services has occurred is that the potential benefits of instituting changes became very large to two groups, the federal government and business. (Government and business developed a "concentrated interest" in cost containment.) As expenditures for medical care kept rising rapidly, the federal government and business had to keep funding these increases. Business found it increasingly difficult to pass these cost increases on in the form of higher prices. The federal government was concerned with having to continually raise Medicare Social Security taxes to pay for hospital benefits under Medicare. The potential savings from more stringent cost-containment policies made such efforts worthwhile to both groups.

Conversely, in those cases where the benefits from regulation have declined, the regulated firms and their associations were not willing to spend a great deal to maintain those legislated benefits. An example of this occurred in the railroad and airline industries. The respective regulatory agencies had set high (compared to cost) prices for both rail and air travel. Profits, however, from these high (compared to cost) prices were eroded by entry of new firms (trucks), and by nonprice competition from existing firms (the airlines). These regulated firms eventually concluded that the benefits of regulation were no longer sufficient to spend the necessary funds to maintain their regulated status. (The reasons for deregulation are discussed more fully in Chapter 5.)

Uncertainty

If the effects of legislative change are uncertain, that is, it is not clear who will benefit and who will lose or what the size of those expected benefits or losses will be, then a group is less likely to organize to achieve favorable legislation or forestall unfavorable legislation. Advocates of the status quo are more often represented than proponents for change because both the size of the benefits and its recipients are more uncertain to those benefiting from the change.

Those benefiting from the status quo are more knowledgeable regarding any change in their status. There is often more information available to the existing firms than to potential beneficiaries or losers. When legislation is proposed that will impose costs on existing firms, for example, mandating pollution control devices on electric utilities, these same firms will be more knowledgeable about the costs of that legislation than will the beneficiaries of the legislation's positive effects. Thus the existing firms are more likely to organize and represent their interests.

Greater certainty about the effects of legislation and about which groups receive the benefits or bear the burden increases the likelihood that those groups will organize to represent their interests. Research that provides information as to the consequences of legislation, and the subsequent publicizing of that information, should increase certainty as to the legislation's effects. This should increase the number of groups organizing to represent their interests.

The following examples illustrate the importance of uncertainty in determining legislative outcomes.

An example of producer groups that have been legislatively successful are the auto industry and the auto union, who were able to impose "voluntary" import quotas on Japanese autos. The auto industry has few firms and one union, the United Auto Workers (UAW). Auto plants are also located in many states, which increases the number of senators who would favor such protectionist legislation. The benefits of such a trade restriction to both the industry and its union are known with fairly high certainty. The costs are diffuse; they are borne by auto purchasers. While the higher auto prices that result from this protection are obvious to some auto buyers, they are not obvious to many others. Further, the proponents of voluntary quotas attempt to create uncertainty about the cost of this protection by claiming that if auto workers are laid off, the public will have to pay increased taxes to care for unemployed workers. Thus the costs to the public of restrictive trade policies are diffuse and uncertain.

Previously, medical societies were successful in having state legislation enacted making it difficult for persons to start prepaid (HMO) health plans. (These plans could not advertise, they had to be nonprofit, they could not exclude any physician from participating, and physicians had to make up a majority of the board.) Organized medicine viewed such organizations as competitors to the solo, fee-for-service physician and wanted to eliminate such competition. There were few of these organizations available before the mid-1970s, thus the public was unaware of the advantages of participating in this form of medical delivery system. The public also had a diffuse interest with regard to medical expenditures. The potential beneficiaries of prepaid plans therefore did not organize to represent their interests. Physician organizations, because they had a concentrated interest in how medical services were both paid for and delivered, understood the potential consequences to their members if prepaid health plans were established.

Another example where current producers are more knowledgeable about the effects of proposed legislation is the issue of preferred provider organizations (PPOs), an organization of providers who have agreed to sell their services at a lower price than that which prevails in the market. To receive the price reductions, patients can only go to those providers who are participating in the PPO. PPOs may be started by insurance companies or by providers themselves. If PPOs did not exist, then patients would not be locked in to a particular set of providers (e.g., dentists). While all dentists are able to join a PPO, they have to accept lower fees to do so. PPOs are therefore a means of stimulating price competition among providers.

The ADA and state dental societies have attempted to prohibit the development of dental PPOs by making them illegal. Aware of the negative effect on their members' incomes if dental PPOs are established, dental societies in various states have lobbied their legislatures to have them prohibited. The beneficiaries of dental care PPOs, namely the patients and purchasers of dental services, generally do not know what PPOs are, let alone know their beneficial effects. This lack of information and uncertainty over the size of the benefits has kept the public out of the controversy and left it up to the dental societies and the insurance companies to determine the outcome of state legislation regarding dental PPOs.

The development of new healthcare delivery systems has been inhibited because of lack of information and uncertainty. Existing providers have a better understanding of the adverse effects on their incomes of new delivery systems, such as HMOs and other forms of prepaid health care, while the beneficiaries—the public—are unaware. Potential new firms are not represented in the legislative arena. Existing physicians and the medical societies that represent them, are already organized and are aware of the effects of innovation on their incomes. It is for this reason that changes in the status quo in medicine have taken so long to occur.

Concluding Comments

It is to be expected that groups with a special interest will lobby for their members' interests before Congress. However, to understand why certain special interest groups are more successful than others in achieving their legislative demands requires an analysis of the organization of an interest group itself. If a group is to be formed, health professionals and firms must find it in their interest to join. If they can be coerced into joining, no one can receive a free ride. If coercion is not possible, then sufficient economic incentives must be provided to make it economically worthwhile to join. Otherwise the organization will not be able to raise sufficient funds to lobby for the group's legislative interests.

In the past, membership in the county medical society was a necessity if a physician was to practice in a hospital and earn an income. At that time it was important for the national organization (the AMA) to convince the local organizations to belong to the national organization. The membership structure of the ADA required membership in the national organization if the individual dentist joined the local society. Traditionally, local associations have been more important to the careers and income goals of health professionals than national associations. Important to the success of the national organization, therefore, is its ability to tie membership in the local society to the national association.

To induce health professionals to join their local society requires that the perceived benefits of membership exceed the professional's costs (dues). The medical society offered the strongest of incentives, a physician's ability to practice. Other societies (and medical societies currently) attempt to sell private services to their members, e.g., journals, educational programs, retirement plans, and malpractice insurance. To the extent these can be offered at a lower price than the individual can purchase otherwise, the individual has an incentive to join. However, the amount of dues that can be raised in this way to support lobbying efforts at the national level depends upon the value to the practitioner of these economic incentives.[16]

American Nurses Association

The nursing associations have had the most difficulty in organizing their members. The interests of their members are not as similar nor as singular as in other professions. There are few incentives for nurses to join their local society, there are a greater number of members to organize, and their members are less aware of the potential legislative benefits of membership. Nursing associations have been ambivalent in acting as a unionizing agent for nurses. However, as other unions have tried to organize nurses, nursing associations have begun to assist in unionizing for fear of losing members. Unless nurse associations can replicate the unions in overcoming the free rider problem, it is unlikely that the reasons for low membership in state and national nursing associations can be easily overcome.

American Dental Association

The ADA has many of the necessary ingredients for a successful health association. Its members are relatively homogeneous and they are required to join the national organization as a condition to joining the local dental society. However, the amount of dues that the local society can charge is limited by the nature of the economic benefits they can provide. The ADA has been relatively successful in the legislative arena. Also, state dental societies have been able to reduce the potential for price competition among dentists by limiting dentists' productivity increases; the tasks that can be performed by nondentists, i.e., dental auxiliaries, have been limited by state law so that productivity increases do not exceed increases in demand for services. Further, potential substitutes such as denturists (dental technicians that sell dentures directly to the public) are legal in only several states, and this only since 1977. Dentists have been relatively successful in reducing—to a great degree, legislatively—their competition.

Although the ADA has many attributes of a successful association, it is concerned over its ability to be the sole representative and voice of the dental profession. Some strains within the profession are beginning to show. In part these concerns are a result of the changing economic situation. There are large numbers of younger dentists as a result of the past expansion of dental schools. There is increased competition among dentists; an increase in the number of corporate dental clinics, advertising, and dental PPOs; greater emphasis by business and insurance companies on cost containment; and some questioning by specialists of the ability of their generalist colleagues. Various groups within dentistry, such as the dental examiners, dental schools, and dental researchers, believe themselves to be underrepresented in the ADA's House of Delegates. There is a growing divergence among dentists in their economic interests, for example, solo-practice dentists are opposed to corporate dental clinics. These concerns led to the formation of a special study group to examine "Fragmentation of the Association and the Profession."[17]

American Hospital Association

The AHA faces difficult times in its role of hospital advocate. The federal government is attempting to limit increases in hospital expenditures under Medicare; there is increased competition among hospitals; many member hospitals may be forced to close; and the growing divergence in economic interests between different types of hospitals, for example, small and rural hospitals, teaching hospitals, and for-profit hospitals, makes it more difficult for the AHA to lobby for legislation beneficial to all its constituencies. Increased legislative benefits for one group of hospitals is likely to come only at the expense of other hospitals.

American Medical Association

While still politically influential, the AMA is unlikely to recover the legislative influence it once had. This decline in influence is due to three reasons. First, its membership has become more heterogeneous with differing economic interests. There are more women and minorities in the profession and more physicians are working as part of large managed care organizations rather than as fee-for-service practitioners. With the rapid expansion in the supply of physicians, physicians are engaged in greater market competition. Favoring one type of delivery system (fee-for-service) over others (capitation), brings the AMA into conflict with physicians that work in these other settings.

Second, the new Medicare physician payment system forced each medical specialty into conflict with every other specialty. The "budget neutrality" of the legislation split the medical profession into specialty groups with opposing concentrated interests. Increased fees for one group can only come at the expense of others. Each specialty was forced to represent its interests in the legislative marketplace.

Given the divergent economic interests within the medical profession, the AMA is being forced to favor the more narrow economic interests of some of its members and thereby limit the AMA's credibility as the sole representative of organized medicine.

Third, the rise of competing groups with a concentrated interest has affected the legislative success of the AMA.[18] Podiatrists and chiropractors have formed their own lobbying organizations, as the potential benefits from organizing have increased.[19] Other professions, such as physician's assistants and nurse practitioners, are also seeking to have greater leeway in the types of tasks they are permitted to perform and to be reimbursed independently of the physician for their services. Being included in public programs, such as Medicare and Medicaid, offers greatly increased incomes to members of these other professions. Changing legislation enabling members of these other associations to perform a greater number of tasks offers large potential rewards to these practitioners.

Other interest groups have also formed to represent their members' interests. Business groups, such as the Washington Business Group on Health, now realize that large savings can be achieved from increased legislative involvement. Businesses are opposed to legislation that would increase their employees' health costs (such as mandating increased health benefits by employers), while favoring legislation (such as HMOs), that offer the potential for reducing the rise in their employees' health insurance premiums. Similarly, the large potential savings to the federal government from reducing expenditures on public medical programs provides the federal government an incentive to represent, legislatively, its own interests more strongly.

An increase in the number of organized groups with divergent economic interests raises the cost and thereby diminishes the likelihood that any one group will be successful in achieving all of its legislative aims. The rise of opposing interest groups diminishes the AMA's political influence.

Study Questions for Chapter 3

1. Why is it necessary for an organization to overcome the "free rider" problem if it is to be successful in achieving its legislative objectives?
2. What are some of the approaches used by health associations to overcome the "free rider" problem?
3. Discuss the characteristics that an association should have if it is to be successful in achieving its legislative agenda.
4. How has the federal government's "budget neutral" financing methods under Medicare (RBRVSs for physicians and DRGs for hospitals) affected the American Medical Association's and the American Hospital Association's ability to represent their constituents' interests?
5. Of the American Dental Association and the American Nurses Association, which organization is more likely to be successful in representing the legislative interests of its members?

Notes

1. Data on internal rates of return to a physician's education from the 1930s through the 1980s are summarized in Paul J. Feldstein. 1993. *Health Care Economics.* New York: Delmar Publishing Co. 356. Data on nurses' incomes compared to those of comparable professions are presented on pages 402–403.
2. James G. Burrow. 1963. *AMA: Voice of American Medicine.* Baltimore: The Johns Hopkins Press. 7–8.
3. If limits were placed on the tasks that physicians could perform, then different educational and licensure requirements would be appropriate. There has never been a career ladder in medicine. All physicians take the same basic four years of college and then four years of medical school and then a residency requirement. It does not matter that the training of a family practitioner can be accomplished in fewer years or with a different curriculum than for a neurosurgeon. Thus a physician can be an anesthesiologist with no additional training, with additional training, or with board certification. They can all charge the same price. A career ladder would make it easier to become a physician; nurses could become physicians with some additional training. It would have been more difficult for the AMA to limit the supply of physicians if advancement were based on tests and additional training.

4. Malpractice should be an effective limitation on the tasks performed by a physician. However, the malpractice system has not always performed up to expectations in this regard.

5. "Current Attitudes in Health Care: Physician Attitude Survey," *Socioeconomic Report*, Bureau of Research and Planning, California Medical Association, 26 (6) 2–3.

6. Ibid., 5.

7. Ibid., 7.

8. John Colombotos and Corinne Kirchner. 1986. *Physicians and Social Change*. New York: Oxford University Press. 105–6.

9. *AHA: Inside Out. A Guide to the American Hospital Association*. Chicago: American Hospital Association. 6–7.

10. For a discussion of the free rider problem, as well as its application to unions, see Mancur Olson. 1965. *The Logic of Collective Action*. Cambridge: Harvard University Press.

11. Ibid., 133. In a study of a large number of interest groups, Walker found that the proliferation of nonprofit interest groups in the last 20 years, (i.e., groups whose constituents were not members of the same occupation), was a result of financial support from outside sources, rather than from the sale of private services to its members. These groups were generally the least homogeneous in membership. Examples of these "citizen" groups are civil rights groups, peace organizations, and groups representing the handicapped. The funding required to start and maintain these groups came from government agencies through grants and contracts, e.g., to increase public understanding, for the training of professionals. The government agencies attempted to further their own political objectives through this funding to outside groups (p. 402). Other sources of funds for such groups came from patrons of political action, e.g., the UAW and aging organizations. Without such outside support these groups would not have been able to overcome the free rider problem and generate sufficient funds to organize. Jack L. Walker. 1983. "The Origins and Maintenance of Interest Groups in America," *The American Political Science Review* 77 (2) 390–406.

12. The Mundt resolution, which was declared unconstitutional in the mid-1960s, required that the entire medical staff of a hospital be members of the county medical society if the hospital was to be approved for intern and residency training. Physicians wanted their hospitals to have interns and residents since they increase physician productivity. Membership in the county medical society was also a prerequisite if a physician wanted to take examinations for various specialty boards. For a more complete discussion of the control mechanisms used by organized medicine over the behavior of individual physicians, see Reuben Kessel. 1958. "Price Discrimination in Medicine," *The Journal of Law and Economics* 1 (October).

13. Membership in the ADA is a three-tiered system. "The system by bylaw, that a dentist must pay dues to the component society, constituent society, and ADA in order to join the local dental society." (*The ADA News*, September 26, 1983, p. 1.)

   In April 1972, four dentists sued the ADA on grounds that the three-tiered membership system violated the antitrust laws. The dentists lost and the ADA's membership system was retained.

14. *The ADA News*, October 24, 1983, 2. At the time the annual dues were $400.

15. Olson, *The Logic of Collective Action*, 66.

16. The less price elastic the demand for these private services, the higher the price at which they can be sold.

17. April 14, 1986 "Final Report of the Special Committee on Fragmentation of the Association and the Profession," *American Dental Association*.

18. According to Becker, the political effectiveness of a group is determined not just by its absolute efficiency (i.e., "its absolute skill at controlling free riding—but by its efficiency relative to the efficiency of other groups.") Gary S. Becker. 1983. "A Theory of Competition Among Pressure Groups For Political Influence," *Quarterly Journal of Economics* 98 (3) 371–400.

19. In addition to a change in the magnitude of benefits (or costs), other reasons an unorganized constituency may become legislatively involved are the ability to overcome the free rider problem and a reduction in both the costs of information and of organizing.

THE DEMAND FOR LEGISLATION BY HEALTH ASSOCIATIONS

The Motivation of Health Associations
Framework for Analyzing Legislative Behavior
    Demand-Increasing Legislation
    Securing the Highest Method of Reimbursement
    Legislation to Reduce the Price and/or Increase the Quantity
       of Complements
    Legislation to Decrease the Availability and/or Increase the
       Price of Substitutes
    Legislation to Limit Increases in Supply
Implications of the Legislative Success of Health Associations

Health interest groups demand legislation that is in their members' interests. It is necessary, however, to go beyond that statement. Health associations, such as the American Medical Association (AMA), have claimed that they are educational organizations, not trade associations representing the narrow economic interests of their members.[1] Further, such associations claim that the legislation they favor is in the public's interest; they are concerned with quality rather than economic interests. Thus it is important to be specific about the types of legislation on which health associations take a position. For example, do health associations such as the AMA favor measures that increase quality regardless of the effect on their members' incomes, or do they favor only those quality measures that increase their members' incomes?

Chapter 4 is adapted from Paul J. Feldstein. 1993. *Health Care Economics*, 4th ed. Albany, New York: Delmar Publishing Inc. 424–54.

It is necessary to use a framework for examining health legislation. The framework lets us understand which types of legislation are in the economic interests of health associations' members. It indicates the types of legislation health associations favor or oppose, since it is not always obvious how certain types of legislation promote the economic interests of association members. The AMA has had a great deal of political influence at both the state and federal level. Understanding which legislation is both preferred and opposed by the AMA explains much of the type of health legislation this country has or has not had, particularly in the period up to the 1980s. This model also helps to predict the types of legislation health associations will favor or oppose in the years ahead.

First it is necessary to describe what is meant by the economic interests of health association members. After all, some health associations, such as the American Hospital Association (AHA) and the Association of American Medical Colleges (AAMC), are representatives of nonprofit organizations. Once the economic interests of health association members are defined it becomes possible to demonstrate how particular legislation works to enhance members' interests. The validity of the proposed framework can be tested by how well it predicts the political positions of the various health associations. Without a definition of interests and a legislative framework, it would not be obvious how specific legislation promotes the economic interests of the members of a health association. The final section of this chapter discusses the implications of the political behavior of health associations on the financing, quality, and organization of the healthcare delivery system.

The Motivation of Health Associations

Health associations demand legislation that serves the interests of their members. Without a definition of those interests, however, it would not be obvious how specific legislation promotes the members' perception of these interests.

Health professionals and health organizations, such as hospitals, have many goals. Even within the same profession, individuals place different weights on what they perceive to be their self-interest. The tendency, therefore, is to make the definition of self-interest complex. However, if the definition is complex, encompassing this diversity, or if different motivations are specified for each piece of legislation, then it is not possible to develop a good predictive model. While it may seem more realistic to develop a complex goal statement, it is easier to evaluate the effects of legislation using a simple one. Besides, unless the membership easily understands the goal that its association is pursuing, the members may be distressed over the activities the association is engaged in. The true test of whether the simply defined goal accurately measures member self-interest is how well it predicts the association's legislative behavior.

The legislative goal of associations with individuals as members—physicians, dentists, nurses, optometrists—is assumed to be to *maximize the incomes of its current members*. Health professionals are no different from other individuals; they will say that they have many goals, of which income is only one. However, income is the only goal that all the members have in common. (Goals such as increased autonomy and control over their practice are highly correlated with increased incomes. Income is thus a more general goal.)

Nonprofit institutions—hospitals, Blue Cross, and medical and dental schools—cannot retain profits. Medical and dental schools are assumed to be interested in maximizing the prestige of their institution. Prestige for a medical school is defined as having students who wish to become professors and researchers themselves, a faculty that is primarily interested in research, and a low student-to-faculty ratio. Little prestige accrues to a medical school that trains students to enter family practice or to practice in underserved areas.

Until the mid-1980s, when hospitals were reimbursed according to their costs, hospitals were also interested in maximizing their prestige, which is indicated by a hospital's size and the number of facilities and services it offers. Administrators of large, prestigious hospitals were held in esteem by their peers and earned higher incomes. Each hospital attempted to become a medical center. The availability of a full range of services also made it easier for the hospital to attract physicians to its staff.

Beginning in the early 1980s, hospital objectives began to change. The payment system for hospital care went from cost-based reimbursement to fixed prices; hospitals engaged in price competition to increase their volume of patients from insurers and HMOs; low-cost substitutes for hospitals, such as outpatient surgery centers, began to reduce hospital utilization, as did utilization review programs.[2] As these changes occurred, hospitals became more concerned with survival than with emulating major teaching institutions. Even teaching hospitals began to act as though their future was in doubt. Hospitals began to minimize their costs, dropped money-losing services and patients, and gave greater consideration to the profitability of their investments. To succeed in a more competitive environment, hospitals attempted to minimize their costs and to act as though they were trying to maximize their profits.

Blue Cross and Blue Shield plans were originally started by hospitals and physicians, respectively. Hospitals provided the initial capital to

Blue Cross plans and controlled the organization. The same was true for medical societies and Blue Shield plans. It was not until the 1970s that these nonprofit organizations separated from the providers that controlled them. Until that time, therefore, the objectives of Blue Cross and Blue Shield plans were to serve their providers' interests.

During the period when Blue Cross and Blue Shield were controlled by their respective providers, their methods of provider payment and their benefit structure were in accordance with the economic interests of hospitals and physicians. These policies also coincided with the interests of the organizations' managers. Nonprofit organizations want to grow. A larger organization provides management with greater responsibility, and that justifies higher incomes. Like any nonprofit bureaucracy, these organizations also have some form of satisficing behavior as a goal; namely, extra personnel, larger facilities, and higher wages than if these organizations were in a very competitive industry.

As the healthcare sector became more competitive in the early 1980s, competition between Blue Cross and Blue Shield plans and commercial insurance companies increased. To survive in this new marketplace, Blue Cross and Blue Shield began to merge. While these organizations remained nonprofit, their behavior became similar to for-profit insurance companies. By attempting to minimize costs, increase market share, and respond to employer demands on benefit design, Blue Cross and Blue Shield acted as though they were attempting to maximize profits. An adversarial relationship began to replace their previously cooperative association with hospitals and physicians.[3] (In the early 1990s, several Blue Cross plans, such as California Blue Cross, actually transformed themselves into for-profit organizations.) In analyzing the legislative behavior of Blue Cross and Blue Shield plans it is important to keep in mind the periods when their objectives differed.

Although differences existed in the objectives of health associations representing health professionals, hospitals, medical and dental schools, and Blue Cross and Blue Shield plans, the members of these associations all tried to make as much money as possible. They would then retain it for themselves, as did health professionals, or spend it to achieve prestige goals, as did hospitals and medical schools; the incomes of employees of prestigious institutions are likely to exceed those of less prestigious institutions. Thus the objective underlying the demand for legislation is the same for each health association. *Each association attempts to achieve for its members through legislation what cannot be achieved through a competitive market, namely, a monopoly position.* Increased monopoly power and the ability to price as a monopolist seller of services was, and is, the best way for the associations to achieve their goals.

Framework for Analyzing Legislative Behavior

There are five types of legislation that health associations demand on behalf of their members. As government policy shifted from increasing to decreasing health expenditures (given the concern over the budget deficit) the emphasis devoted to each of these types of legislation by health interest groups has changed over time.

There are several caveats to this model. The above model should predict an association's political position on legislation according to the earlier definition of its members' interests. However, it may occasionally be observed that the association takes a political position different than expected. Before concluding that the above framework is inaccurate, the following must be determined.

Is the association's preferred position no longer politically possible? No health professional association favors reexamination for licensure. Some of its members may not be able to pass the exam. If the examination is made so simple that all members can pass, then nonmembers would claim they should be allowed to enter the profession because they could pass the examination. If there is a great deal of pressure from the media, for example, for reexamination, the profession may propose a less costly alternative—continuing education. The association would not normally propose continuing education, because it imposes some costs on its members. However, to forestall an even more costly policy the association comes out in favor of it. Thus the association's policy on continuing education, while not its preferred position, is consistent with the model's predictions.

Another example where it may appear that the political position of an association diverges from its members' interests occurs when the cost of taking a position exceeds its potential benefits. The AHA's position on the applicability of minimum wage laws to hospital employees is an example. Minimum wage laws increase the cost of labor to hospitals. For many years the AHA was successful in exempting hospitals from such legislation. As hospital wages began to increase, most hospital employees earned in excess of the minimum wage. Thus its applicability to hospitals would have had a small effect. When removal of the hospital exemption was once again proposed, the AHA decided not to oppose it. Not only would the effect have been small, but the AHA determined that the legislation would have passed over its objections. The AHA decided that it would be a needless loss of political capital to oppose it.

Except for these caveats mentioned, health associations are expected to act in accordance with their members' economic interests. The five types of legislation each association either favors or opposes are based on the above economic framework.

Demand-Increasing Legislation

An association favors demand-increasing legislation since an increase in demand, with a given supply, will result in an increase in price, an increase in total revenue, and, consequently, an increase in incomes or net revenues.

The most obvious way to increase the demand for the services of an association's members is to have the government subsidize the purchase of insurance for the provider's services. Health providers, however, do not want the government insuring everyone. Instead, the providers' demand for insurance subsidies was always discussed in relation to specific population groups within society, i.e., people with low incomes. The reason for selective government subsidies is twofold: first, people with higher incomes presumably have private insurance coverage or can afford to purchase the provider's services; therefore, the greatest increase in demand would result from extending coverage to those unable to pay. Second, extending government subsidies to those currently able to pay for the services would greatly increase the cost of the program to the government. A greater commitment of government expenditures would result in the government developing a concentrated interest in controlling the provider's prices, utilization, and expenditures. Thus when demand subsidies were favored by health associations, they are always in relation to specific population groups or services rather than to the population at large.

Examples of the above approach were the AMA's position on national health insurance, Medicare, and Blue Shield. The AMA successfully defeated President Truman's national health insurance proposal in 1948 because subsidies would have been provided to all regardless of income level. The AMA's opposition to Medicare was also based on the fact that all aged, regardless of income, were to be subsidized (see Chapter 9). Instead, the approach favored by the AMA was a system of tax credits for the purchase of health insurance, which would decline as a person's income rose.

In more recent years, as concern with the federal deficit has increased and federal funds to subsidize those with low incomes were unlikely to be available, the AMA has favored an employer mandate, whereby employers are required to purchase health insurance on behalf of their employees. An employer mandate would increase the demand for physician services by requiring the working uninsured to have private coverage. It would also move low-income employees and their families off Medicaid onto private insurance, which also reimburses providers at a higher rate. (The AMA's position on President Clinton's health reform is discussed more completely in Chapter 10.)

In the 1930s and 1940s when medical societies developed (and controlled) Blue Shield, it only provided coverage for physician services (not for physician substitutes) and paid the physician's bill in full only if the patient's income was below a certain level (originally $7,500 a year). A low-income person purchasing Blue Shield would increase their use of physician services and not be concerned with which physician had a lower price. (The demand for physician services was increased and physicians did not have to compete on price for that business.) If the subscriber's income exceeded $7,500, the physician was permitted to charge the patient an additional amount above the Blue Shield payment (referred to as "balance billing"). Higher-income patients could afford to pay more.

The American Dental Association's (ADA) major demand-increasing effort has been to expand private insurance coverage for dental services. Insurance is generally purchased for events that are very expensive, such as hospital care and in-hospital physician services, and that have a low probability of occurring. Dental expenditures, which are relatively small, expected, and not catastrophic, are therefore not insurable in the same sense as hospital or surgical services; in fact, dental prepayment is not really insurance but a form of forced savings.

If special incentives to purchase dental insurance did not exist, most people would just pay for dental care when they needed it. The use of dental services is also highly related to income.[4] Thus a major reason for the growth in dental insurance has been the favorable tax treatment of employer-paid health insurance premiums. Such contributions are not considered part of the employee's income; the employee does not have to pay federal, state, or Social Security taxes on employer-paid health benefits.

During the 1970s, when the demand for dental insurance grew rapidly, the top income tax bracket was 70 percent. In addition, the person would have to pay Social Security and state income taxes on additional earned income. For middle-income and high-income people, the after-tax value of a $1,000 raise would be reduced by these three taxes, leaving the individual with perhaps one-half of that amount to spend on out-of-pocket medical payments, dental care, vision benefits, etc. If instead the employer used the $1,000 to purchase more comprehensive health insurance for the employee, the employee could receive $1,000 worth of health benefits.

The exclusion of employer-paid health benefits from the employee's taxable income results in a large revenue loss to the federal and state governments. The lost tax revenue (excluding state taxes) from this tax exclusion in 1994 was estimated to be $74 billion dollars.[5] The beneficiaries of this tax exclusion are clearly those in the upper-income groups. Eliminating or "capping" the amount of employer-paid health benefits that are excluded from taxable income has been proposed in some healthcare reform proposals as a means of raising revenues to finance health benefits for those with low incomes. Economists have also favored eliminating or reducing this tax subsidy for the purchase of health insurance because it would make employees more cost conscious in their choice of health plans, selecting a more expensive health plan would have to be paid with after-tax dollars.

The ADA's major legislative strategy in the last several years has been to defeat any such tax cap. If a tax cap were passed, employees would want less comprehensive health benefits because they would have to pay for additional benefits with after-tax dollars. The ADA believes, and rightly so, that if the tax discount for purchasing dental insurance were eliminated, the incentive for employees to purchase such insurance would decline. With less dental insurance, consumers would have to pay the full price of dental care. The demand for dental care would decline and consumers would be more inclined to "shop" among dentists for the lowest price.

Additional approaches used by the ADA to increase the demand for dental care involve lobbying to include dental benefits in federal employees' health benefits; permitting dependents of military personnel to have free choice of civilian dentists even though military dental clinics are available; including dental benefits as part of Medicare Part B, as well as lobbying for increased funding of dental benefits as part of state Medicaid programs; and promoting the inclusion of dental care as part of the benefits of health maintenance organizations.[6]

The American Nurses Association (ANA) has favored three types of demand-increasing legislation. The first are proposals that increase the demand for medical services. An example is the ANA's support for national health insurance. Increases in demand for medical services would increase the demand for institutions in which RNs are employed, thereby increasing the demand for RNs. However, since health insurance coverage for hospital care is more extensive than for any other delivery settings (and two-thirds of nurses work in hospitals), nurse associations have also favored other demand-increasing proposals. For instance, the ANA has favored requiring minimum nurse staffing ratios in institutions for certification purposes, such as mandating that there be a minimum number of RNs on the staffs of nursing homes and home health agencies.

Second, nurse associations have opposed hospital attempts to substitute lower-paid nurse aides to perform more of the RNs' tasks, which would decrease the demand for RNs.[7]

A third type of demand-increasing proposal favored by nurse associations is one that widens the nurse's role, that is, increases the number of tasks nurses are legally able to perform. The nurses' value to the institution increases as they are permitted to perform more, and higher valued, tasks. The demand for their services will increase, with a consequent increase in their incomes. In attempting to increase their tasks, nurses have come in conflict with the AMA, which is fearful that changing state laws that limit the scope of what nurses with advanced training can do would decrease the demand for physicians.[8]

As nurses work to increase their roles, they wage a struggle in the legislative marketplace to prevent other health professionals, such as licensed practical nurses (LPNs), from performing tasks previously reserved for RNs. The ANA is also in competition with physician assistants (PAs) over which profession will be able to perform tasks previously reserved to physicians.

The health professional association that is successful in enabling its members to increase their role, while preventing other health professionals from encroaching upon their own tasks, will be able to increase the demand for, and hence the incomes of, its members. Examples of the legislative conflict over state practice acts are the attempts by optometrists to increase their role at the expense of ophthalmologists—as well as the struggles of psychologists vs. psychiatrists, obstetricians vs. nurse-midwives, and podiatrists vs. orthopedic surgeons.

The initial approach used by hospitals to increase the demand for their services was the establishment and control of Blue Cross. When hospitals started Blue Cross, Blue Cross only paid the costs of hospital care. Even if it was less expensive to perform diagnostics in an outpatient setting, for the patient with Blue Cross coverage it was less expensive to have it performed in the hospital. The patient with Blue Cross did not have to pay any additional hospital costs, thus high-cost hospitals were not at a price disadvantage with low-cost hospitals, thereby precluding price competition for Blue Cross patients. Further, every Blue Cross plan had to have at least 75 percent of the hospitals in its area participate in Blue Cross. This requirement precluded Blue Cross from contracting with only a lower-cost panel of hospitals.

As the price of hospital care became free to the Blue Cross subscriber, hospital use increased. Hospitals were reimbursed generously by Blue Cross for their services.

Legislatively, the AHA favored government subsidies to stimulate the demand for hospital services by the aged and the poor. Medicare, which provided generous hospital coverage for the aged, increased the demand for hospitals by a high-user group with generally low incomes.

Hospitals have been in the forefront of lobbying efforts to receive federal subsidies for "uncompensated care"; that is, hospital care to the poor for which hospitals are not reimbursed. In the 1990s debate over national health insurance, the AHA has favored an employer mandate, which would increase the demand for private health insurance by those who are uninsured and by those whose hospital bills are being paid by Medicaid.

The Association of American Medical Colleges has favored legislation, at both state and federal levels, that provide such schools with unrestricted operating subsidies. Such subsidies would increase the demand for medical and dental schools by enabling them to set tuition levels greatly below the actual costs of education. With artificially low tuition levels and limits on the number of students schools would accept, there would be an excess demand for their spaces. As long as there is an excess demand for a medical education—and the schools do not willingly expand their spaces to satisfy this demand—then the schools can determine the type of educational curriculum that comes closest to meeting their (and the AMA's or ADA's) preferences.

Without excess demand for a medical education, the schools would have to respond, that is, compete for applicants as would any other supplier, by providing the type of service that demanders were willing to pay. These schools have a monopoly over the provision of medical and dental education. By charging tuition levels that were so low as to encourage excess demand for such an education, the schools are able to select the type of students they prefer. The schools are thereby able to establish the training times and educational requirements for entering the profession. These policies are also in the economic interest of physicians and dentists since they lead to higher incomes.

Securing the Highest Method of Reimbursement

Regardless of whether the association member's goal is income, prestige, or growth, the method by which the provider is reimbursed is crucial to attainment of that goal. High prices, resulting in large net revenues, increase incomes and enable institutions to achieve their objectives through the expenditure of those revenues. The method of reimbursement, or the method used by the provider to charge for their services, has been crucial to understanding provider economic behavior.

Two basic approaches have been used by health associations to achieve the highest possible reimbursement for their members. The first has been to try to eliminate price competition among their members. The ability to engage in price competition is more important to new practitioners or firms desiring to enter a market. New competitors must be able to let potential patients know (through advertising) they are available and new surgeons must be able to provide primary care physicians with an incentive (fee splitting) to switch their surgical referrals away from established surgeons.

To prevent price competition from occurring, health associations have termed the elements of price competition, such as advertising and fee splitting, "unethical behavior" and have prohibited such behavior in their state practice acts.[9] The medical and dental professions have used strong sanctions against practitioners who engaged in unethical behavior. A physician could have his or her license suspended and be assessed financial penalties. Previously, medical societies were able to deny hospital privileges to physicians who advertised or engaged in price competition.[10] Without hospital privileges a physician could not offer patients complete medical service. Since physicians new to an area had the greatest incentive to engage in such "unethical" behavior, they were given probationary membership in the local medical society. They were thereby placed on notice that they could lose their hospital privileges if they engaged in such behavior. (Since the application of the antitrust laws to healthcare in 1982, such anticompetitive behavior by medical societies is no longer permitted.)

A number of studies have shown that restrictions on advertising raised the price of optometric services from 20 to 50 percent.[11] (Most of the studies on advertising in the health field have been conducted on prescription drugs and optometric services.) The American Optometric Association (AOA) has claimed (without offering evidence) that higher prices reflect higher-quality services. In 1980, the Federal Trade Commission (FTC) attempted to resolve the issue of quality and advertising. The FTC took seven people with similar visual conditions and trained them at two optometric schools with regard to the optometric exam. When these seven subjects went to specified optometrists, they recorded the price charged, the amount of time spent by the optometrist, and specific information on the tests and procedures performed. These subjects went to cities where advertising was prohibited as well as to cities where it was permitted. In cities that permitted advertising, they visited optometrists who advertised as well as those who did not.[12]

The conclusion of the study was that removing advertising restrictions would cause prices to decline by more than 20 percent. Further, nonadvertising optometrists *in markets where advertising occurs* provide service of superior quality to those of optometrists in nonadvertising markets. Optometrists who do not advertise (in markets where other optometrists advertise) compete by lowering their price—but not by as much as optometrists who advertise, and by spending more time with their patients. Thus optometric services are lower in price and, on average, higher in quality where advertising is permitted than where it is prohibited.

Price competition and advertising are not necessarily related to the provision of low-quality services. Defining such practices as unethical could only be interpreted as a means of preventing price competition.

As a result of the FTC's successful suit against the AMA (upheld by the U.S. Supreme Court in 1982), state medical and other professional societies can no longer penalize their members if they advertise or engage in other anticompetitive activities. All professionals are now permitted to advertise. As a last attempt at forestalling competition, the AMA, ADA, and other professional groups that are regulated at the state level then tried to have Congress grant them an exemption from the FTC's jurisdiction, but were unsuccessful. Anticompetitive behavior in healthcare is now subject to the antitrust laws.

The second approach used by health providers to secure the highest possible payment for their services is to engage in price discrimination, which means charging different patients or payers different prices for the same service. These different prices do not result from differences in costs, but from the patients' or their payers' abilities to pay. Charging according to ability to pay results in greater revenues than a pricing system that charges everyone the same.

The desire by organized medicine to maintain a system whereby physicians could price-discriminate influenced the financing and delivery of medical services for many years. Once medical insurance was introduced, organized medicine attempted to retain the physician's ability to price-discriminate. For example, when medical societies started Blue Shield plans, the physician's fee was paid in full for those subscribers whose incomes were below a certain level. Physicians were permitted to charge higher-income patients an amount in addition to the Blue Shield payment. The Blue Shield income limits were eventually eliminated as the large majority of subscribers' incomes exceeded the income limit. Blue Shield insurance was not worth as much to high-income people if they had to pay a significant amount each time they went to the physician, in addition to the annual premium. As Blue Shield organizations dropped their income limits so as to be able to enroll more high-income subscribers, some medical societies dropped their sponsorship of the Blue Shield plans.

Once the income limits were removed, physicians could still maintain some ability to price-discriminate by deciding when they wanted to participate in Blue Shield and when they wanted to charge the patient directly. In the latter case, the patient would then receive payment from

Blue Shield for an amount less than the physician's charge. For persons with higher incomes, physicians would charge the patient directly, which would provide them with a higher payment than if the physician participated in Blue Shield.

The physician payment system under Medicare was based on the same principle. Physicians could decide to participate in Medicare on a case-by-case basis. If they thought they could make more money by charging the patient directly, they would do so. When they accepted the Medicare fee, the patient was responsible for a 20 percent copayment. When the physician chose not to participate, the patient had to pay the physician's fee, which was greater than the Medicare fee, and the patient was responsible for the difference in the fees as well as the copayment. By having the option of participating when they wanted to, physicians were assured of payment from low-income persons, while still being able to charge a higher price to the higher-income patient. The method of pricing and flexibility of physician participation under Blue Shield and Medicare was crucial to their acceptance of these plans.[13]

Organized medicine's desire to maintain the physician's ability to price-discriminate limited the growth of prepaid health plans. HMOs charge patients the same premium regardless of income level. When fee-for-service physicians charge higher-income patients a higher fee, then a plan that charges all persons the same premium is a form of price competition; it limits the physician's ability to price-discriminate.

In his classic article, "Price Discrimination in Medicine" (1958), Reuben Kessel describes how county and state medical societies attempted to forestall the development of prepaid group plans.[14] When physicians moved into an area with the intention of joining a prepaid plan, local medical societies prevented them from receiving hospital privileges. Unless the plan had its own hospital, which was unlikely, this effectively eliminated competition. There were several successful antitrust suits brought against medical societies for this behavior.[15] (Such suits are, however, costly and take years to resolve.) Medical societies were subsequently successful in having restrictive legislation enacted at a state level that effectively limited the growth of these plans. For example, one such restrictive statute permitted only the medical profession to control and operate such plans. In 1976, Blue Shield of Spokane, Washington, agreed to discontinue their practice of discriminating against physicians who offered their services through an HMO. Blue Shield ended its boycott only after the FTC ordered it to do so on the grounds that it was anticompetitive.

In the mid-1980s, the federal government offered to pay HMOs an annual capitated price for each Medicare enrollee (referred to as "Medicare Risk contracts"). HMOs that enroll those eligible for Medicare are reimbursed 95 percent of the average area per capita cost (AAPC) of the combined amounts of Parts A and B of Medicare. HMOs can keep the difference between the amount the government pays them and the costs of providing care for their aged enrollees. This approach increases the choices available to the Medicare patient. To attract Medicare patients from the fee-for-service system, HMOs offer additional benefits. The AMA opposed this approach and attempted to delay its implementation.

Dental societies have acted similarly with respect to advertising and price competition. Until the successful FTC suit against the AMA, dental societies included bans on advertising in their state practice acts. Since the FTC suit, a number of cases have been brought against dental societies for their failure to eliminate anticompetitive behavior. Certain dental societies have prohibited advertisements on quality, prohibited practice by a dentist under a trade name (which would adversely affect corporate dental chains), and placed restrictions on prepaid dental plans.[16]

An important recent legislative activity of many state medical and dental societies has been to enact "any willing provider" legislation, which seeks to ensure that all patients have free choice of any provider. HMOs and preferred provider organizations (PPOs) use closed panels of providers to deliver medical and dental services. Providers included in these closed panels are willing to discount their fees and practice cost effectively in return for receiving a greater volume of patients. HMOs and PPOs are thereby able to offer their services to insurers and employers at premiums lower than those prevailing in the area. Providers who are not a part of these closed panels do not have access to the HMOs' and PPOs' patient population. Providers in closed panels are engaged in price competition with providers who are not in the closed panels. By enacting "any willing provider" legislation, medical and dental societies remove providers' financial incentive to discount their fees in return for more patients. If providers in closed panels have to share their patients with providers who are not in closed panels, providers are unlikely to join closed panels and discount their fees.

If closed-panel plans are not in violation of the antitrust statutes, why is further legislation necessary to protect the public?

To enable dentists to charge what the market will bear, the ADA has favored dental insurance but not the use of insurer fee schedules. The ADA has proposed that the dentist charge the patient, with the patient being reimbursed by the insurer. In this manner the dentist would be able to raise prices. Several years ago, the Pennsylvania Blue Shield (PBS) won an antitrust suit against the Pennsylvania Dental Association (PDA) on just such an issue. Pennsylvania Blue Shield claimed that the

PDA boycotted PBS because the Blue Shield dental plan paid dentists according to a fee schedule. The PDA wanted dentists to be able to charge the patient an additional amount if they so desired.

Similar to the above, the ADA has also opposed the practice of insurance companies reimbursing a patient a lower amount if they go to a nonparticipating dentist. The ADA has called for legislation prohibiting insurance companies from this payment approach. (The dentist is not prohibited from participating with the insurance company. However, they would prefer not to participate, to receive the same amount as participating dentists, as well as to be able to charge the patient an additional amount.)

The ANA has been in favor of permitting advanced practice nurses to bill fee-for-service, which has been used with such success by physicians, dentists, and other health professionals. Registered nurses are striving to become independent practitioners, such as nurse practitioners and nurse-midwives, who will then be able to bill the patient on a fee-for-service basis. The ANA has attempted to secure such direct reimbursement for nurses through government programs, such as Medicare. Fee-for-service payment to a health professional, which in most cases is reimbursed by the government or private insurance, is the most direct way for a health professional to increase income and to work independently of physicians.

Another legislative approach pursued by the ANA to increase nurses' income was to require that the concept of "comparable worth" be used in setting nurses' wages. Equal pay for equal work has already been enacted into law. Proponents of comparable worth go beyond that; they want equal pay for work of comparable value. If a registered nurse does work that is comparable in value to that of an electrician or a family physician, then the nurse should receive a comparable (the same) income.[17] Comparable worth proponents seek to substitute fact-finding commissions for the marketplace, since the marketplace determines wages through the forces of supply and demand. The only way comparable worth can be implemented is to legislate it.

The AHA has favored two concepts in the design of payment systems for its member hospitals. The first was to eliminate any incentive for hospitals to engage in price competition. When hospitals started Blue Cross, the plans were required to offer their subscribers a service benefit plan, which provides the hospitalized patient with services rather than dollars, a characteristic of an indemnity plan. By guaranteeing payment to the hospital for the services used by the patient, the service benefit policy removes any incentive the patient (or the hospital) may have regarding the cost of hospitalization. Since the patient does not have to make any out-of-pocket payments, the prospective patient has no disincentive to enter the most expensive hospital, which may or may not be the highest-quality hospital. Under a service benefit policy, hospitals cannot compete for patients on the basis of price.

When Medicare was enacted, the AHA proposed a method of hospital payment, which was adopted by the government, that paid hospitals for providing care to Medicare patients based on each hospital's costs plus 2 percent. Once the patients paid a deductible, they were not assessed any copayments. Not only did this method of payment eliminate any incentive for patients to select less costly, more efficient hospitals, but it provided hospitals with an incentive to *increase* their costs.

The second concept underlying hospitals' preferred method of payment is to be able to engage in price discrimination, that is, to be able to charge different payers different prices. Hospitals prefer having several different purchasers, rather than one major purchaser, of their services. With multiple payers, hospitals can charge each a separate price, based on willingness to pay. An example of this strategy was hospitals that gave Blue Cross a 20 percent discount compared to what commercial insurers were charged. This discount enabled Blue Cross to offer a more expensive policy (a service benefit) that was in the hospitals' interest. The discount was also a competitive advantage for Blue Cross and enabled them to increase their market share over the commercial companies.

Hospitals did very well financially under the initial Medicare payment policy. The government was anxious for hospitals to participate in Medicare and therefore accepted many of the AHA's payment proposals. Not only were hospitals able to negotiate a 2 percent addition to their costs of serving Medicare patients and receive favorable treatment for depreciating their assets, but the manner in which hospital costs were calculated gave hospitals additional payment. Because hospitals could not separate the actual costs of serving Medicare patients from those of other patients, the method used to calculate Medicare costs was to use a ratio of what hospitals charge for Medicare patients to the charges for non-Medicare patients. That ratio was then used to determine the portion of the hospitals' total costs that should be paid by Medicare. The effect of this policy was to provide hospitals with an incentive to raise charges on those services used predominantly by the elderly, such as bed rails. By raising the proportion of their charges for the aged, a greater portion of the hospitals' total costs were paid by the government. The hospital would then be able to make a higher profit on its charges to commercial insurance companies.

As Medicare began to reduce the amount it paid to hospitals over the years, the AHA proposed to Congress (in 1982) that hospitals be able to decide each year whether or not they wanted to accept Medicare payment as payment-in-full for services provided to a Medicare patient. If a hospital decided it did not want to take Medicare patients "on assignment," then the hospital could charge the Medicare patient an additional amount. This approach, which was being used by physicians serving Medicare patients, would have enabled hospitals to price-discriminate; higher-income aged could be charged more than lower-income aged. In rejecting this approach, Congress was concerned with the political reaction of the elderly.

Hospitals were also able to price-discriminate by setting a higher price:cost ratio for those services for which there was a greater willingness to pay, that is, services that were less price-elastic. Ancillary services, such as lab tests and x-rays, had higher price:cost ratios than the hospital's basic room charge. Once a patient was hospitalized, he or she had little choice on the use or price of ancillary services. Patients who paid part of the hospital bill themselves could, before they entered a particular hospital, more easily compare charges for obstetric services and room rates. Consequently, the charges for these services were much closer to their costs.

Medical and dental schools, as discussed above, seek unrestricted federal and state subsidies rather than charge their students the full cost of their education. Charging tuition that is below actual costs and limiting the number of admissions results in an excess demand.

The method by which public medical and dental schools receive their subsidies is also very important. Subsidies go directly to the school, as do government funds distributed for loans and scholarships. Under this arrangement, the student receives a subsidy (tuition less than costs) only by attending a subsidized school. This method requires that students compete for medical and dental schools. If government subsidies went directly to the student, then the schools would have to compete for students. As with subsidies, medical and dental schools prefer to distribute loans and scholarships themselves rather than have students apply directly to the government for such financial assistance. If the students received the subsidies and loans directly, then they would have an incentive to shop and select a school based on its tuition rates and reputation. The current system provides a competitive advantage to schools receiving subsidies. Needless to say, private schools would prefer that the subsidies go directly to the students.

The methods used by health professionals and health institutions for pricing their services has enabled these providers to maximize their revenues. The health associations representing each provider group have had, in negotiating with the government, in establishing their own insurance organizations, and in proposing legislation, a clear appreciation for which pricing strategies are in their members' economic interest. As a result, it is difficult to believe that the distinction between profit and not-for-profit has any meaning with regard to which group can provide services at a lower price.

Legislation to Reduce the Price and/or Increase the Quantity of Complements

A registered nurse may be a substitute or a complement to the physician. It is difficult to determine when an input, such as a nurse, is a complement or a substitute based only on the task performed. A nurse may be as competent as a physician in performing certain tasks. If the nurse works for the physician and the physician receives the fee for the performance of that task, then the nurse has increased the physician's productivity and is a complement. If, however, the nurse performs the same task and is a nurse practitioner billing independently of the physician, then the nurse is a substitute for the physician providing that service. The essential element in determining whether an input is a complement or a substitute is who receives the payment for the services provided by that input. Whoever receives the payment controls the use of that input.

The state practice acts are the legal basis for determining which tasks each health profession can perform and under whose direction health professionals must work. A major legislative activity for each health association is to ensure that the state practice acts work to their members' interests. Health associations that represent complements (e.g., nurses and denturists), attempt to have their members become substitutes. Health associations whose members control complements seek to retain the status quo.

In the past, almost all the health professions and health institutions were complements to the physician. That situation is now changing. The physician is no longer the sole entry point to the delivery of medical services. Hospitals and HMOs try to attract their own patients and subscribers. These organizations may then use nurse anesthetists, nurse practitioners, and salaried physicians to serve those patients. Other health professionals, such as nurse-midwives, are similarly seeking to be able to practice independently from physicians.

Providers can increase their incomes if an increase in demand for their services is met through greater productivity than through an increase in the number of competing providers. The providers' income can be increased still further if their productivity increases are subsidized and they do not have to pay the full cost of the increased productivity.

The following are several examples of legislation that has subsidized providers' productivity. The AHA lobbied for passage of the Nurse

Training Act in the belief that federal educational subsidies would increase the supply of RNs available to hospitals. With a larger supply of nurses, nurses' wages would be lower than they otherwise would have been. For similar reasons, the AHA favored educational subsidies to increase the supply of allied health professionals. The AHA was a strong proponent of the Hill-Burton program, which provided capital subsidies to modernize hospitals. But the AHA opposed legislation that would have increased the cost of inputs to hospitals. It also opposed the extension of minimum wage legislation to hospital employees and has called for a moratorium on the separate licensing of each health professional. (Separate licensing limits the hospital's ability to substitute different health professionals in the tasks they perform and to use such personnel in a more flexible manner.) Conversely, separate licensing is demanded by each health professional association so as to increase the demand for its members' services by restricting the tasks that other professions can perform.

The AHA has opposed proposals for a flat-rate income tax, which would reduce marginal tax brackets by eliminating a number of deductions. The AHA was concerned that any elimination of the charitable contribution deduction might adversely affect hospitals. The AHA was also concerned that lowering income tax brackets would make hospitals' tax-exempt bond financing less attractive to investors.

The AMA has also favored subsidies to hospitals. When a patient demands a treatment for a medical problem, the physician decides on the combination of resources and settings to use in the provision of that treatment. Hospital care was often the most costly component of that treatment. Before hospital insurance was so widespread, the physician was concerned over the cost of hospital care. The more the patient paid for hospital care, the less there would be available to pay for the physician's services. Similarly, the AMA favored subsidies to increase the supply of nurses, since it lowered hospitals' costs of inputs. The AMA has, however, opposed the increased educational standards that the ANA wanted to impose on nursing institutions as a condition for receiving funds under the Nurse Training Act. Higher educational standards for nurses do not necessarily increase the productivity of nurses, but they do limit the supply of nurses. Financial support for graduate level training of nurses also increases the nurses' qualifications to be a physician substitute for some tasks.

The AMA has favored internship and residency programs in hospitals. Interns and residents are excellent complements for physicians; they can take care of the physician's hospitalized patients and relieve the physician from serving in the hospital emergency room and from being on call. The more advanced the resident is, the closer the resident is to being a potential substitute for the physician. Residents, however, are complements since it is the physician that bills for the service. For this reason the AMA has favored the use of foreign medical graduates to serve as interns and residents. Once they graduate, however, they become substitutes to existing practitioners. The AMA has, therefore, favored the return of foreign medical graduates to their home country once their residencies are completed.[18] (The AMA advocated a time limit on how long foreign medical graduates can remain in the United States as well as the requirement that they be out of the country two years before returning.) The AMA has also favored increased training times for U.S. medical graduates. Not only does longer training time increase the time each graduate serves as a complement but it also delays the time when they become competitors.

A telling example of the AMA's attitude toward new health professionals was its position on the physician assistant (PA). If PAs practiced independently, they would become a substitute to some physicians (family practitioners). Thus the main concern of the AMA toward emerging health professionals was to ensure that these types of personnel become complements to, not substitutes for, the physician. Thus, whether there is direct or indirect supervision of the PA by the physician is less important to the AMA's political position than who gets the fee for the PA's service.

Another important determinant of the AMA's position toward the introduction of PAs was whether PAs would create excess capacity among physicians in the community. Excess capacity causes increased competition among physicians for patients. If physicians faced insufficient demand for their services, then increased productivity, through the introduction of new types of personnel, would make it even more difficult for those physicians who would like to be busier. Indicative of this concern by its membership was the AMA's 1972 recommendation that all states enact legislation to empower state boards of medical examiners to approve, on an individual basis, a given physician's request to employ a PA and the proposed functions to be performed by that PA.[19] Unless there was sufficient demand per physician in an area, permission to use a PA would not be granted, regardless of the PA's training.

Particularly during the period from the late 1950s through the early 1970s, when demand for physicians and dentists was increasing, state practice acts were relaxed to permit greater delegation of tasks. As excess capacity among physicians and dentists increased in the 1980s, medical and dental societies began to oppose further delegation of tasks (to, e.g., expanded function dental auxiliaries). Growth in productivity among health professionals, paid fee-for-service, was related more to demand conditions facing physicians and dentists than to the competency of the new personnel.

The latest legislative attempt by physicians and dentists to lower the cost of their inputs has been action at both the federal and state level to limit increases in malpractice premiums. There are many reasons why malpractice premiums have risen.[20] One important reason however is the incompetency of some physicians. "There have been estimates that as many as 5 to 15 percent of doctors are not fully competent to practice medicine, either from a deficiency of medical skills or because of impairment from drugs, alcohol, or mental illness."[21] Professional associations have been more willing to seek legislation to place limits on the size of malpractice awards than to make a concerted effort to eliminate unqualified practitioners.

Up until the mid-1980s (at which time large employers placed pressure on insurance companies to reduce their premiums), the Blue Cross premium consisted almost entirely of the costs of hospital care. Its main cost therefore had been the cost and quantity of hospital care used by its subscribers. Commercial insurance companies had broader coverage (although it included deductibles and cost sharing), and therefore hospital care was a smaller portion of the total premium. Thus to remain competitive against commercial insurance companies, Blue Cross had to keep the cost of hospital care (both hospital use and cost per unit) from rising so rapidly. Under the service benefit policy, however, patients, their physicians, and the hospital had no incentive to be concerned with cost or use. In fact it was in the hospital's interest to add facilities and services and pass the costs on to Blue Cross. As more hospitals added facilities and services in a race to determine who could be more prestigious, there was a great deal of duplication of costly facilities and services and, consequently, low use. Blue Cross, however, was committed to pay. To limit the increase in these costly facilities, Blue Cross favored legislative restrictions on hospital investment.

Given the control hospitals had over Blue Cross, Blue Cross was not aggressive in trying to limit the rapid rise in hospital costs, such as by limiting what they would pay hospitals. Blue Cross and the major hospitals favored an indirect approach that prevented smaller hospitals from expanding their beds and facilities and the entry of new hospitals. To receive Blue Cross (and Medicare) reimbursement for capital expenditures, a hospital had to receive the approval of a planning agency for its investment. Existing large hospitals either had the latest facilities or were the likeliest candidates to receive approval from the planning agency, whose criteria favored large, full-service hospitals. These large institutions also favored the development and strengthening of planning agencies because it limited competition.

Blue Cross relied on controls to hold down hospital investment and rising Blue Cross premiums. Hospitals, however, had different objectives and cost control was not one of them. All studies have shown that controls on capital investment were not effective in holding down either hospital investment or the rise in hospital costs.[22] It was not until Blue Cross began to experience strong competitive pressures, sufficient to affect its survival, that it finally undertook more direct means of lowering the costs of its major input. At that time Blue Cross began including lower-cost substitutes to hospitals as part of its benefits, instituting utilization control programs, and changing the method by which it pays hospitals.

Legislation to Decrease the Availability and/or Increase the Price of Substitutes

All health associations try to increase the price of services that are substitutes to those provided by their members. (Similar to increasing the price of a substitute is decreasing its availability.) If the health association is successful in achieving this, then the demand for its members' services will be increased.

Health associations use three general approaches to accomplish this objective. The first is to simply have the substitute declared illegal. If substitute health professionals are not permitted to practice, or if substitutes are severely restricted in the tasks they are legally permitted to perform, then there will be a shift in demand away from the substitute service. The second approach, used when the first approach is unsuccessful, is to exclude the substitute service from payment by any third party, including government health programs. This approach raises the price of the substitute. The third approach is to try and raise the costs of the substitutes who must then raise their own prices if they are to remain in business. The following examples illustrate the behavior of health associations for each of these approaches.

For many years the AMA regarded osteopaths as "cultists." It was considered "unethical" for physicians to teach in schools of osteopathy. Unable to prevent their licensure at the state level, the AMA tried to deny osteopaths hospital privileges. (A physician substitute is less than adequate if that substitute cannot provide a complete range of treatment.) As osteopaths developed their own hospitals and educational institutions, medical societies decided the best approach to controlling the increase in supply of these physician substitutes was to merge with the osteopaths, make them physicians, and then eliminate any future increases in their supply. An example of this approach, which was used in California until it was overturned by the state Supreme Court, was to allow osteopaths to convert their D.O. degree to an M.D. on the basis of 12 Saturday refresher courses. (By 1966, 15 states had similar merger agreements between the medical and osteopathic societies.) After the merger between the two societies occurred in California, the Osteopathic Board of Examiners was no longer permitted to license osteopaths.

Medicare has been the vehicle for much legislative competition. The AMA has lobbied for only covering physician services under Medicare Part B while excluding nonphysician services. By including only physician services, the prices of substitute providers to the aged are effectively increased relative to those of physicians. For example, optometrists and chiropractors are potential substitutes for ophthalmologists and family physicians, respectively. By including physician services under Medicare, but excluding payment for nonphysicians, the price of nonphysicians is increased relative to physicians. An aged person with Medicare Part B pays less for a physician's services, since the out-of-pocket price to the aged of physician services has been lowered. The AMA has similarly opposed direct payment of nurse anesthetists under Medicare.[23]

In one case the intervention of the courts prevented physicians from artificially raising the price of a substitute. In Virginia, Blue Shield did not reimburse psychologists as providers of psychotherapy. Psychiatrists' services were therefore less expensive than psychologists' to a patient with Blue Shield. The psychologists brought a successful antitrust case against Blue Shield in 1980 claiming discrimination of nonphysician providers.

Other examples of the AMA's attempts to adversely affect substitutes was to oppose payment for chiropractic services under veterans' benefits and under the Civilian Health and Medical Program of the Uniformed Services (CHAMPUS) program (health benefits for dependents of military personnel). The AMA has also opposed federal funding for advanced nurse training for fear that nurses would become independent nurse practitioners. The AMA's House of Delegates approved a resolution to recommend to all hospital staffs that only physicians take histories and perform physicals. The floor debate indicated that the resolution was directed at PAs, registered nurses, and dentists.

One medical society effectively eliminated competition from two independent nurse-midwives when the malpractice insurance of the backup obstetrician was cancelled. The insurance company was controlled by the medical society. The backup obstetrician had to leave the state to get new insurance.

An example of the legislative behavior of dental societies toward substitute providers is illustrated by dentistry's actions toward denturists. "Denturism" is the term applied to the fitting and dispensing of dentures directly to patients by people not licensed as dentists. Independently practicing denturists are a threat to dentists' incomes since they provide dentures at lower prices. Denturists are legal in most of Canada. As a result of their political success in Canada, denturists in the United States became bolder by forcing referendums on the issue and by lobbying for changes in the state practice acts. Until recently, dental societies had been successful in having denturism declared illegal nationwide. Since 1977, however, seven states have passed laws legalizing denturism.[24]

Occasionally denturists have sold dentures directly to patients illegally. To eliminate this competition and to prevent its increase, local dental societies, such as in Texas, have responded in two ways: first, they offered to provide low-cost dentures to low-income persons; second, they pressured state officials to enforce the state laws against illegal denturists.

A special ADA commission studied the threat of denturists and reported that the number of persons who are edentulous is much greater in the lower-income levels. It is among this population that denturists have met with great success in selling low-cost dentures. An ADA editorial (1976) commenting on this special study commission's report proposed:

> Organized dentistry should set up some system for supplying low-cost dentures to the indigent or the near-indigent all over the country, but especially in those states where the legislatures are considering bills that would allow dental mechanics to construct dentures and deliver them directly to the patient . . . this is the type of program that would have a favorable impact on the public—not to mention legislators. . . . The supplying of dentures to low-income patients by qualified dentists at a modest fee (or even at no fee in special cases) and in quantities meeting the public demands would go a long way toward heading off the movement of legalized denturists.[25]

It is only the threat of competition that results in the dental profession's offer to provide low-cost dentures to the indigent or near-indigent. If the denturists' competitive threat is eliminated through dentistry's successful use of the state's legal authority, the net effect will be to cause the public, particularly the poor, to pay higher prices for dentures.

The ADA is also concerned that dental hygienists remain complements to, not become substitutes for, dentists. Several state dental hygienist associations have attempted to change the state practice act to permit hygienists to practice without a dentist's supervision and to become independent practitioners. In 1986, the hygienists were successful in achieving this goal in Colorado. The ADA views this activity by hygienists as a "war"[26] and has challenged the constitutionality of the Colorado legislation. Further, the ADA has filed a Friend of the Court brief against individual hygienists who challenged their state's requirements that they must be supervised by dentists.

One of the most important substitutes for registered nurses is foreign-trained registered nurses. Nurses' salaries are considerably higher in the United States than in other countries, providing a financial incentive for foreign nurses to enter this country. The ANA has been successful in decreasing the availability of a low-cost substitute for U.S. registered nurses by making it more difficult for foreign-trained RNs to enter the country. The ANA has proposed that foreign RNs desiring to enter the United States be screened by examination in their home country before being allowed to immigrate. Once a foreign-trained RN enters the United States, the nurse is screened again by taking a state board exam. As of 1978, both the U.S. Department of Labor and the Immigration and Naturalization Service require that a foreign nurse graduate pass a screening exam—in English—that measures proficiency in both language and nursing before a work permit and a labor preference visa will be issued.

The ANA's position on entry screening is consistent with a policy of reducing the inflow of foreign nurses. If the screening exam were administered only in the United States, then foreign-trained RNs could still work in some nursing capacity in this country even if they did not pass the exam. The foreign-trained nurse could then retake the exam in the future. As it is, the screening exam is an additional barrier for foreign nurses to pass before they can enter the United States; if they do not pass the exam, they are unlikely to emigrate.

There are two additional legislative approaches that the ANA has used to raise the cost of substitutes for RNs. The first is to favor increases in the wages of other health professionals. A great deal of substitution for RNs by licensed practical nurses (LPNs) has occurred. The larger the wage increase of LPNs, the less likely it is that LPNs will be used instead of RNs. The disparity between RN wages and those of other health professionals would be diminished.

The second legislative approach used by the ANA is to prevent other personnel from performing tasks performed by the RN. The ANA has opposed permitting physicians to decide which personnel can perform nursing tasks; the ANA has opposed permitting LPNs to be in charge of skilled nursing homes, otherwise there would be substitution away from RNs (who receive higher wages) currently performing such functions. The California Nurses Association opposed a bill that would have authorized firemen with paramedic training to give medical and nursing care in hospital emergency departments. As a means of preventing PAs from assuming a role that the RN would like, the ANA has favored a licensing moratorium. A moratorium would prevent any new health personnel from being licensed to perform tasks that RNs do or would like to perform.

The AHA opposed the growth of freestanding ambulatory surgicenters.[27] Surgicenters are low-cost substitutes for hospitals; performing surgical procedures in a surgicenter decreases the use of the hospital and its revenues. To limit the availability of these low-cost substitutes, hospital associations have argued that surgicenters should be permitted only when they are developed *in association* with a hospital. The hospital would then be able to control the growth of this competitive source of care. As the number of surgicenters increase, the hospitals would receive increased revenues. Denying Blue Cross reimbursement to freestanding surgicenters and including surgicenters under certificate-of-need (CON) legislation were approaches favored by hospital associations. Hospitals have had a great deal of influence in the CON process. If approval was to be given for a surgicenter, it was more likely to be given to a hospital wishing to start one than to a freestanding one. (Previously, when hospitals were reimbursed according to their costs by both Blue Cross and Medicare, Blue Cross opposed surgicenters on the grounds that surgicenters raised the cost of care since hospitals are left with excess capacity, which third-party payers then have to cover.)

Health maintenance organizations were also included in state CON legislation for the same reason, since they decrease the use and revenues of hospitals. Several large HMOs were able to persuade Congress that CON legislation was inhibiting their ability to compete, and they were able to receive an exemption from the federal CON legislation in 1979. Many states, however, still use CON to limit entry by new health facilities, even by home health agencies, which have virtually no economies of scale and could not be considered to raise costs by duplicating existing medical services.

The value of CON legislation has not been lost on other groups. As occupancy rates have fallen, hospitals have tried to convert those empty beds into long-term-care beds ("swing beds"). To do so usually requires either CON or state permission. Opposing the hospitals are nursing home associations who are concerned that hospitals will take business away from them, particularly from private pay rather than Medicaid patients.

Hospital associations have used several methods to raise the prices charged by their competitors, for-profit hospitals. They opposed the granting of tax-exempt status to for-profit hospitals, thereby raising their costs. They successfully lobbied for reducing the return on equity of for-profit hospitals under Medicare reimbursement. And hospitals opposed granting for-profit hospitals Blue Cross eligibility. Being ineligible for Blue Cross payment precludes the use of the hospital by patients with Blue Cross coverage.

Blue Cross competes against several substitutes. Commercial insurance companies were for many years the most important competitor to the Blues. To increase the cost of commercial insurers, Blue Cross opposed granting them the same tax-exempt status that Blue Cross plans enjoyed. Commercial insurance companies generally paid higher state taxes on their premiums than Blue Cross. (Blue Cross's federal tax exemption has since been removed, a political success for commercial insurers seeking to increase Blue Cross's costs.) Blue Cross plans also opposed state rate regulation of hospitals that would enable all insurers to pay the same price for hospital care. Such policies would have removed the cost advantage of Blue Cross, since they received a hospital discount.

Substitutes for American medical and dental schools are foreign schools whose graduates (who may be U.S. citizens) want to practice in the United States. To reduce the likelihood that foreign medical schools will substitute for U.S. medical schools, the AAMC has favored strong restrictions on the number of foreign medical graduates who can enter the country. In the past, the AAMC has had limited success. Many U.S. citizens attend a foreign medical school and then seek a residency in the United States. Until recently, Congress has been reluctant to limit residency opportunities for U.S. citizens trained overseas. While the AMA has favored the return of alien foreign medical graduates to their home country once they have finished their U.S. residency, the AMA did not want to restrict residency opportunities for foreign-trained medical graduates, since residents increase physician productivity. Also important to the AMA's political position on this issue is the fact that approximately 20 percent of U.S. students studying abroad are the sons and daughters of U.S. physicians.[28]

A number of factors are changing, making it likely that the AAMC will be more successful in decreasing the availability of a substitute supply of medical students. The increased supply of physicians has made the AMA concerned with the influx of foreign-trained U.S. graduates. Congress is concerned with reducing expenditures under Medicare. (Medicare pays teaching hospitals for graduate medical education, and one method of reducing Medicare expenditures is to reduce the number of medical graduates that Medicare supports.) The AAMC has been a strong proponent for eliminating Medicare payments for residents trained in foreign medical schools, since this would be a sufficient incentive for these hospitals not to accept such graduates. Given the large growth in the number of U.S. medical school graduates, this policy should have little adverse effect on teaching hospitals.

The ADA and the Association of American Dental Schools have been more successful in reducing the attractiveness of a foreign dental education. Practicing dentists do not use residents as do physicians. Therefore their interest is solely with decreasing the supply of dentists. There are increased time requirements for a foreign-trained dentist wishing to practice in the United States. A minimum number of years of training in the foreign country is required, as well as a license to practice in that country. (For a U.S. citizen, this would mean learning a different language.) And once foreign-trained dentists enter this country, additional requirements are then imposed upon them. They are required to take the last two years of dental school in an accredited U.S. dental school. They may also be required to take additional examinations before the licensing exam.[29] To date, such restrictive practices have raised the cost of a U.S. dental license for foreign-trained dentists (both U.S. and non-U.S. citizens). The consequence has been a decreased demand for a foreign dental education as a substitute for a U.S. dental education. The measure of how successful the dental profession and the dental schools have been is that less than 3 percent of all practicing dentists in the United States are foreign-trained.

The concept of interest groups seeking political action to increase the price of substitutes is not reserved solely for providers of medical services. Large companies and unions, for example, have lobbied state and federal legislatures to enact mandated employer health insurance, whereby the employer must pay a majority of the employees' health insurance premium. Large firms and their employees typically have health insurance, thus small firms and their employees would be primarily affected by such legislation. Mandated employer health insurance would increase the cost of low-wage labor to small firms and would cause these firms to increase their prices, thereby increasing the demand for substitute suppliers, namely large firms and their union employees.

Legislation to Limit Increases in Supply

Essential to the creation of a monopoly are limits on the number of providers of a service. Health associations, however, have justified supply control policies on grounds of quality. Restrictions on entry, they maintain, ensure high quality of care to the public. These same health associations, however, oppose quality measures that would have an adverse economic effect upon existing providers (their members). *This apparent anomaly—stringent entry requirements and then virtually no quality assurance programs directed at existing providers—is only consistent with a policy that seeks to establish a monopoly for existing providers.*

If health associations were consistent in their desire to improve and maintain high-quality standards, then they should favor all policies that ensure quality of care, regardless of the effect on their members. Quality-control measures directed at existing providers, such as reexamination, relicensure, and monitoring of the care actually provided, would adversely affect the incomes of some providers. More importantly, such "outcome" measures of quality assurance would make entry or "process" measures less necessary, thereby permitting entry of a larger number of providers.

A test of the hypothesis that entry barriers are primarily directed toward developing a monopoly position rather than improving quality of care would be as follows: Does the health association favor quality measures, regardless of the effect on its members' incomes or does it only favor those quality measures that enhance members' incomes? If the health association only favors those quality measures that have a favorable impact on its members' economic position, then it can be concluded that the real intent of those quality measures is the improvement of its members' competitive position rather than the assurance of quality care in the most efficient manner.

The following examples illustrate health associations' positions on quality. Quality programs that are in its members' interests are expected to be favored while those that would have an adverse impact are expected to be opposed.

Health associations always favor state licensure. The profession is the group that lobbies for and demands licensure laws. The profession then controls the licensure process by having its own members appointed to the licensing board and by having them establish the requirements for licensure. Licensure, by itself, is not a sufficiently strong barrier to entry, so additional requirements are then imposed. The major additional requirement is educational. Before any person can take a licensing exam he or she must have had a specified education, for a minimum number of years. (The number of years is continually increased.) Further, the specified education must take place in an educational institution approved by the profession or by its representatives. The number of educational institutions is kept limited so that, as in medicine and dentistry, there is a continual excess demand for admission. (Medical and dental schools, as well as optometric, veterinary, and similar schools, favor such supply control policies since it provides them with an education monopoly.) Placing limits on the number of educational spaces and specifying educational requirements in excess of the skills necessary to practice reduces the number of persons that can take the licensing exam.

If the licensure requirements merely specified passing an examination, then potential applicants for the exam could receive the necessary knowledge in a number of ways, in different institutions, and in different lengths of time. Under such circumstances, the number of persons that could potentially take the exam and pass it would be much greater than if those applying were limited by the number of approved educational spaces.

The above approach to quality has been used by both the AMA and the ADA, as well as other health professions. In 1904 the AMA formed its Council on Medical Education, whose purpose was to upgrade the quality of medical education. To receive greater public acceptance of its work, the council induced the Carnegie Foundation to survey existing medical schools. The result was the Flexner report, which recommended closing many medical schools and upgrading educational standards. "Flexner forcefully argued that the country was suffering from an overproduction of doctors and that it was in the public interest to have fewer doctors who were better trained."[30]

As a result of the Flexner report, state medical licensing boards imposed the requirement of graduation from an approved medical school before a person could take the licensure examination. Medical schools were to be approved by the AMA's own Council on Medical Education. As a result, the number of medical schools steadily declined from 162 in 1906 to 69 in 1944. The graduates of schools that were closed continued to practice; they were not required to rectify their educational deficiencies. *Whenever standards are raised, grandfather clauses protect the rights of existing practitioners, regardless of their abilities.*

The ADA followed in the footsteps of organized medicine. A licensure requirement followed by an educational requirement still left dentistry with "too many" practitioners. Dental schools were effectively able to license their own graduates. The number of dental schools grew, from 10 in 1870 to 60 by 1902.[31] Many of these new schools were for-profit businesses. Limits were placed on for-profit schools to control the growth in the supply of new graduates. State and local dental societies, as well as nonprofit dental schools, lobbied state legislatures to change the dental practice acts. Under the new state practice acts, the state board of dental examiners mandated that all dental graduates would have to take a licensing examination, and that only graduates from approved schools would be permitted to take the exam.

The ADA produced the Gies report in 1926, its own version of the Flexner report. Approval of dental schools as a requirement for licensure was to be determined by the ADA's Council on Dental Education. Indicative of the control the ADA has had on its Council on Dental Education is one of the duties of the council—according to the ADA's bylaws: " . . . to accredit on behalf of this association dental schools and schools in related fields of dental education *in accordance with requirements and standards approved by the House of Delegates* [italics added]."[32] The result of these requirements was that the number of schools and spaces declined and the educational requirements for becoming a dentist increased. Educational requirements became standardized and the for-profit dental schools went out of business. As with physicians, practicing dentists, whose interests were served by the ADA, were always grandfathered as requirements increased.

In recent years there has been a growing concern among dentists (as well as among other health professions) that there are too many practitioners. As would be expected, rather than relying on market forces to determine the number of dentists, the ADA approach is to reduce the number of dental school spaces. Indicative of this approach is the ADA's statement (1984), "Resolved, that public statements made by the American Dental Association . . . include the recognition that a surplus of dentists does exist to meet the current demand for dental services, . . . [and that] the ADA encourage and assist constituent societies in preparing legislation that may be used to petition state legislatures and governmental bodies with respect to private schools to adjust enrollment in dental schools."[33]

Optometrists have also followed the same supply control policies as medicine and dentistry. By the early 1900s, optometrists were able to secure licensure in all states. However, there were many private schools for training optometrists. By the 1920s the American Optometric Association was successful in disqualifying 20 of the 30 optometric schools and in raising educational requirements. Optometry requires six years of education in an approved optometric school and at least three years (most applicants have completed four years) of traditional undergraduate college education.[34] Increasing educational requirements for a profession involves not just increasing the number of years of professional training but also requiring more years of undergraduate training. (It is not intuitively obvious why a professional must also have a traditional college education.)

Nursing is also moving toward requiring more stringent educational requirements. Previously, most nurses graduated from diploma schools of nursing (90 percent in 1955). These programs were operated in conjunction with hospitals and generally lasted two years. By 1992, the percentage of practicing nurses that graduated from diploma schools had declined to 30 percent. Other practicing nurses received either an associate degree (AA) from a two-year college (31 percent graduated with an AA degree) or a four-year BSN degree (31 percent), the remaining 8 percent have advanced degrees.[35] The growth in demand for an AA degree was related to their high rate of return, whereas a nurse with a BA received a similar income but was required to take an additional two years of education. The marketplace did not place a sufficiently high return on the additional two years of education to make it worthwhile for most nurses to seek a four-year degree. Since the four-year degree did not meet the market test, the profession decided to impose it.

The ANA has proposed and has lobbied their state legislatures that nursing education take place only in colleges that offer a BA.[36] Only four-year nurse graduates would be referred to as professional nurses, otherwise the nurse would be a technical nurse. By proposing an increase in the educational requirement of two-thirds of the nurse graduates, the ANA must be well aware that the result will be a decrease in the number of nurse graduates. Any increase in an educational requirement increases the tuition that the student must pay as well as the forgone income a student could have earned during those additional years. The consequence of this policy, however, will be a much smaller increase in the supply of registered nurses, increased wages for RNs, and higher costs of healthcare. With an increased educational requirement, the ANA will also try to justify an increase in tasks that nurses are able to perform. The effect of increased education and an increase in nursing tasks would be an increase in the incomes of existing nurses, who would be grandfathered in as professional nurses.

It is unlikely one would ever observe a health association proposing increased educational requirements that are then applied to its existing members. Only to forestall more stringent requirements proposed by others would a health association favor additional training requirements for its existing members. Health associations do not favor relicensure or reexamination requirements for their current members, even though increased knowledge is the basis for requiring additional training for those entering the profession. Reexamination and relicensure would lower the incomes of their members, since they would have to take the time to study for the exam. Current practitioners also may not be able to pass the exam. No health association proposes that the time required to prepare a person to enter their profession be reduced.

Various medical school deans have suggested that one way to reduce the rising cost of a medical and dental education is to reduce the number of years required, for example, one less year of college and/or professional school.[37] A person would be willing to pay higher tuition levels for the years they are in school if they could enter practice one to two years earlier. However, the only direction with regard to the number of years of education required is the ADA's proposal that each dental graduate take an *additional* one-year postdoctoral program, which includes hospital experience.[38]

As medical and dental knowledge increases and educational requirements for new graduates lengthen, the public is led to believe that all persons in a profession are equally (or at least minimally) qualified. This is unlikely to be the case, particularly for those practitioners who were trained 30 years ago and have not maintained their knowledge.

At times the health professions have imposed requirements on new entrants that are blatant barriers. For example, foreign medical and dental graduates were required to be U.S. citizens before they were allowed to practice in some states.[39] Further, a dentist desiring to practice in Hawaii, for example, no matter how well-trained or how long in practice in another state, is required to complete a one-year residency requirement before being allowed to practice.[40] Such requirements cannot be remotely related to the profession's concern with quality.

If the members of a profession are concerned with quality, then they should favor monitoring quality among themselves. Yet associations have opposed any attempts by others to review the quality of care practiced by their members. Health associations that have proposed continuing education for their members have done so in response to demands by those *outside* the profession. These requirements are made easy to achieve and at a low cost to the members of the profession.

An indication of the lack of quality control in the health professions is provided by evidence over time on the number of disciplinary actions taken against physicians by state licensing boards. One such study, conducted in 1969, found that in the preceding five years a total of 938 formal actions had been taken. These disciplinary actions varied from revocation of licenses to simple reprimands. Given the number of physicians involved in patient care during those years, these disciplinary actions amounted to 0.69 per 1,000 physicians per year. Another study through 1972 resulted in an annual disciplinary rate of 0.74 per 1,000 physicians. These numbers include a number of states that had taken no disciplinary actions. Over the period 1980–1982, the disciplinary rate rose slightly to 1.3 per 1,000 physicians. The author of these studies, Dr. Robert Derbyshire, asks, "Does organized medicine adequately discipline unethical physicians? The answer is no."[41]

The Florida Board of Medical Examiners was reorganized in 1979 and a layperson appointed as director. The impetus for this change was a belief that the Florida medical licensing board was not performing its function.

There was widespread media coverage of Florida physicians who had harmed their patients or violated the law but were still in practice. As a result, Florida strengthened the regulatory process. (A new governor was elected at that time and the state's medical practice act came up for renewal under the state's sunset law provisions.) In 1982, there were 147 disciplinary actions against physicians in Florida. This included revoking and suspending licenses. These actions represented a threefold increase from a prior period. Since there were more than 20,000 physicians in Florida, these disciplinary actions affected 7.4 per 1,000 physicians.

Other states had widely varying rates of disciplinary actions. In 1982, Pennsylvania recorded only 0.5 disciplinary actions per 1,000 physicians; New York had 1.1; California, 2.8. Seventeen states reported 3.0 or greater. The author of the above study, Dr. Feinstein, asked, "It is difficult to believe that in any given year any state or territory would not have at least one physician per thousand who posed a threat to the health and safety of its citizens, and yet in 1982, 14 states reported less than that number of disciplinary actions. Has the balance of interests in these states tipped too far in the direction of protecting the profession to the detriment of its citizens?"[42]

In more recent years there has been an increase in the number of disciplinary actions against physicians. During 1994, 3,685 physicians, or 0.5 percent, of approximately 650,000 physicians were disciplined (5.67 per 1,000 physicians).[43] The increase in the number of disciplinary actions has most likely resulted from increased publicity about the inadequate performance by state medical licensing boards. Yet the performance of state licensing boards still varies greatly among the different states. As of 1994, the number of actions per 1,000 practicing physicians was 11.37 in Florida, 3.87 in Michigan, 5.67 in New York, 3.32 in Pennsylvania, and 3.76 in California.

It is also unfortunate that physicians who lose their license in one state can then move to another state and practice again. Only 12 states (as of 1995) permit their licensing boards to take action solely on another state's findings. And the Government Accounting Office has recommended that physicians losing their license in one state not be able to collect from Medicare and Medicaid as they move from state to state.

The AMA acknowledged in 1986 that physician peer review programs have not been performing as well as they should. "Because of the fear of personal liability, physicians are reluctant to report colleagues to state medical boards, and adverse hospital review determinations too often stay within the hospital. Peer review can be more careful, vigorous, and uniform."[44] A likely reason for this acknowledgment by the AMA's Board of Trustees on its plans to improve self-regulation among its members is that both government and business are demanding an accounting on quality assurance. Stan Nelson, Chairman of the AMA's board of trustees, stated, "Some big businesses, as payers for care, are realizing that they cannot only look at cost. They have to look at quality and they are demanding that the information be available to them."[45]

The current method of quality assurance for health professionals is aimed solely at entry into the profession rather than at monitoring the quality of care given. The inadequate performance of state licensing boards in disciplining their members is evidence of this practice. Further, little communication exists between state licensing boards to check the credentials and status of a physician moving in from a different state. The public is less protected against unethical and incompetent practitioners than it has been led to believe. The public will become better protected, not as a result of the good intentions of the profession, but when the health professions are forced to respond to the demands for quality from those outside the professions.

Hospitals and Blue Cross plans have also been advocates of supply control policies. These institutions have realized that the first step in achieving monopoly control is to limit entry. Large hospitals have favored certificate-of-need legislation and bed reduction programs. CON was used to limit investments by smaller hospitals and to prevent entry by potential competitors, such as for-profit hospitals. In the late 1980s, as hospital occupancy rates have fallen and price competition has increased, large hospitals favored government-sponsored bed reduction programs. Eliminating excess beds reduces incentives for hospitals to compete among themselves.

Blue Cross plans were established so as not to compete with one another. They were required to sign up 75 percent of the hospitals and beds in an area. This requirement precluded more than one Blue Cross plan from being established within any one market, and so Blue Cross had a virtual monopoly over the type of product it was selling, a service benefit policy for hospitalization. (No other insurance company could have competed with Blue Cross on a similar product since they would not have received the hospital discount given to Blue Cross.)

To compete with Blue Cross, commercial insurance companies had to offer a different product, such as payment of a fixed-dollar amount for hospital care. To offset the Blue Cross hospital discount, the commercials also had to include lower-cost substitutes to hospital care. The result was that commercial insurance companies innovated the concept of major medical insurance. Major medical did not cover all the costs of hospital care but it provided medical insurance against large expenditures, both in and outside the hospital.

As the health insurance market has become more competitive, other types of insurance plans, such as HMOs, have taken market share away from the traditional health insurers. Blue Cross plans have had to adapt to this new environment. They have changed their product, offering care in settings other than just the hospital; they have established their own HMOs; and some Blue Cross plans are entering other Blue Cross plans' markets. As Blue Cross plans compete among themselves, the monopoly that a Blue Cross plan has over the use of the Blue Cross name will be eroded. Such a trend presents great problems for the Blue Cross Association.

Since the 1980s, much of the diminished political power and economic benefits enjoyed by organized medicine has been the result of (1) the rise of opposing concentrated interests, in part because diffuse costs increased to where they became concentrated, and (2) the applicability of the antitrust laws to the health field. The federal and state governments have developed a concentrated interest in reducing the rise in Medicare and Medicaid expenditures. Otherwise taxes would have to be raised or politically popular programs cut back. Large employers and their unions have a great interest in reducing the rise in their employees' health insurance premiums, otherwise their product prices must be increased and employee wages reduced.

Implications of the Legislative Success of Health Associations

Health professionals and health institutions do not exhibit characteristics of a natural monopoly, that is, large economies of scale for a given size of market sufficient to preclude entry of competitors. Because these professionals and institutions cannot achieve a monopoly position through the normal competitive process, they seek to achieve it through legislation. The first step toward increasing their monopoly power is to erect barriers to entry. The next is to limit competition among their members. They then attempt to improve their monopoly position by further demanding legislation that will increase the demand for their services, permit them to price as would a price-discriminating monopolist, lower their costs of doing business, and disadvantage their competitors either by causing them to become illegal providers or by forcing them to raise their prices.

Health professionals, particularly physicians and dentists, have been successful in the legislative marketplace, as evidenced by the design of public programs to pay for their services and by their relatively high incomes. However, three types of "costs" are imposed on the rest of society as a result of the restrictions that cause a redistribution of wealth to members of health associations that have achieved legislative success.

The first type of "cost" is higher prices. The more successful a health association is in achieving their members' goals, the higher will be the price of their members' services. However, once price competition occurs between members of different health associations, the lower will be the prices of both groups' services. The establishment of low-cost denture clinics by state dental societies is an example. When competition is reduced, as when state dental societies apply pressure to have the laws against denturists enforced, the price of dentures will once again increase. Allowing freestanding surgicenters to compete with hospitals lowers the cost to the patient for minor surgical procedures (through reduced insurance premiums). Other tactics used by health associations to prevent price competition among their members included prohibitions against advertising, limiting productivity increases to prevent excess capacity, preventing physicians in HMOs from having hospital privileges, and requiring free choice of provider under both public and private insurance plans. These restrictions have resulted in healthcare prices being higher than they would be otherwise.

The beneficiaries of restrictive policies that maintain high healthcare prices are, of course, the healthcare professionals themselves. These higher prices, which are not visibly attributed to these legislative policies, are borne by patients and by taxpayers who finance government programs.

The second implication of successful legislative behavior by health associations is that the public is provided with a false assurance with respect to the quality of the medical care it receives. The state has delegated its responsibility for protecting the public to the individual licensing boards, which in turn have been controlled and operated in the interests of the providers themselves. The approach toward quality assurance used by both the profession and by licensing boards is needlessly costly and inefficient. It has been more concerned with the process of becoming a health professional, such as entry into the profession, than with monitoring the care provided. As such, state licensing boards have devoted too few resources to investigating complaints against and removing incompetent or unethical providers. Too rarely do state licensing boards take disciplinary action against their members.

The movement toward a competitive market in medical services has resulted in a new emphasis on quality of care. Large employers are pressuring HMOs to provide information on their enrollees' medical outcomes, preventive measures undertaken, and health status indicators of their subscriber population. It is through actions by such large purchasers that HMOs are developing "report cards." Employer emphasis on "outcome" measures is forcing HMOs and medical groups to reexamine how medical care is provided. It is doubtful that this new approach toward quality would have occurred had market competition not developed.

The third effect of legislative success by a health association is that innovation in the delivery of medical care has been inhibited. Innovation provides benefits to consumers; they have greater choice, higher quality, and lower costs. Innovation, however, threatens the monopoly power of a protected provider group, and is therefore opposed. Medical and dental societies have been protectors of the fee-for-service delivery system. These organizations have delayed the introduction of alternative delivery systems, such as HMOs and PPOs. Rather than being pro-competitive, "any willing provider" laws and "free choice of provider" have been used by the professions to eliminate competition from "closed" provider panels. HMOs and PPOs cannot negotiate volume discounts with closed panels of providers if they have to offer their subscribers free choice of any provider. HMOs and managed care organizations are able to offer lower premiums than traditional insurance because they are able to impose restrictions on the types of participating providers and by instituting medical management programs. Legislative restrictions against closed panels, such as by requiring free choice of provider, prevents managed care organizations from successfully competing against traditional insurance plans.

Medical and dental societies have inhibited the development of new types of health personnel, such as nurse-midwives, nurse practitioners, and expanded function dental auxiliaries, because they might become substitutes. The determination of which tasks a health professional is able to perform is related more to their economic impact on another health profession than to the professional's qualifications and training.

Hospital associations have sought, through certificate-of-need legislation, to stifle innovations such as the growth of freestanding surgicenters. It was the commercial insurance companies that introduced major medical insurance, a distinct innovation that also increased their share of the health insurance market. The process of receiving a professional education (medical, dental, and optometric) has changed little over time (except for an increase in years required) because it has remained under the auspices of accredited schools and their professions. It is very likely that the necessary knowledge could actually be provided to students in a shorter period of time, thereby decreasing the total cost of such an education.

Innovation offers the hope of greater productivity, lower costs, and an increase in quality. The political activities of health associations should be viewed in their proper perspective, namely, to benefit their members while imposing a cost on the rest of society. Past reliance on professional regulation to protect the patient has reduced incentives for innovation.

The movement toward market competition in the delivery of health services does not, however, negate the need to be concerned with quality. Large employers and the formation of business coalitions wield sufficient purchasing power to force managed care organizations to monitor quality of care within their organizations and to compete on such measures. It is, however, among those population groups not monitored by large employers, such as those on Medicaid and Medicare, that concerns remain over the quality of care received. State and federal authorities will still have to be responsible for the care provided to these more vulnerable populations. The question remains whether government oversight will improve so as to provide the same quality of care protection that occurs when providers compete for large, well-informed purchasers.

Study Questions for Chapter 4

1. Provide examples of the types of "demand-increasing" legislation favored by different health associations.
2. What do you expect would be health insurers' and the American Dental Association's political position on proposals to limit the amount of employer-paid health insurance that is excluded from taxes?
3. What methods has the American Medical Association used in the past to discourage price competition among its members?
4. How did the initial benefit structure that hospitals designed for Blue Cross eliminate any possibility of hospitals engaging in price competition for patients?
5. Explain why health professionals (e.g., a nurse practitioner), can either be viewed as a complement or a substitute, depending upon who receives the fee for the service (e.g., the nurse practitioner or the physician).
6. What are some different approaches medical associations have used to decrease competition from substitute providers?
7. Did hospital and registered nurse associations favor an increase in the number of foreign-trained registered nurses to alleviate nurse shortages?
8. With reference to specific approaches that have been used to increase the quality of health professionals, such as graduation from an approved medical school, increased educational requirements, etc., discuss the following statement, "Health associations only favor those quality measures that enhance their members' incomes, not

all quality measures regardless of the effect on their members' incomes."

9. With the increase in managed care competition, in what ways is quality assurance of both health professionals and medical services changing?

Notes

1. In 1975, the Federal Trade Commission charged that the American Medical Association, the Connecticut State Medical Society, and the New Haven County Medical Association restricted the ability of their members to advertise. The AMA claimed that the FTC did not have jurisdiction over them because they were a not-for-profit organization. The approach used in this chapter and in an earlier book by the author, 1977. *Health Associations and the Demand for Legislation: The Political Economy of Health.* Lexington, MA: Ballinger Publishing Company, with its applications to the AMA, was the basis for testimony by the author on the jurisdictional issue to demonstrate that the AMA acted in the economic interests of its members. The administrative law judge found in favor of the FTC on both the advertising and jurisdictional issues. These decisions were upheld on appeal and in 1982 the U.S. Supreme Court, by a tie vote, upheld the lower court rulings.

2. A more complete discussion of the change to market competition, as well as the reasons for this change, is provided in Chapter 6.

3. The antitrust laws were also used to ensure that the interests of Blue Shield and medical societies were kept separate. The Federal Trade Commission investigated physician control of Blue Shield plans and brought a successful suit against the Michigan State Medical Society (MSMS). MSMS bargained with Blue Shield on behalf of its physician members. Medical societies are no longer permitted to do this since a physicians' boycott against Blue Shield would be illegal.

4. It has been estimated that the income elasticity of demand for dental services is approximately 2; that is, a 10 percent increase in income would lead to a 20 percent increase in expenditures on dental services. Charles Upton and William Silverman. 1972. "The Demand for Dental Services," *The Journal of Human Resources 7* (Spring) 250.

5. Congressional Budget Office. 1994. *The Tax Treatment of Employment-Based Health Insurance.* Washington, D.C. 48.

6. One demand-increasing proposal is reputed to have had an adverse effect on patients' oral health. In 1974 the Federal Social Court in Germany ruled that false teeth should be included in the country's compulsory health insurance programs. "Fillings went out of fashion and prevention was ignored as vast quantities of teeth were pulled and replaced. By 1980, German dentists were using 28 tons of tooth gold a year, one third of the world total." Dentists' incomes soared, exceeding those of physicians by 30 percent. The sickness funds reported a huge deficit, forcing them to raise the level of compulsory contributions. "Dentists Gnashing Teeth in West Germany," *The Wall Street Journal,* December 26, 1985.

7. "Nurses Decry Cost-Cutting Plan That Uses Aides to Do More Jobs," *The Wall Street Journal,* January 20, 1994.

8. "Doctors Group Denounces Nurses' Demand for Power," *The Washington Post*, December 7, 1993.

9. Fee splitting occurs when a physician refers a patient to a surgeon and in return receives part of the surgeon's fee. Fee splitting is an indication that the surgeon's fee is in excess of his or her cost; the surgeon can still make a profit though rebating part of the fee. If the fee was not in excess of the costs (including the opportunity cost of the surgeon's time), the surgeon would be unwilling to split the fee. The state practice acts permit surgeons to act as a cartel by preventing any one surgeon from engaging in this form of price competition. Fee splitting is a way of eroding the surgeons' monopoly power. Surgeons opposed to fee splitting consider it unethical because the referring physician has a monetary incentive to select the surgeon. Any concern the medical profession has with the quality of surgeons or with the ethical behavior of physicians should be addressed directly through examination and monitoring procedures and not by prohibiting price competition. Unfortunately, as will be discussed, the medical profession has not favored reexamination nor monitoring. For a more complete discussion of fee splitting, see Mark V. Pauly. 1979. "The Ethics and Economics of Kickbacks and Fee Splitting," *The Bell Journal of Economics* 10 (1) 344–52.

10. Reuben Kessel. 1958. "Price Discrimination in Medicine," *The Journal of Law and Economics* 1 20–53.

11. See, for example, Lee Benham and Alexandra Benham. 1975. "Regulating Through the Professions: A Perspective on Information Control," *The Journal of Law and Economics* 421–47.

12. John E. Kwoka, Jr. 1984. "Advertising and the Price and Quality of Optometric Services," *The American Economic Review* 74 (1) 211–16.

13. The physician's fee for Medicare, Blue Shield, and private pay patients is supposed to be the same. The fee is based on the physician's "usual, customary, and reasonable" fee. Blue Shield and Medicare maintain physician fee schedules in their computers. However, Blue Shield pays physicians' fees if they are under a certain percentile limit; Medicare has limited the annual increase in physicians' fees for a number of years. Therefore the physician's fee to a private patient is usually higher than the fee paid by Medicare and Blue Shield.

14. Kessel, "Price Discrimination in Medicine."

15. Group Health Association in Washington, DC, was one such case cited in the Kessel article.

16. The FTC brought a case against the Indiana Federation of Dentists on grounds of boycotting an insurer for requiring submission of radiographs by dentists. The U.S. Supreme Court in 1986 upheld the FTC by unanimous decision, thereby agreeing with the FTC that the Indiana Federation of Dentists had engaged in an illegal conspiracy. Other state dental boards have undergone similar FTC review. "The Federation argued that if insurers are allowed to determine whether they will pay a claim for dental treatment on the basis of x-rays, they might decline erroneously to pay for necessary treatment and deprive the patient of fully adequate care. The court strongly objected to this argument, likening it to the argument, also rejected in a separate case, 'that an unrestrained market in which consumers are given access to the information they believe to be relevant to their choices will lead them to make

unwise and even dangerous choices.'" "U.S. Supreme Court Upholds FTC Order," *The ADA News*, June 16, 1986.

17. For a discussion of comparable worth as it applies to nursing, see Joanne Disch and Paul Feldstein. 1986. "An Economic Analysis of Comparable Worth," *Journal of Nursing Administration* 16 (6) 24–31.

18. For a review of immigration policies toward the foreign medical graduate during this time period, see Alfonso Mejia, Helena Pizurki, and Erica Royston. 1980. *Foreign Medical Graduates*. Lexington, MA: Lexington Books. Appendix, "Immigration and Licensure Policies."

19. *AMA House of Delegates Proceedings*, 121st Annual Convention, June 20–24, 1972, Report Z. Chicago: American Medical Association. 115. For an excellent study of state legislation authorizing and regulating the practice of physician assistants, see Stephen C. Crane. 1981. *The Legislative Marketplace: A Model of Political Exchange To Explain State Health Regulatory Policy*, doctoral dissertation, School of Public Health, University of Michigan. In his extensive study of the determinants of state PA policy, Crane states, "It is clear that the single variable that best accounts for PA policy restrictiveness is the policy preferences of special interest groups" (p. 332).

20. Patricia M. Danzon. 1985. *Medical Malpractice: Theory, Evidence and Public Policy*. Cambridge, MA: Harvard University Press.

21. Richard J. Feinstein. 1985. "The Ethics of Professional Regulation," *New England Journal of Medicine* 312 (12) 801–804.

22. David S. Salkever and Thomas W. Bice. 1979. *Hospital Certificate-of-Need Controls: Impact on Investment, Costs, and Use*. Washington, D.C.: American Enterprise Institute.

23. *Statements of the American Medical Association*. 1983, 1984. Compendium of Statements to the Congress and Administrative Agencies, Department of Federal Legislation. Chicago: American Medical Association.

24. The seven states are: Maine (1977), Arizona (1978), Colorado (1979), Oregon (1980), Idaho (1982), Montana (1984), and Washington (1994). Colorado also enacted a bill permitting the independent practice of hygienists. This unprecedented action was attributed, by the Colorado Dental Association's executive director, to the state's sunset laws which gave an opportunity for the bill's proponents to lobby for it. The proponents were feminists (since most hygienists are women), consumer advocates, and a large number of deregulators in the state legislature. The political influence of these groups also changed the composition of the state dental board, making dentists a minority. *The ADA News*, May 19, 1986, p. 5.

25. "Action Urgently Needed on 'Denturist' Movement," editorial. *Journal of the American Dental Association* 92, 665.

26. Dale F. Redig. 1986. "Which Side of this War Are You On?" *The ADA News* 4.

27. AHA Board of Trustees policy statement. 1973. Reported in *Hospitals, Journal of the American Hospital Association*. 47 (15) 132.

28. John K. Iglehart. 1985. "Reducing Residency Opportunities for Graduates of Foreign Medical Schools," *New England Journal of Medicine* 313 (13) 835.

29. "In the [American Dental] Association's view, testing alone cannot provide adequate assurance of competence. Therefore the Association recommends that a foreign-trained dentist be required to complete supplementary education programs in an accredited dental school of at least two years' duration as a precondition to

licensure." *Dentistry in the United States.* Chicago: American Dental Association, 1985. 27.

30. Kessel, "Price Discrimination in Medicine," 27.

31. Kenneth C. Fraundorf. 1984. "Organized Dentistry and the Pursuit of Entry Control," *Journal of Health Politics, Policy and Law* 8 (4) 759–81.

32. *Constitution and Bylaws*, revised to January 1, 1963 Bylaws Section 1110B. Chicago: American Dental Association.

33. *1984 House of Delegates Resolutions*, October 25, p. 537. This resolution follows a previous one (124H-1981) where the ADA was to encourage their "constituent dental societies to utilize these reports (on dentist supply) in petitioning their legislative bodies to consider by lawful means the number of dentists that should be trained." *Transactions*, 125th Annual Session, October 20–25, 1984. Chicago: American Dental Association.

34. James W. Begun. 1981. *Professionalism and the Public Interest: Price and Quality in Optometry.* Cambridge, MA: The MIT Press. Also see, James W. Begun and Ronald C. Lippincott, "A Case Study in the Politics of Free-Market Health Care," *Journal of Health Politics, Policy and Law* 7 (3) 667–85.

35. Evelyn B. Moses. 1994. *The Registered Nurse Population: Findings from the National Sample Survey of Registered Nurses, March 1992.* Washington, D.C.: U.S. Department of Health and Human Services. 52.

36. For a more complete discussion of this proposal, see Andrew K. Dolan. 1978. "The New York State Nurses Association 1985 Proposal: Who Needs It?" *Journal of Health Politics, Policy and Law* 2 (4) 508–30.

37. Robert H. Ebert and Eli Ginzberg. 1988. "The Reform of Medical Education," *Health Affairs* 7 (2) Supplement 5–38. The authors state, "We believe it is feasible to reduce significantly the time it takes to prepare a primary care physician (or a specialist) without sacrificing quality."

38. 1984. "Dentistry's Blueprint for the Future," *Journal of the American Dental Association* 108 (1) 20–30.

39. Many states adopted the citizenship requirement for foreign medical graduates after the AMA's House of Delegates passed such a resolution in 1938. Five states continued such a requirement as late as 1975. Although citizenship is no longer required in any state, all foreign medical graduates, excluding those from Canadian schools, are required to take an exam prior to entering a residency program.

40. Another entry barrier used in dentistry is restrictions on interstate mobility. Various studies have shown that dentists graduating from a dental school within a state have a greater chance of passing that state's licensing exam than dentists from other states. Unlike medicine, most states do not permit reciprocal licensing for dentists. See, for example, Lawrence Shepard. 1978. "Licensing Restrictions and the Cost of Dental Care," *The Journal of Law and Economics* 21 187–201. See also, B. Friedland and R. Valachovic. 1991. "The regulation of Dental Licensing—The Dark Ages," *American Journal of Law and Medicine* 17 (3) 249–270.

41. Robert C. Derbyshire. 1974. "Medical Ethics and Discipline," *Journal of the American Medical Association* 228 (1) 59–62. Also see, Robert C. Derbyshire. 1969. *Medical Licensure and Discipline in the United States.* Baltimore: Johns Hopkins University Press. Robert C. Derbyshire. 1984. "Medical Discipline in Disarray: Offenders and Offenses," *Hospital Practice* 98a–98v.

42. Feinstein. "The Ethics of Professional Regulation," p. 803. In view of the poor record of state medical boards in disciplining physicians, the comments by Dr. James Sammons, executive vice president of the AMA, were all the more revealing. In opposing mandatory reevaluations for relicensing, Dr. Sammons stated, "There are better ways to measure competency. [Reviews in hospitals and state medical boards] are best able to weed out incompetent physicians." "Cuomo's Plan for Testing Doctors Is Part of Growing National Effort," *New York Times,* June 9, 1986.

43. Communication with the Federation of State Medical Boards of the United States, Fort Worth, Texas.

44. "AMA Adopts New Self-Regulation Plan For MD Profession," *The ADA News,* November 17, 1986, 18. Also see, "AMA Initiative on Quality of Medical Care and Professional Self-Regulation," 1986. *Journal of the American Medical Association* 256, 1036–37.

45. Ibid.

THE REASONS FOR DEREGULATION

I t is clear why existing firms in an industry would want to be regulated. Through regulation, they can achieve rewards unattainable in a competitive market. Yet, starting in the 1970s, a number of industries were deregulated: railroads, trucking, airlines, banking, telecommunications, and securities. The health sector also changed from a heavily regulated industry to one characterized by market competition.

Was the deregulation brought about because it was in the public interest? Was there a recognition among legislators that the costs of regulation, in terms of higher prices and a smaller output to consumers, exceeded its benefits? Political support maximization, as an approach for explaining legislative outcomes, must be able to explain not only why industries seek regulation and are able to control the regulatory process but it also must explain why some of those same industries are deregulated. Deregulation presumably destroys the economic wealth of regulated firms, so those firms would be expected to oppose it. Regulated industries are likely to offer an amount of political support up to the value of their regulatory benefits. Who would be able to offer more?

While deregulation occurred among some industries during the 1970s and early 1980s, other industries maintained their regulatory protection. And in some industries government regulation actually increased.

The following discussion attempts to explain why deregulation occurred in some industries and not others. It is shown that the reasons for deregulation are consistent with the hypotheses of self-interest and that legislators seek to maximize their political support. First is a brief discussion of some of the deregulated industries. Second, the similar characteristics of deregulated industries are examined to suggest reasons for deregulation. The reasons for deregulation are then used in the next chapter to explain the change to market competition in the health industry.

Examples of Deregulated Industries

Freight Transportation

The classic case of a regulatory agency serving the economic interests of those being regulated is the Interstate Commerce Commission (ICC). Federal regulation of railroads began in 1887 with the passage of the Interstate Commerce Act, which established the ICC. The two interest groups favoring this act were shippers and the railroads themselves. The railroads wanted to end the frequent rate wars and secret concessions given by some railroads to shippers. The shippers also wanted less rate instability but were concerned because they were being charged more to ship freight short distances than long distances. (Prices were higher for short hauls because there was less competition.)

Subsequent federal legislation empowered the ICC to set maximum rates, control entry and exit into the industry, and perform many of the tasks necessary for operating the industry. This resulted in the industry performing as a cartel.[1] The method used by the ICC to establish fixed rates was to set rates generally proportional to the distance traveled, rather than to cost. This resulted in raising long-haul rates rather than lowering short-haul rates as the shippers wanted.

With federal regulation, investment returns in the railroad industry improved and investor risk was reduced. Employee wages were also increased. Federal regulation enabled the railroads to achieve rates of return above those achievable in a competitive environment.

In the 1920s, two new unregulated competitors came on the scene, buses and trucks, which decreased the benefits of regulation to railroads. There were few economies of scale and the number of bus and truck firms increased rapidly. The profitability of railroads declined as trucks undercut the high fixed rail rates for short hauls. Railroads countered this competitive threat by bringing both trucking and buses under state regulation. In the late 1920s, however, two Supreme Court decisions negated the states' authority to regulate interstate trucking and buses. As a result, the railroads sought federal regulation to protect their interests. Shippers, on the other hand, opposed the extension of the ICC's jurisdiction over these low-cost alternatives. Truckers, however, favored federal regulation. Existing truckers saw regulation as a means of protecting themselves from newcomers.

Both railroads and truckers achieved what they had sought. The Motor Carrier Act of 1935 set minimum prices and established entry controls on trucks. Railroads were protected from price competition by low-cost substitutes (trucks), and truckers received the benefits of a cartel, control over prices and entry into their industry. Including another producer group, common-carrier trucks, under the ICC's jurisdiction, however, would eventually result in a decline in the relative political influence of railroads.

Railroads began to lose their profitability by the 1950s. Rates proportional to distance resulted in railroad rates that were below cost for short hauls (and low-density markets) and above cost in long-haul, high-density markets. Railroad rates were set so high in long-haul markets that truckers, whose costs were generally higher than railroads for long-haul freight, found it worthwhile to compete. A number of railroads went into bankruptcy, including the Penn Central, in large part because of losses in the short-haul market and increased competition in the long-haul market.

Regulation was no longer working to the benefit of the railroads. Despite rate regulation, they were losing their market share to the truckers. Improved technology and the interstate highway system benefited the truckers; trucking costs were reduced and motor carrier service became faster and more reliable. As a cartel for establishing rates, the ICC was now hurting rather than helping the railroads. The Association of American Railroads complained that unless the ICC granted greater rate and route flexibility to the railroads, they would end up "dead in the water."[2] Other interests, such as the truckers' association, the Teamsters, and users of regulated services were representing their interests before the ICC and offering political support to legislators. The ICC had other interests and their political support to consider when making decisions.

The railroads saw their salvation in greater price flexibility so they could compete with the truckers. Railroad profitability was also adversely affected by their being required to provide money-losing services, such as passenger service, and the requirement that they serve certain passenger and freight routes. Railroads had to receive ICC approval to drop these services. However, those benefiting from these services wanted them continued. Regulation had given these beneficiaries a valuable right which they did not want to lose. But to return to profitability, the railroads needed greater flexibility in both prices and services.

On the side of the railroads were the major shippers. Greater price flexibility meant lower prices to shippers. The National Association of Manufacturers was in the forefront of the deregulation movement.

In the 1970s several railroads went bankrupt. The political choices were to either nationalize the railroads and subsidize them or to permit deregulation. The Carter administration favored greater flexibility for the railroads; they were concerned that the bankruptcy of more railroads would mean continued large government subsidies.[3] (Conrail lost $1.4 billion in its first four and one-half years.) The railroads also preferred deregulation to nationalization.

Several changes were made in railroad regulation in the 1970s. The trend toward deregulating the railroads culminated in the Staggers Rail Act of 1980, which permitted greater price and service flexibility.

As a result of partial deregulation, railroads were able to compete favorably against truckers. They raised their short-haul rates and lowered their long-haul rates. Railroads, which are very efficient (i.e., low cost, in transporting large volumes of freight over long distances), were able to increase their market share over truckers in the long-haul market by lowering prices. Rates for some products, such as grain, declined by more than 30 percent.[4] Piggyback methods, which combine the flexibility of trucks in local pickup and delivery with the long-haul efficiency of railroads, and previously prohibited by the rate structure of the ICC, were introduced. The result was an integrated transportation system. Market share of railroads, compared to truckers, increased; for example, shipping of fruits and vegetables by rail nearly doubled between 1979 and 1983.[5]

Service quality on the railroads also improved. Accidents on poorly maintained tracks, which had been increasing prior to deregulation, were reduced. From the shippers' perspective, their costs of maintaining inventories (logistic costs) were reduced as rail service became more reliable. Railroads were now able to negotiate delivery times and other services with shippers, whereas formerly they were prohibited from doing so by the ICC because it was viewed as a form of price cutting.[6] Railroads were now permitted to abandon unprofitable branch lines. Rather than reducing service on these lines, new railroads operated them using nonunion labor; with lower operating costs, service continued and these lines served as feeder traffic into the larger railroads.

The consequence of these actions was that railroad profitability increased. Profits more than doubled between 1978 and 1981.[7] Federal subsidies to railroads declined from more than $500 million in 1980 to $66 million in 1985.[8]

Labor, however, was a big loser in deregulation. Previously, railroads faced detailed labor work rules and labor protection provisions. After deregulation, railroads were able to make sizable reductions in their workforce—a decrease of 40 percent between 1980 and 1985.[9] Because of these adverse effects, in 1986 labor attempted, unsuccessfully, to subject the railroads once again to regulation.

In 1980, the Motor Carrier Act was passed. This act replaced earlier legislation governing the trucking industry, allowing for ease of entry and removal of pricing restrictions. There was, however, an important distinction between deregulation of the railroads and the Motor Carrier Act. Railroads wanted to be free of previous regulatory restrictions; truckers and the Teamsters wanted the restrictions affecting trucking to remain in place. The regulated firms in trucking were in a different situation than the railroads. They were not going bankrupt. In fact, deregulation of trucking was strongly opposed by the Teamsters and by the American Trucking Association, the two beneficiaries of continued regulation. Why then was trucking also partially deregulated?

An important reason for this change was a court case. P.C. White Truck Line requested that the ICC permit it to enter new markets. The ICC turned them down. The applicant then appealed its case to the District of Columbia Court of Appeals. In 1977, the court ruled in favor of the applicant, stating that in deciding on entry requests the ICC should not only consider whether existing trucking services are adequate, but take into account the beneficial effects that increased competition might have on the public.[10] The significance of this case was that unless the ICC considered the beneficial effects of competition when judging new applications, the courts would reverse their decisions.

In subsequent decisions, the ICC placed greater emphasis on the beneficial effects of competition to the public. In the *Liberty Trucking Co.* case (1979) the ICC found that increased competition outweighed any harm that might occur to existing carriers. As a result of these decisions, the number of applications to enter trucking markets expanded by tenfold over the previous decade. The entry barriers were being removed as a result of the 1977 District of Columbia Court of Appeals judicial decision.

During this period, the ICC commissioners were slowly being replaced with market-oriented commissioners. Presidents since Kennedy had favored some form of trucking deregulation, though all were unsuccessful. In the 1970s President Ford again raised the visibility of deregulation as a political issue, promoting it as a means of reducing the rate of inflation, an important concern at the time. Oil prices had increased sharply and there was opposition to these cost increases being passed on in the form of higher shipping costs. President Ford, however, was unsuccessful in deregulating the trucking or any other industry. President Carter also saw deregulation as a partial means to combat high oil prices and stagflation in the economy; he continued to raise the visibility of deregulation as a political issue. (He was also attempting to establish his leadership on deregulation and thereby preempt his political rival, Sen. Edward Kennedy, from receiving credit for this issue.) The initial success that either administration had was to appoint regulatory commissioners who were more market-oriented. These new appointees were in favor of the court rulings (*P.C. White* and *Liberty*) that liberalized entry into trucking.

When the new appointees achieved a majority in the ICC, the ICC announced (in 1979) that they were going to reevaluate the method that had been used in establishing trucking rates (rates were set collectively, not competitively). At this point, the trucking association and the Teamsters decided it would be in their own best interest to push for legislation that would stop the movement toward competition in both entry and in pricing.

The trucking industry was successful in introducing legislation favorable to their interests in the House of Representatives. Trucking companies operate in all congressional districts; and the Teamsters and truckers' association were providing political support to many legislators. However, the administration opposed the bill as did the press, which made this restrictive legislation very visible. The press emphasized the waste and inefficiency resulting from trucking restrictions, such as truckers not being able to carry full loads both to and from their destinations. The Teamsters were also receiving bad publicity during this period; the president of the Teamsters went to jail for attempting to bribe Sen. Howard W. Cannon, the Chairman of the committee with jurisdiction over the deregulation bill, and the issue had become too visible. President Carter threatened to veto the House bill if it became law.

The Senate passed a bill that permitted the reforms in trucking to continue. Senators do not need campaign funds as frequently as representatives. Further, the size of a political contribution to a senator or representative from any one political action committee is limited by law; since Senate races require a great deal more money than races for the House, political contributions from any one group are a small percentage of a senator's total contributions. Given their broader constituencies and their needs for greater amounts of money, senators are generally less responsive than representatives to small special interest group demands. With respect to trucking legislation, however, senators up for reelection were more likely to vote for three restrictive amendments desired by the truckers and Teamsters than those senators not running for reelection.[11] Once the restrictive amendments were defeated, those senators running for reelection also voted for passage of the final bill. In this way they could say they were "pro-consumer," they had voted for deregulation.

The House went along with the Senate and the Motor Carrier Act was passed. Since 1980 was also an election year, the president, in signing this legislation, used it as an indication of his political leadership. It was believed to be important to consumers.

The big losers under partial deregulation have been the Teamsters; they had been earning approximately 50 percent more than they would in a competitive environment: in the first year after deregulation they lost half that amount.[12] Another loser was the regulated trucking firms. There has been a tremendous increase in the number of new trucking firms; between 1980 and 1982, the number of firms increased by 42 percent.[13] Price competition by the new firms, some that are owner-operated and others that use nonunion labor, has reduced the profitability of the previously protected trucking firms. One indication of the monopoly profits received by a trucking firm during regulation is the value of a trucking licen∂e, which was $530,000 in 1977 and subsequently declined to $13,000 in 1981 with increased entry. As competition increased, prices declined by approximately 25 percent between 1977 and 1982. As prices and profitability declined, the percentage of firms going bankrupt increased. As shipping prices declined, entry increased and profitability declined; Teamsters' wages declined as well. In their opposition to deregulation, the Teamsters clearly foresaw its consequences.

These consequences of competition, however, did not result in any decline in quality. According to surveys of shippers, quality either improved or stayed the same. Further, complaints by shippers to the ICC declined.[14]

The opponents of deregulation, the trucking firms and their unionized employees, continued their battle at the state level, where they have had more influence than at the federal level. The federal act deregulating interstate trucking did not preempt state laws regulating intrastate trucking. Thus only six states fully deregulated trucking during the period 1980–1991. Most states continue to regulate the movement of intrastate goods, thereby maintaining artifically higher intrastate rates.

To overcome the trucking firm's political advantage at the state level, large shippers, such as Federal Express and United Parcel Service, have continued to press for federal legislation ending state rate regulation.

Airlines

For many years, domestic air transportation policy was based on the Civil Aeronautics Act of 1938 and the Federal Aviation Act of 1958. The regulation of the industry was placed in the hands of the Civil Aeronautics Board (CAB).[15] The CAB controlled entry into the industry, not permitting a single new trunk carrier from 1938 through the 1970s. It also determined the routes that each airline could fly; regulated air fares; and exercised control over the airlines' service competition, even to the extent of regulating the amount of meat that could be served in a sandwich.[16] The CAB's primary concern in setting air fares was airline profitability. Any carrier seeking to enter another market had to prove it would not harm the carrier currently serving that market.

Some of the consequences of airline regulation were: (1) fares were approximately 50 percent higher than fares in unregulated markets (i.e., intrastate travel), such as within California and Texas; (2) there was extensive nonprice competition between the airlines, such as frequency of flights and the rapid introduction of new equipment, leading to higher operating costs; and (3) fares were set proportional to distance traveled, when in fact cost per mile was less on long-distance than short-distance flights. Cities that were less frequently traveled to were subsidized by the busier routes.

In the late 1960s, the airlines had converted their fleets to jet aircraft. In addition, the airlines competed among themselves on frequency of flights. The consequence was that airline capacity increased faster than the growth in demand. Faced with rising costs and declining profits, the airlines kept asking the CAB for increased fares.

In 1975, at the recommendation of new staff member Stephen Breyer, Senator Kennedy decided to hold hearings on airline regulation. It was believed that deregulation would be a visible consumer issue that would provide Senator Kennedy with political support.[17] Media coverage of the hearings showed that consumers were being denied the benefits of airline competition, such as lower prices. During the 1975 hearings, the airlines were opposed to any form of deregulation. However, the hearings performed an important service.

The hearings made clear that regulation was not really working for two of the major proponents of continued regulation—small cities and the airlines themselves. Certain small cities (and consequently their legislators) were concerned that air travel to their cities would be sharply curtailed under deregulation. At Senator Kennedy's hearings it was determined that few cities would actually lose their air service. Most cities did not require subsidies to have continued air service. Small aircraft, less than 30 seats, had been exempt from CAB entry limits. Exempt firms had been increasing the number of flights, and scheduling them at more convenient times, to small communities just as the CAB-regulated major airlines, with their larger planes, were decreasing service to small communities.

The hearings also showed that regulation was not working for the airlines. The protected airlines were not making monopoly profits. They had been using up the excess profits they made on their most profitable routes because of nonprice competition. Therefore the industry did not have that much to lose under deregulation. At the same time, the deregulated airlines, those flying in the intrastate markets of California and Texas, were quite profitable. At the hearings, evidence of the benefits of lower air fares to the airlines was presented. Intrastate airlines were shown to have higher load factors and increased profitability as a result of reduced fares.

In late 1975 another important event occurred. The District of Columbia Court of Appeals overturned an earlier CAB decision on the denial of a route to Continental Air Lines. After almost nine years of litigation, the court stated that the CAB's rejection of competition was not in accord with the public interest. (This was the same court that in 1977 would rule in favor of competition in trucking in the *P.C. White* case.) Although the court's decision was not a signal for unlimited entry, it was the beginning of the elimination of barriers in the airline industry's profitable cartel markets.

Faced with this criticism of its policies (and the subsequent appointment of more competitively oriented board members), the CAB permitted over the next several years a little more flexibility for air charters as a low-cost substitute to scheduled air service. American Airlines, recognizing the threat of low-cost charters serving the New York-to-California market, offered discount fares. The results were surprising; air traffic surged. The success of this fare flexibility, and its profitability for the airlines, encouraged the CAB to continue and expand fare flexibility. The airlines' profitability increased dramatically. Fares declined (adjusted for inflation), air traffic increased at a faster annual rate than in the previous ten years, and public support for airline deregulation grew.

As a result of increased information, opposition to deregulation among the airlines changed. The industry was split over the benefits of continued regulation. United, the largest domestic carrier, favored deregulation because it believed that it would have a greater chance to grow and gain market share. Under regulation it was unlikely to be awarded new routes. Pan Am, an international carrier, also favored deregulation because it wanted domestic routes but had not been able to receive any under CAB regulation. Other airlines that had competed vigorously in intrastate competition with the major airlines, PSA (California) and Southwest Airlines (Texas), believed their only chance to compete in interstate markets was in a deregulated industry.

The association representing airline interests had members with conflicting interests. Within the association, large carriers had different economic interests than the small carriers. Each airline provided its own political support to legislators; the association itself was able to provide very little. In subsequent hearings before the House, the carriers were split in their opposition to deregulation and the association did not testify.

Indicating the importance of information in changing the airlines' perceptions of the profitability of deregulation was the comment in 1986 by Frank Borman, chairman of Eastern Airlines: "I think I was most surprised by how much traffic is generated by cutting fares. Deregulation saved the industry. It turned it from what would have become a moribund, stagnant industry like the Europeans' into a vibrant, growing industry."[18]

As this perception of potential profitability spread, opposition to deregulation within the industry decreased. To alleviate the concerns of some small communities, the only potential losers under deregulation, a separate subsidy program was proposed. Legislators therefore had little to lose by supporting deregulation. They could be pro-consumer, airline opposition was no longer an important concern, and small communities would not be hurt. It was not until after all this had occurred that a deregulation bill was feasible.

In October 1978, the airline industry was deregulated. The congressional action continued what the CAB had started. The flexibility shown by the CAB and the resulting increase in air traffic and airline profits limited the opposition by the airlines to legislation officially deregulating the industry. There were no large monopoly profits to be protected by returning to the previous heavily regulated system. The public favored lower fares. Several of the major carriers (and the intrastate airlines) saw opportunities in deregulation. And the small cities, and their representatives in Congress, realized they would not be hurt by deregulation. By the time the bill came before Congress in the fall of 1978, "there was little opposition and the bill passed by a large majority."[19]

The deregulation of the airlines led to a complete reversal in the structure of the industry; after being a regulated cartel the industry felt the full force of market competition within a relatively short time period.

As a result of airline deregulation, the structure of fares changed. Prices more closely approximated costs of service. Thus air fares in long-distance and high-density markets declined up to 40 percent.[20] As fares declined, airline load factors increased. Long-distance air travel proved to be very responsive to lower prices; nonbusiness travel increased substantially. (As load factors have increased, passenger comfort has decreased. However, passengers have apparently chosen less comfort since first-class travel has fallen sharply.) An important reason for the reduction in air fares in high-density markets has been the entry of new and regional airlines. These carriers offered large discounts, created price competition, and increased their market share, which went from 12 to 30 percent between 1978 and 1982.[21]

Those airlines initially protected by the CAB had higher operating costs than their new competitors. The new entrants did not use unionized labor, paid their pilots perhaps one-third as much as the established airlines, and did not have restrictive work rules. To compete on price, the older airlines had to reduce their labor costs so that they were comparable to those of their new competitors. Unionized labor in the airlines industry had, with good reason, been opposed to deregulation. Airline employees faced difficult times; they were forced to renegotiate their wages downward. Several of the original trunk carriers had financial difficulties; Braniff went out of business and Continental declared bankruptcy (enabling it to hire nonunion employees and to change its work rules).

The structure of the industry changed after deregulation. Airlines developed a hub-and-spoke method of delivery. The major airlines encouraged regional and local airlines to serve smaller cities (the spokes), to feed more traffic into the hubs.

Throughout deregulation, quality, as measured by airline accidents and fatalities per passenger mile, improved.[22]

New York Stock Exchange

The New York Stock Exchange (NYSE) was founded in 1792 and was operated as a cartel until 1975. The NYSE had a fixed number of members, and it fixed the prices members could charge for selling and purchasing stocks. The Securities and Exchange Commission (SEC) was the government regulatory agency that enforced the economic interests of the NYSE. The monopoly power of the NYSE was based on the fact that it handled more than 80 percent of all stock trading. The NYSE also undertook a number of regulatory functions to minimize the financial irresponsibility of its members and to set minimum standards before a company could list its stock for trading on the exchange.[23]

The commission (price) charged for the purchase and sale of stock was fixed and did not reflect the actual costs of the transaction. For small orders, the commission was below the actual cost; for large orders the commission was greatly in excess of costs. There was thus a cross-subsidy from large volume traders to the small traders.

Before 1960, less than 2 percent of the volume on the NYSE was attributed to large block sales by institutions. By 1976, large institutional firms accounted for 44 percent of the NYSE volume (and 54 percent of the dollar value) of shares traded.

A new group of traders had arisen, large institutional traders with a definite economic interest in paying the lowest commissions for their trades. NYSE member firms, with fixed commission rates set by the exchange, were not permitted to engage in price competition for the business of these large traders. Instead, they engaged in nonprice competition (such as "free research") for large institutional traders, which increased their costs and thereby decreased the profitability of regulated prices. In response to the search by these large institutional traders for lower commissions, nonmember firms appeared to arrange large block sales and purchases. Such a firm would match large buy-and-sell orders for institutional traders and the sale would be consummated off the NYSE, at lower commissions. The NYSE cartel began to collapse. Large institutions also started using regional stock exchanges to place their orders. As the volume of large trades fell, the NYSE allowed its member firms to give discounts for large trades.

The elimination of fixed commissions by the Securities Acts Amendments of 1975 was a recognition of economic realities: fixed commissions were no longer economically viable.

The rise of large institutional traders, the development of (lower-cost) substitute exchanges to serve the large traders, the loss of volume by the NYSE to these substitute exchanges, and the decline in profitability of NYSE member firms that did not compete for the business of large traders, led to de facto deregulation. The change in the securities laws merely ratified what was occurring. No longer could member firms receive monopoly profits through fixed commission rates and therefore there was little economic value left to protect by maintaining fixed commissions.

Deregulation brought increased volume back to the NYSE and, as in a competitive market, commissions became more closely related to the cost of executing trades. Commissions on small trades increased by approximately 12 percent, while for large institutional traders commissions were reduced by more than 50 percent.[24] And as the cost of trading declined, volume increased. It is also believed that the lower cost of large trades increased the growth of institutional ownership of stocks through mutual funds.[25]

Brokerage firms that could only survive in a regulated environment had to merge as price competition increased. The firms were forced to take advantage of economies of scale in their operations. Previously, larger, more efficient firms had to compete at the same price as smaller firms. Larger brokerage firms favored deregulation because they believed that with their economies of scale they would be able to increase their market share at the expense of small brokerage firms. The other effect of deregulation was the emergence of discount brokers. Brokers began to unbundle their services. Previously, because large trades were so profitable, brokers competed on nonprice factors, such as research services to clients. With the rise of price competition, some customers decided to purchase their research services separately and pay just for the trading services they used. Discount brokers have captured approximately 20 percent of the retail sales market.

Brokerage firms have also diversified; revenues from commissions account for approximately 20 percent of the total revenues, down from 50 percent in 1975.[26] Brokerage firms have established related businesses in insurance, money market funds, and real estate operations.

Banks and Savings Institutions

Banking and savings and loan (S&Ls) institutions are among our most heavily regulated industries. Limits are placed on the amount of interest these institutions can pay to their depositors, on the interest they can charge on some types of loans, on who can establish new banks, and on the activities in which these institutions can engage. However, in recent years, particularly since 1980, there has been a great deal of change. Some of these changes permit banks to engage in branch banking, to operate in other states, and to pay market interest rates to customers. While the industry continues to be quite heavily regulated by federal and state authorities, deregulation has been occurring. To illustrate the reasons for partial deregulation in this industry, only one regulatory change will be examined, namely, interest paid on savings accounts.[27]

In 1933, the Federal Reserve Board promulgated Regulation Q, which established maximum interest rates (2.5 percent) that commercial banks could pay to depositors on savings accounts. These maximum rates were permitted to rise to reflect market rates until 1966. As inflation increased in the 1960s, interest rates rose (so as to provide lenders with a "real," that is, an inflation-adjusted, rate of return). The S&Ls had their assets in long-term mortgages that paid low rates of interest to the S&Ls. To attract and keep depositors, the S&Ls would have had to raise their interest rates on deposits. However, this policy would result in the S&Ls

paying more to their depositors than they were receiving on their mortgages. The S&L's solution was for Congress to extend Regulation Q to S&Ls.

Since 1966, the maximum rates paid depositors had been set below the market rate of interest. The effect of doing so was to provide S&Ls with a source of funds at a price that was below the price at which they could loan these funds. Profitability of S&Ls increased. (A reason given for setting rates to depositors below market rates was that by making S&Ls more profitable, they would increase their housing loans at lower than market rates of interest. In fact, this did not occur. Two-thirds of mortgages were written by mortgage bankers, insurance companies, and others that did not have access to this cheap source of funds. Mortgage rates were determined by the overall market.)[28]

Establishing maximum interest rates adversely affected the small saver. Savers with funds of $100,000 or more were exempt from these maximum rates after 1970. (Commercial banks, fearful that they would lose their large depositors, were allowed to pay market interest rates on large deposits.) Savers with smaller sums, $10,000 to $25,000, could invest those funds in Treasury bills and bonds and thereby receive the higher market rates of interest. It was only the small saver who did not have a substitute source for their savings that was adversely affected by having to accept the lower rates. To ensure that small savers did not withdraw their funds from S&Ls and invest in Treasury bills, the regulators increased the minimum size of Treasury bills, from $1,000 to $10,000 in 1970.

There were an overwhelming number of small savers and so the cost of this regulatory policy was diffuse; the foregone interest each saver lost was small and spread out over many individuals. The cost of organizing and representing their interests was not worth the effort.

As market interest rates continued to rise and the spread between those interest rates and the amount paid to S&L depositors increased, S&Ls had to engage in nonprice competition to attract savers. S&Ls offered radios, TV sets, and other prizes to depositors. Since this policy raised the cost to the S&Ls of attracting depositors, having the same effect as increasing interest on new deposits, it was in the S&Ls' combined interest to limit such competition. The regulators responded by setting limits on such prizes.

As a result of increasing market interest rates and regulated bank rates, money market mutual funds were formed in the early 1970s and expanded rapidly. The development of these money market mutual fund accounts drew savings from the S&Ls. However, as was initially the case with railroads, rather than rid themselves of regulations and compete, the S&Ls sought to have the money market funds placed under the same maximum rates. But they were unsuccessful in overcoming the opposition of the commercial banks and money market firms. The money market funds increased their market share as smaller depositors began to leave the S&Ls in search of higher rates of interest.

In 1978 some decontrol over maximum rates occurred. Credit unions were permitted to pay market rates to their depositors, and new types of savings accounts were established that permitted higher rates of interest. Yet complete decontrol did not occur until years later in 1986.

The S&Ls favored the continuation of maximum rates because, although they lost savers to competitors, maintaining the maximum rates was still very profitable. Even though they were losing business, S&Ls in 1982 still held almost $500 billion in savings accounts, while paying below-market rates of interest. These funds were being loaned out at market rates of interest.

The effect of partial decontrol clearly benefited the small saver; they could now receive increased interest rates on their savings. "It was estimated that decontrol would increase interest payments to depositors by at least $20 billion per year."[29] The big losers were the S&Ls. To compete, they now had to pay more for their money. They also lost customers to substitute savings sources.

The economic value of interest rate regulation to the S&Ls decreased as small depositors were able to receive higher interest rates by switching to unregulated competitors that had developed, such as mutual funds.

The gap between regulated interest rates and market rates provided an incentive for innovation to occur outside the regulated market. These competitors grew as they were able to exploit this difference in interest rates. Money market mutual funds and commercial banks also had a sufficiently strong economic interest to be able to compete successfully in the political as well as economic arena with S&Ls.

Telecommunications

Through the 1950s AT&T was a fully regulated monopoly. Large economies of scale existed in the provision of local telephone service and the Federal Communications Commission (FCC) prevented entry into the market. Local telephone services were provided by AT&T or by other local telephone companies with no effective competition. Long-distance service provided by AT&T also had the characteristics of a natural monopoly, namely, large economies of scale. Local and long-distance service used common equipment. AT&T also had a monopoly on telephone equipment, even though this market lacked the characteristics of a natural monopoly. The break-up of AT&T occurred because of changes in the equipment and long-distance markets.[30]

There was no economic reason why the equipment segment of the industry could not have been competitive. However, AT&T had the monopoly and wanted to keep it. Competition began only as a result of a successful court case against AT&T.

Hush-A-Phone was a nonelectrical, cuplike device that could be placed on the telephone to provide greater privacy. AT&T informed distributors and customers of Hush-A-Phone that this device was illegal since AT&T prohibited the attachment of any non-AT&T devices to telephones. On appeal by Hush-A-Phone, the FCC upheld AT&T's claim that it could not be used with AT&T equipment. Hush-A-Phone then appealed the decision to the Appeals Court and won. The court stated that as long as the device did not harm telephone subscribers it was permissible.

As a result of that court precedent, another innovation, Carterfone, was marketed. Carterfone connected mobile radiotelephone systems to the telephone network. When AT&T objected, the FCC, following the court-established precedent, permitted it. Once these decisions had been made, the precedents were established that ultimately severed the terminal equipment market from the rest of the AT&T monopoly.

AT&T's pricing structure and the development of new technology led to deregulation of long-distance rates. AT&T was the only provider of long-distance service. Large economies of scale existed in the provision of this service. Telephone rates were regulated so that the price of a call was approximately proportional to the distance of the call. (A similar pricing principle was used by the ICC and the CAB.) The cost of serving telephone users, however, was not proportional to the distance of their calls. The actual costs for long-distance calls fell sharply as distance increased. Thus charges were much higher than costs for long-distance calls, while local calls were priced much closer to cost and, in some cases, less than cost. This uniform pricing strategy, price being proportional to distance rather than cost, resulted in long-distance users subsidizing local-service users.

By the mid-1970s, new technology resulted in competition for AT&T's long-distance markets. The costs of microwave and satellite communications were below AT&T's traditional technology for providing long-distance telephone service. Since the price:cost ratio was highest in the long-distance market, this was also the most profitable market for the use of the new technology. Since microwave technology was not subject to large economies of scale, private firms could have their own long-distance service. Using subsidized local calls to connect their microwave system, private firms could have lower long-distance costs than AT&T's high long-distance rates. Large users of long-distance service had an incentive to purchase microwave systems given the high regulated long-distance rates.

AT&T vigorously opposed competition and the FCC protected AT&T's position by denying entry to new competitors. The courts, however, said that the FCC had to show that protection of AT&T's monopoly position was in the public interest. Unable to do so, the FCC was forced to allow competition for long-distance telephone service.

AT&T, however, controlled the local telephone markets, which were still a natural monopoly. All long-distance telephone users had to be connected to the local telephone company. AT&T's strategy was to reduce its long-distance charges to meet the competition, and raise local charges to the competitors. As long as AT&T was able to maintain monopoly power in any one of the three necessary components of telephone service—that is, equipment, long-distance service, or local service—it could maintain its monopoly position in any of the three markets. (A monopolist in any one of these markets has as much power as a monopolist of all three markets.) Although there was now competition in the equipment and long-distance markets, long-distance users had to be connected to local service, and AT&T's control over local telephone service gave it monopoly power over all three markets. AT&T could charge a sufficiently high price for local service to maintain its profits, while making it unprofitable for competitors.

In 1975 the Justice Department filed a major antitrust suit against AT&T on the grounds that AT&T had monopolized each of the three interrelated markets. The Justice Department wanted AT&T to divest itself. In that same period, there were 35 private antitrust suits filed against AT&T. AT&T's competitors claimed that they could not get equal access to AT&T's local service, thereby placing them at a competitive disadvantage.

AT&T was concerned that if it lost the antitrust suit, it would then be liable for triple damages in all the private antitrust suits that were (and that might potentially be) brought against them. (The private plaintiffs would not have to bear the expense of proving an antitrust violation but merely prove the size of their damages.) AT&T therefore decided to settle the case by separating the ownership of the competitive markets from the monopolized market. To avoid losses, local telephone services were to become a separate business. AT&T was to continue in the competitive long-distance and telephone equipment businesses.

Once the courts permitted firms using new technology to compete with AT&T in its most profitable markets, it was inevitable that long-distance charges would decline. Conversely, the price of local service, which was subsidized, increased as price:cost ratios became uniform across local and long-distance markets.

The introduction of new technology in long-distance markets changed prices for users and produced winners and losers. Users of long-distance service benefited, while users of local service paid increased charges. As the cross-subsidy between local and long-distance service disappeared, local prices increased sharply, approximately 100 percent higher than before deregulation, while long-distance prices similarly declined.

Another loser under deregulation has been management and labor. In the period immediately preceding divestiture, AT&T reduced its workforce by 6 percent and a freeze was placed on the salaries of its managers; after divestiture, AT&T continued to reduce its employees by the tens of thousands. The number of employees per manager at AT&T was only one-half those of its competitors (4 to 1 vs. 9 to 1). The pay for AT&T employees was also twice as high as its major competitors.[31] To become price-competitive, AT&T had to reduce employees, increase productivity, and renegotiate its labor contracts so that wages were comparable to its major competitors.

The regulated pricing structure for long-distance service provided large users of such services with an incentive to adopt new technology, which was not subject to large economies of scale. These users and the eventual application of this technology to smaller users would have ultimately eroded the economic value of AT&T's monopoly using more costly traditional long-distance equipment. The intervention of the courts, however, made deregulation occur much more rapidly.

The Reasons for Deregulation

Regulated industries are characterized by limited entry, fixed prices that benefit the regulated firms, employees who receive higher wages than in a competitive industry, and politically important constituencies who benefit from cross-subsidies. These three groups favor continued regulation: the regulated firms that are receiving monopoly prices, and presumably, monopoly profits; the users of subsidized services whose cross-subsidies would disappear if prices were to reflect their costs of service; and union members in the regulated industry, whose wages would be reduced if they were in a competitive industry.

Not all regulated industries have been deregulated, and some of the industries that have been deregulated have been only partially deregulated. There are, however, certain similarities among those industries that have experienced deregulation.

Increased Regulatory Costs to Groups with a Concentrated Interest

For the same reasons that firms are able to achieve regulatory benefits, an industry may lose those benefits. Regulation affecting a group will change when a change occurs in the relative political support offered by opposing groups. Regulation imposes costs on others. As these costs increase and become substantial, they provide an incentive for others to organize and provide political support so as to lessen these costs. Those bearing the costs of regulation face a simple cost-benefit calculation. For an industry adversely affected by regulation, there are costs of ascertaining the effects of regulation on their profitability, of organizing their members (and of overcoming any free rider problems), and of providing political support. The benefits are the lessened costs of regulation.

An increase in regulatory costs imposed on others is not a sufficient condition to set in motion the forces to overturn the costs of regulation. If imposed on the public in a diffuse manner, it is unlikely that individuals will find it in their interest to learn of these costs, to bear the costs of organizing, and to raise political support. An example of these large regulatory costs are federal agricultural price supports. Maintaining high farm prices costs many billions of dollars in taxes; further, the prices paid by consumers for farm products are greater than what they would be without such regulation. The cost per consumer or per taxpayer, however, is relatively small. Import restrictions (tariffs or quotas) on items such as textiles also raise the price; however, the cost to consumers is not sufficiently high to cause them to lobby Congress.

Before change can come about, large regulatory costs have to be imposed on groups with a concentrated interest in having them reduced. Firms in an industry are less costly to organize than large numbers of individuals. Firms are also more aware of policies that affect their costs and revenues. When regulatory costs become sufficiently large, it will then be worthwhile for a group to organize and raise the political support to overcome them. Money market funds and commercial banks would not have been able to raise large sums of savings had they not opposed the S&Ls on maximum interest rates. Institutional traders could not have achieved large savings on their commission rates if they had not bypassed the NYSE and developed alternative trading sources, e.g., regional exchanges. These concentrated interests saw either increased profitability or reduced cost as their benefits from deregulation.

The federal government itself (the administration) develops a concentrated interest when the financial commitments imposed on it require cutbacks in other politically popular programs or necessitate a tax increase. It was for this reason that the administration proposed greater rate and service flexibility for the railroads; it wanted to forestall additional railroad bankruptcies. The government would have had to bear large costs if they had to provide subsidies to railroads in financial difficulty. During the 1970s when inflation was increasing, deregulation was proposed by various administrations as a means of reducing the rise in prices; otherwise more politically costly measures to reduce inflation would have had to be used.

Erosion of Monopoly Profits

Another reason for deregulation is a decline in the regulated firm's profitability. Regulation was meant to achieve what the regulated firm was not able to achieve in a competitive market, namely, monopoly profits. If monopoly profits are no longer attainable through regulation, then the regulated firm has little economic incentive to support continued regulation. This was particularly true in the case of railroads, airlines, and the NYSE. As the economic value of regulation declines, so does the necessary political support offered by the firms to maintain regulation. In fact, some regulated firms actively promoted deregulation in their belief that their economic returns would be improved.

The value of regulatory benefits also declined for certain constituents of airline regulation, thereby leading to their loss of support for its continuance. Small communities became less concerned that they would lose air service if deregulation occurred.

The decline in the economic value of regulation may occur for several reasons. One reason is entry by new firms. Since the number of firms in regulated industries is limited, substitute industries arise to take away the regulated industry's monopoly profits; new firms typically enter by introducing new technology. In the case of railroads, trucking was one such innovation; with regard to the commissions on securities, regional exchanges and off-floor trading eroded the volume and profitability of the NYSE; money market mutual funds grew rapidly at the expense of the S&Ls; and microwave and satellite technology enabled new firms to enter AT&T's profitable long-distance markets.

The incentives for entry and innovation are greatest in those regulated markets where profitability is greatest, that is, where prices are highest in relation to cost. In regulated industries, prices are not set proportionate to cost; instead prices are often established proportionate to distance, volume, or some other criterion. Since unit costs in regulated industries decline as distance or volume increases, profitability is highest in long-distance or large-volume markets. With railroads, airlines, and telecommunications, profitability was greatest in the long-distance markets; in the NYSE it was large trades; in banking it was large deposits.

The initial response by the regulated industry to innovation is to reduce competition by encompassing the new competitors within the regulatory agency's jurisdiction. This occurred with railroads and it was attempted with telecommunications and banking. The truckers' association accepted regulation because they saw it as a means of limiting entry to new truckers. In telecommunications, the FCC tried to exclude new competitors but was unable to do so as a result of court intervention. In some instances, the competitors are sufficiently organized and the economic advantage of deregulation so large, that they are willing to invest the necessary political support to bring about deregulation. This was the case in banking (the commercial banks) and in securities trading (the large institutions desiring lower commissions).

When new competitors enter the regulated firm's markets, they decrease the regulated firm's market share and profitability.

The other reason for erosion of monopoly profits in regulated industries is intensive nonprice competition. Since prices are fixed and above costs, regulated firms compete for market share by offering additional services or amenities. The airlines introduced jet aircraft and increased the number of scheduled flights. The S&Ls offered prizes to new depositors, and securities firms offered research services to attract customers. Eventually the regulatory agency has to establish limits on nonprice competition, which raises costs and reduces profitability. Profitability of airlines and railroads increased when price flexibility became permissible.

Courts and Antitrust

The antitrust laws are another important reason why industries have been deregulated. The federal judicial system is less in need of political support, hence less subject to political pressures than Congress or the regulatory agencies. Consequently, the federal courts are more likely to act without regard to a specific industry's economic interest when applying the antitrust laws. While it is possible for a concentrated interest group to receive congressional exemption from the antitrust laws, it has been very difficult to do so. (There are a few exceptions—labor unions are one.) For an industry to receive an exemption requires a much higher degree of political support (i.e., a higher cost), than is required to achieve regulatory benefits for an industry where those costs are diffuse and less visible.

It was the prospect of losing an antitrust case, with its consequent economic losses, that convinced AT&T it should settle with the government. Previously, there had been several successful court appeals by competitors that enabled them to enter AT&T's protected markets. Had it not been for the judicial system and the applicability of the antitrust laws, AT&T would have been able to retain its monopoly power. The courts were also important in permitting increased entry in trucking and airlines.

The basis of the antitrust laws is that competition will achieve economic efficiency and thus may be said to be in the public interest. The development of new technology that provides a low-cost substitute to the service provided by a regulated industry threatens the regulated industry's revenues. The regulated industry will at first try to include that technology under the regulatory agency's jurisdiction. In that way the regulated industry can control the introduction of low-cost substitutes. However, if antitrust suits are brought against the regulated industry, it is likely that the courts will rule that competition will be in the public interest. At that point the regulatory agency will have to accommodate the new competitors. The ultimate effect, which usually takes a number of years to play out, will be a loss of revenues for the regulated industry and its eventual deregulation. The federal judicial system may be society's best method of assuring the introduction of new technology.

Deregulation is most likely to occur in those circumstances where low-cost substitutes erode the market share and profitability of the regulated firms. There is then little economic value remaining for the regulated industry to protect. As profitability decreases, so does the amount of political support that firms are willing to provide to maintain regulation. When the courts become involved because of antitrust claims, then the regulated firms are unable to prevent erosion of their profits.

When the courts are not involved, as in those cases where Congress provides explicit mandates to the regulatory agency, then attempts at deregulation are less certain. The power of opposing interests will determine the outcome. If the regulated firms still receive large economic benefits from regulation, then they will strongly oppose deregulation. For example, the truckers' association and the Teamsters were able to maintain regulatory benefits at the state level long after interstate trucking was deregulated.

When the regulated firms continue to receive large economic benefits and the costs of regulation are diffuse, opposing interest groups are unlikely to arise, and deregulation is unlikely to occur. It is for these reasons that many industries retain their regulatory benefits, for example, dairy price supports and maritime shipping rates.

The deregulation trends of the 1970s occurred because of the rise of opposing interest groups, lower-cost substitutes, decline in profitability of the regulated firms, and the jurisdiction of the federal courts. It was not because it was an idea whose time had come.

Study Questions for Chapter 5

1. What were some of the dissatisfactions with the public interest theory that led to the development of the economic theory of legislation?
2. What would the public interest and the economic theory predict would be the legislative position of regulated industries toward attempts to deregulate their industry?
3. Why did the railroad industry seek deregulation?
4. Critique the "An Idea Whose Time Has Come" theory to explain deregulation during the 1970s and 1980s.
5. What are alternative explanations for the industries that were deregulated during the 1970s and 1980s?

Notes

1. The discussion in this section is based on Sam Peltzman. 1989. "The Economic Theory of Regulation After a Decade of Deregulation," *Brookings Papers: Microeconomics 1989*. Washington, D.C.: The Brookings Institution. 1–41. (Also see the comments by Roger Noll on Peltzman's paper, 48–59). Marcus Alexis. 1983. "The Political Economy of Federal Regulation of Surface Transportation," *The Political Economy of Deregulation*, edited by Roger G. Noll and Bruce M. Owen. Washington, D.C.: American Enterprise Institute. 115–31; Marcus Alexis. 1982. "The Applied Theory of Regulation: Political Economy at the Interstate Commerce Commission," *Public Choice* 39 (1) 5–27; Thomas G. Moore. 1986. "Rail and Trucking Deregulation," in Leonard W. Weiss and Michael W. Klass, *Regulatory Reform: What Actually Happened*. Boston: Little, Brown and Company. 14–39; Theodore E. Keeler. 1984. "Theories of Regulation and the Deregulation Movement," *Public Choice* 44 (1) 103–45; Ann F. Friedlaender. 1981. "Equity, Efficiency, and Regulation in the Rail and Trucking Industries," in Leonard W. Weiss and Michael W. Klass, *Case Studies in Regulation: Revolution and Reform*. Boston: Little, Brown and Company; Martha Derthick and Paul J. Quirk. 1985. *The Politics of Deregulation*. Washington, D.C.: The Brookings Institution.
2. Moore, "Rail and Trucking Deregulation," 20.
3. Ibid., 22.
4. Christopher C. Barnekov. 1987. "The Track Record," *Regulation* 11 (1) 19–27.
5. Elizabeth E. Bailey. 1986. "Price and Productivity Change Following Deregulation: The U.S. Experience," *The Economic Journal* 96 (381) 1–17.
6. Ibid., 22.
7. Thomas G. Moore. 1983. "Rail and Truck Reform—The Record So Far," *Regulation* 37–47. Also see John C. Taylor. 1994. "Regulation of Trucking by the States," *Regulation* 2, 37–47; Thomas G. Moore. 1995. "Clearing the Track: The Remaining Transportation Regulations," *Regulation* 2, 77–87.

8. Barnekov, "The Track Record," 19.

9. Ibid., 26.

10. *P.C. White Truck Line, Inc. v. Interstate Commerce Commission and United States of America,* 551 Federal Reporter, 2d Series, 132.

11. Derthick and Quirk, *The Politics of Deregulation,* 134.

12. Moore, "Rail and Truck Reform—The Record So Far," 39.

13. Ibid., 37.

14. Ibid., 40.

15. The discussion in this section is based on Alfred E. Kahn. "Deregulation and Vested Interests: The Case of Airlines," in Noll and Owen, eds., *The Political Economy of Deregulation*; Daniel P. Kaplan. "The Changing Airline Industry," in Weiss and Klass, *Regulatory Reform: What Actually Happened.* 40–77. Theodore E. Keeler. "The Revolution in Airline Regulation," in Weiss and Klass, eds., *Case Studies in Regulation: Revolution and Reform*; Derthick and Quirk. *The Politics of Deregulation.*

16. Noll and Owen, *The Political Economy of Deregulation,* 156.

17. Derthick and Quirk, *The Politics of Deregulation,* 40–41.

18. "Frank Borman on Deregulation, Unions, Managing—and Borman," *The Wall Street Journal,* June 11, 1986, 33.

19. Leonard W. Weiss. "Introduction: The Regulatory Reform Movement," in Weiss and Klass, *Regulatory Reform: What Actually Happened.* 10.

20. Bailey. "Price and Productivity Change Following Deregulation: The U.S. Experience," 6. Also see Thomas G. Moore. 1986. "U.S. Airline Deregulation: Its Effects on Passengers, Capital, and Labor," *The Journal of Law and Economics* 29 (April) 10.

21. Bailey, "Price and Productivity Change Following Deregulation: The U.S. Experience," 12.

22. Kahn, "Deregulation and Vested Interests: The Case of Airlines," 148.

23. This discussion is based on Gregg A. Jarrell. 1984. "Change at the Exchange: The Causes and Effects of Deregulation," *The Journal of Law and Economics* 27 (2) 273–312; and Hans Stoll, "Revolution in the Regulation of Securities Markets: An Examination of the Effects of Increased Competition," in Weiss and Klass, *Case Studies in Regulation: Revolution and Reform.*

24. Bailey. "Price and Productivity Change Following Deregulation: The U.S. Experience," 5.

25. Ibid.

26. Ibid., 11.

27. The discussion in this section is based on Andrew S. Carron. "The Political Economy of Financial Regulation," in Noll and Owen, eds., *The Political Economy of Deregulation;* and Lawrence J. White. "The Partial Deregulation of Banks and Other Depository Institutions," in Weiss and Klass, editors, *Regulatory Reform: What Actually Happened.*

28. Carron, "The Political Economy of Financial Regulation," 71.

29. Ibid., 73.

30. The discussion in this section is based on Gerald W. Brock. "The Regulatory Change in Telecommunications: The Dissolution of AT&T," in Weiss and Klass, *Regulatory*

Reform: What Actually Happened, 210–33; Keeler, "Theories of Regulation and the Deregulation Movement," 103–45; and Sam Peltzman, *Deregulation: The Expected and the Unexpected,* Selected Paper No. 61, Graduate School of Business, University of Chicago, April, 1985.

31. Bailey, "Price and Productivity Change Following Deregulation: The U.S. Experience."

THE EMERGENCE OF MARKET COMPETITION
IN THE U.S. HEALTHCARE SYSTEM

Since the mid-1980s, the delivery of medical services in the United States has changed dramatically. Rather than moving in the direction of increased regulation, which was the trend during the 1970s, market competition has become the dominant force affecting hospitals and health professionals.

Hospitals and physicians are joining forces and becoming part of an integrated delivery system. As hospitals have experienced dramatic declines in their occupancy rates and competition is increasingly on the basis of which hospital can offer lower prices to insurers, hospitals have become more efficient and have begun to merge with other hospitals in an attempt to gain market power over insurers. After years of concern over shortages of physicians, nurses, and dentists, surpluses of health professionals, particularly among specialists, has become a problem as capitated payment systems use more primary care providers and fewer specialists to deliver medical services. These problems were not anticipated.

Why did these changes occur? The U.S. healthcare system was highly regulated and there was apparently no reason to assume a change in trends. The economic motivation of existing providers was to maintain the status quo; market competition threatens their economic well-being. In such circumstances change is unlikely to occur.

Once many of the regulatory constraints on the medical care system have been removed, what are the implications of market competition for healthcare providers? And is the public likely to be worse off as a result of market competition?

U.S. Medical System Before Market Competition

Goal of Increased Access to Medical Care

In 1966 Medicare and Medicaid were started. Medicare is a federal program to finance the medical costs of the elderly, with well-defined benefits and beneficiaries. Under Medicaid certain minimum benefits and classes of beneficiaries are defined, however the individual states have flexibility to increase those benefits and expand eligibility for those considered to be medically indigent. The federal government assists the states in paying for the programs.

To ensure that hospitals and physicians participated in these public programs, hospitals were required by the federal government to accept Medicare patients (but not Medicaid patients). In turn the federal and state governments generously paid hospitals according to their costs (plus 2 percent under Medicare) and paid physicians fee-for-service, according to their usual and customary fees. These financial inducements resulted in high participation rates by hospitals and physicians in both programs. As a result of Medicare and Medicaid, the aged and the medically indigent increased their use of hospitals and physicians.[1]

Rising inflation during the late 1960s (to finance the Vietnam War) served to further stimulate the private demand for health insurance. As incomes increased due to inflation, employees moved into higher income tax brackets and unions bargained for increased health benefits. Employees preferred to receive health insurance as a fringe benefit, since fringe benefits were not taxed. The tax advantages of employer-purchased health insurance increased as the employees' incomes rose and they moved into higher marginal tax brackets. (Until 1981 the highest marginal tax bracket was 70 percent.)

As insurance coverage in the private sector increased, consumers' out-of-pocket price for medical services decreased and their concern over rising medical costs diminished. Price competition among third-party payers (i.e., Blue Cross and commercial insurers), in the private sector was limited as employees became less price sensitive. The Blues had a competitive advantage over the commercials in that they received large discounts from the hospitals (which provided their initial capital and controlled them). And certain unions, the largest of which was the United Auto Workers, would not contract with commercial insurers. Commercial insurers did not use aggressive cost-containment methods, such as utilization review, in part because of concern that physician organizations would boycott their plans.

With the increase in insurance coverage, from both the private and government sectors, an "erosion of the medical marketplace" began.[2] Out-of-pocket medical prices to consumers diminished and providers sharply increased their prices with little fear of diminished demand. With increased demand for medical services and rising medical prices, health insurance premiums increased rapidly. Part of the increased cost of health insurance premiums were paid by employees in the form of lower wage increases and the remainder were passed on by the employer in the form of higher prices for their goods and services. In a growing economy with increasing inflation, higher prices and lower wage increases due to higher insurance premiums were less noticeable to both the worker and the public.

There was a great deal of satisfaction with the healthcare system during this period. The aged and the poor received increased access to mainstream medical care. Congress consistently voted for increased health expenditures, medical research, increased benefits under Medicare, inclusion of new beneficiary groups under Medicare, and expansion of health manpower training programs. Health programs were politically popular with both consumers and health providers.

During this period, physicians had medical responsibility for the care of their patients, but were not fiscally responsible for the costs of treatment. Each provider was paid separately by the third-party payer. Patients had limited financial incentive to be concerned with their treatment costs. Physicians had the financial incentive to provide more services since they were paid a fee for each service. Hospitals were being reimbursed, for the most part, according to their costs, and this gave them a strong incentive to expand their services. Hospitals competed, but it was for physicians and prestige. Blue Cross and Medicare did not pay for out-of-hospital services, thereby providing patients with the incentive to have all their medical needs attended to in the most expensive setting, the hospital.

The determination of the number of health providers and the size of their practices was not based on which size firm was most efficient, as is the case in competitive industries. Instead, provider preferences and state regulation were the determining factors. Small and large hospitals, whose facilities and services were little used, were able to survive and even grow. Physicians were able to remain as solo practitioners or join groups according to their preference. State practice acts placed limits on the tasks permitted to different health professions. Advertising was considered to be unethical and was banned by medical societies or by state practice acts. There were sanctions on fee splitting and prohibitions against the corporate practice of medicine, e.g., prepaid health plans.

Pressures for Change

The large increases in demand from both the public and private sectors, together with the declining portion of the bill paid for by the patient, led to rapidly rising prices and expenditures for medical services. The cost of those services most covered by insurance, such as hospital care, increased fastest. Out-of-pocket payments by the public for all medical services declined from 52 percent in 1965 to 18 percent in 1993. For hospital care the decline in the portion of the bill paid out-of-pocket was more significant, falling from 17 percent in 1965 to about 5 percent. In 1965 patients paid 62 percent of the bill for physician services themselves; in 1985 they paid less than 20 percent of the bill.[3]

As a consequence, federal expenditures for Medicare and Medicaid increased enormously, from $3.6 billion in 1965 to $31.4 billion by 1975, to more than $112 billion by 1985, and to $230 billion in 1993. State expenditures under Medicaid also increased sharply, from $4.3 billion in 1965 to $42 billion in 1993. Expenditures in the private sector went from $31 billion a year in 1965 to $500 billion in 1993. The more rapid increase in public expenditures (federal and state) increased the overall portion of the health sector that was paid for by public funds, from 22 percent in 1965 to 45 percent in 1994.[4]

These massive increases in health expenditures from both the public and private sectors greatly exceeded the economy's rate of inflation. Healthcare as a percent of GNP went from 5.9 percent in 1965 to about 15 percent currently. *These expenditures were equivalent to a huge redistribution program, from the taxpayers to those working in the health sector and to the beneficiaries of these programs.*

Early attempts to reduce the rise in health expenditures came from the federal government. Original expectations were that Medicare would cost only $2 billion a year and reach $9 billion per year by the early 1990s. However, Medicare was an entitlement program and its benefits and beneficiaries were defined by law; no limit was placed on its overall expenditures. Unless the rise in Medicare expenditures was reduced, the Medicare Trust Fund would be bankrupt. Successive administrations developed a concentrated interest in halting Medicare's rapidly escalating expenditures. However, any administration asking Congress to change the law by imposing a greater contribution on the aged would have lost a great deal of political support from the aged and their supporters. Thus the federal government had only two alternatives for limiting the increase in Medicare expenditures, which were rising by approximately 15 percent a year. These alternatives were either to continue to increase the Medicare tax on employee wages or to limit payments to providers.

Both choices, increasing the Medicare tax and paying providers less, was troublesome (politically) for an administration. But less so than reducing benefits or increasing contributions from the aged.

The federal government started chipping away at the cost-based reimbursement of hospitals in 1969, when it removed the plus 2 percent from the cost-plus formula. In 1971, because of rising inflation, President Nixon placed the entire U.S. economy under a wage and price freeze (the Economic Stabilization Program). The rest of the economy was removed from this freeze after one year. However, the health sector remained under price controls until April 1974. In the first year following their removal, physician and hospital expenditures increased very rapidly, 17.5 percent and 19.4 percent, respectively.

Additional regulatory methods were used to limit these rapid expenditure increases. Each one failed. Physician fee increases under Medicare were limited by the Medicare fee index; the result was that increasing numbers of physicians declined to participate in the Medicare program, while physicians who did participate charged for additional services, thereby negating the effect of the fee freeze. Congress passed the National Health Planning and Resources Development Act (certificate of need) in 1974, which placed limits on hospitals' capital expenditures. Certificate of Need (CON) was supposed to limit both the number of hospital beds and the number of expensive, but little used, facilities and services in an area. Researchers have since shown what many expected, that the CON legislation had no effect on decreasing the rate of increase in hospital expenditures.[5] Utilization review programs (Professional Standards Review Organizations, or PSROs) for Medicare patients were passed by Congress in 1972. Again empirical studies failed to find significant savings in hospital use or expenditures as a result of these programs.[6]

In 1979 President Carter made hospital cost containment his highest legislative priority. His proposed legislation would have placed limits on the annual percent increase in each hospital's expenditures. The regulatory approach moved from the use of indirect methods, such as limits on capital expenditures (CON) and utilization (PSROs), to placing direct controls on hospital expenditures.

President Carter suffered an important legislative defeat. The American Medical Association (AMA) and hospital associations were instrumental in providing political support to defeat the proposed legislation.[7] The proposed cost-containment legislation was too direct a threat to hospitals' goals and revenues. Previous regulation, such as CON, was not only ineffective in preventing hospitals from expanding but it was also used to protect those same hospitals from competition.[8] Federal efforts to control the rise in federal health expenditures were stymied.

Meanwhile a number of states began implementing their own rate review programs. These programs were, in many cases, assisted in implementation and design by the state hospital associations themselves. Rather than have stringent rate controls imposed at the federal level, many hospital spokespersons believed that their influence would be greater at the state level and that state rate review programs would be more considerate of individual hospital differences.[9]

By the late 1970s, it appeared that pressures to contain the rise in health expenditures would result in increased regulation. Rather than eliminate previous regulations (such as CON) proven to be ineffective, additional regulations were proposed. Hospitals were to be subject to controls on their use, on their capital, and on their operating expenditures, as well as on their ability to enter other hospital markets; they began to be talked about as if they were "public utilities."

Emergence of Market Competition

A number of events provided the preconditions for market competition, namely, federal legislation that unintentionally created excess capacity among physicians and hospitals and, second, businesses that developed a concentrated interest in holding down their employees' health insurance premiums. However, it was the application of the antitrust laws that made it possible for competition to occur.

Federal Initiatives

Increased supply of physicians. For approximately 15 years, through the 1950s and early 1960s, the supply of physicians in relation to the population remained constant, at 141 physicians per 100,000. During this period physicians' incomes were rising (compared to those of other occupations) as were the number of applicants to medical schools.[10] As the demand for physicians' services continued to grow, stimulated by the passage of Medicare and Medicaid and the growth of private health insurance, an increased number of foreign medical graduates came to the United States.

During this period there was constant talk of a physician shortage. Many qualified U.S. students who could not gain admission to medical school went overseas to receive their education. Many middle-class families were concerned that their sons and daughters would not become physicians while, at the same time, there was increased immigration by foreign medical graduates. Congress responded to these constituent pressures and passed the Health Professions Educational Assistance Act. Senator Ralph Yarborough stated the reasons for the passage of the act in 1963. "It was when we were trying to give more American boys and girls a chance for a medical education, so that we would not have to drain the help of other foreign countries." And again, "To me it is just shocking that we do not give American boys and girls a chance to obtain a medical education so that they can serve their own people."[11] It took a number of years before the full magnitude of this act took effect. New medical schools were built and existing schools were given financial incentives to increase their spaces. (The same occurred for other health professions.)

By 1980 the supply of physicians had reached 200 per 100,000, almost a 50 percent increase from the early 1960s, when it was 141 per 100,000. Continuing to rise rapidly, the supply of physicians exceeded 250 per 100,000 by the early 1990s.[12]

Contrary to what many believed, the market for physicians does follow the laws of supply and demand. With the rapid increase in the supply of physicians, physicians developed excess capacity. As a result, there has been an increase in the number of physicians participating in Medicare, physicians relocating to areas previously short of physicians,[13] and physicians willing to discount their fees in return for greater volume.

In response to their constituents' interests and over the objections of the AMA, Congress enacted legislation that eventually created excess capacity among physicians. Although it was not the intent of Congress to create competition among physicians, their actions in passing the Health Professions Educational Assistance Act set the stage for it.

The HMO Act.   In the early 1970s, President Nixon wanted a health initiative that would not be very costly to the federal government. His proposal (developed by Paul Ellwood) was to stimulate the growth of prepaid health plans, renamed health maintenance organizations (HMOs).

When Congress passed the HMO Act in 1973, it included two provisions helpful to the development of HMOs and one that was a hindrance. First, firms with 25 or more employees had to offer their employees an

HMO option if there was a federally qualified HMO available. Second, federally qualified HMOs were exempt from restrictive state practices. (A reason often mentioned by survey respondents for not choosing an HMO was a lack of information about how such an organization delivers care.[14] Mandating an HMO option through the workplace enabled a federally qualified HMO to provide this information in a low-cost manner.)

In the initial HMO legislation, federally qualified HMOs were required to offer a set of benefits that generally exceeded the benefits offered by their competition, such as the traditional Blue Cross plans, thereby raising their premiums. This requirement proved a hindrance in that few existing HMOs opted to become federally qualified. This restriction was eased in subsequent amendments to the HMO Act.

HMOs initially had a small competitive effect. They represented a small percent of the market and there was limited premium competition. HMOs generally set their premium equal to that of Blue Cross (which was the amount employers were willing to pay on behalf of their employees) and tried to attract subscribers by offering additional benefits. By not offering lower premiums, employers did not save when their employees joined the HMO. HMOs, however, achieve their savings by decreasing the use of hospitals. As more people joined HMOs, the decreased hospital usage of HMO subscribers contributed to hospitals' excess capacity.

The 1979 amendments to the CON legislation. The initial CON legislation established planning agencies whose purpose was to limit the increase in hospital capital expenditures. HMOs needed access to a hospital to provide a full range of medical services. Some HMOs had hospitals they wanted to expand, while other HMOs wanted to construct hospitals. HMOs began to complain to Congress that CON legislation was being used to block their growth, since they were viewed as a competitive threat by physicians and existing hospitals. HMOs decreased the use of hospitals and locked patients into the HMO delivery system, thereby making them inaccessible to providers not participating in the HMO. "HMOs were subjected to more extensive controls than fee-for-service providers. Although financing plans and provider organizations of other kinds could be established without government approval, establishment of an HMO was subject to planning agency review."[15]

In 1979 Congress amended the CON legislation so that the act could not be used to inhibit competition. While these amendments did not grant all HMOs a complete exemption from the CON act, they loosened the restrictions.[16] The large HMOs fared better in the legislation than the smaller, newly developing ones. The larger HMOs, located in states with rapid HMO growth such as California, used their political influence to provide themselves with a competitive advantage over the small HMOs, which did not receive the same exclusion from planning agency review.

Even after Congress loosened the anticompetitive restrictions of the CON act, many states continued to use CON in an anticompetitive manner, denying entry to freestanding surgicenters and attempting to reduce the bed capacity of small, lower-cost hospitals.

Except for the change in the CON legislation and the enactment of the HMO Act and its amendments, it was difficult for Congress to develop a consensus with the various health interest groups as to what legislative approach, if any, should be proposed to resolve the problem of rising federal health expenditures.

Some opponents of President Carter's cost-containment legislation, such as Representatives Richard Gephardt and David Stockman, began to propose an alternative approach—the use of market competition. Various academics, such as Alain Enthoven, wrote on the virtues of market competition.[17] Health interest groups, however, such as the AMA, the American Hospital Association (AHA), the insurance companies, the Blues, and the unions, all testified against competitive approaches.

Elimination of "free choice" of provider under Medicaid. It was not until several years later, under President Reagan, that additional cost-containment legislation was enacted. In 1981 Congress amended the Medicaid Act to provide states with greater flexibility in how they pay providers. States were no longer required to offer their medically indigent "free choice" of medical provider. This meant that states could take bids and negotiate contracts with selected providers for the care of their medically indigent. Although states were a potentially powerful market force in the Medicaid program, many moved slowly. By 1994, 24 percent of the Medicaid population was enrolled in managed care.[18]

New hospital payment system under Medicare. Then, early in the Reagan administration, a revolutionary method was introduced to pay hospitals under Medicare, that of diagnosis-related groups (DRGs). The hospital and medical associations were powerless against a Republican administration intent on reducing federal expenditures for hospitals.

Payment to hospitals according to DRGs was phased in over a five-year period starting in September 1983. Hospitals were now paid a fixed price per admission for the care of their Medicare patients. The incentives facing hospitals changed. It was now in their economic interest to provide less rather than more service. Lengths of stay for the elderly began to decline. Medicare patients, who represented approximately 40 percent of hospitals' patient days, began to be discharged earlier. The average length of stay for the aged declined from 9.9 days in 1983 to 8 days in

1994. More dramatic than the decline in the length of stay was the decline in total patient days per 1,000 Medicare enrollees. These declined from 3,842 days per 1,000 in 1983 to 2,473 in 1994.[19]

By the time hospitals began to experience the effect of DRGs on their occupancy rates, however, the move toward market competition had already started. DRGs reinforced the competitive pressures on hospitals stimulated several years earlier by declining occupancy rates.

Private Sector Initiatives

Approximately two-thirds of the population has private health insurance coverage, most of which is purchased through the workplace. The stimulus for competition started in the private sector.

In 1981 the nation was faced with a severe recession. In addition, the automobile and steel industries faced increased import competition from foreign producers. These were also the same industries that had the most comprehensive health insurance programs for their employees. The recession led to unemployment, loss of income, and a decrease in health insurance benefits, resulting in a decline in elective hospital admissions. The recession also lowered tax revenues for states. Consequently, many states cut back on their Medicaid benefits, decreased the numbers eligible for Medicaid, and instituted cost-containment measures, such as prior authorization for admission. As a result of these factors, the hospital admission rate for those under 65 years of age started to decline in late 1981.

Once the recession ended, industry was still concerned with labor costs. Those industries engaged in competition with foreign producers found that the strength of the U.S. dollar relative to other currencies forced them to reduce their costs to remain competitive.

Industry began to examine ways in which they could contain the increase in their employees' health insurance costs. Greater pressure was placed on health insurers to hold down their premium increases and to institute new cost-saving programs. Also, an increasing number of business firms started their own self-insurance plans. The firms believed that they, rather than insurance companies, would be better able to control their employees' healthcare use. Other firms joined healthcare coalitions in their area. These coalitions collected data on the use rates and charges of different providers to determine which providers were more costly. Businesses also imposed deductibles and coinsurance requirements on their employees' health plans, thereby increasing their employees' price sensitivity. This trend has continued.

One of the most important changes firms (or insurance companies on their behalf) introduced was a change in the benefit package. Insurance coverage for lower-cost substitutes to hospitals was introduced. Previously, even though it was less costly to perform surgery in an outpatient setting, if this service was not covered by insurance it then became less costly to the employee to have the surgery performed in a hospital. Thus by adding outpatient surgery to the benefit package the insurance premium paid by the business could be reduced.

Private sector initiatives had two effects. First, as purchasers of healthcare benefits the private sector demonstrated that it was concerned with healthcare costs. This concern was transmitted to the health insurers and resulted in insurers becoming more concerned with utilization review of providers. Preauthorization for admission, concurrent review, and second opinions for surgery were instituted as means of reducing the insurance premium. Insurers, particularly the Blues, began to change their relationship with providers and became more adversarial. They began to place greater pressure on hospitals to limit their cost increases. As competition among insurers increased, so did the types of plans that they offered. Insurers formed preferred provider organizations (PPOs) and HMOs. PPOs and HMOs restrict the employees' choice of provider in return for either increased benefits or lower insurance premiums.

The second consequence of businesses' concern with employee health costs was that hospitals developed excess capacity. The efforts to reduce hospital utilization, such as utilization controls, the growth of HMOs, and coverage of care in nonhospital settings, were succeeding. Hospital utilization rates started to decline. As a result, occupancy rates in nonfederal, nonprofit, short-term general hospitals declined from 76 percent in 1980 to 64 percent by 1985 and to 60 percent currently.[20] During this time, a number of hospitals have also closed. As excess capacity increased, hospitals participated with HMOs and PPOs. Subscribers to HMOs and PPOs were locked in to using only participating providers. Providers not participating in HMOs and PPOs had access only to a declining population base. With increased excess capacity, hospitals began forming their own PPOs and joining HMOs.

Practices associated with traditional forms of market competition soon started, such as hospital discounts to HMOs, PPOs offering businesses lower prices, and advertising by providers as well as by HMOs and insurers.

The new approach used by Medicare—paying hospitals by DRGs—and private contracting by Medicaid reinforced the incentives facing hospitals in the private sector to lower their costs. The pressure on hospitals to compete was reinforced as utilization by the elderly and the poor declined.

Enforcement of Antitrust Laws

Concern by business with employees' healthcare costs and the creation of excess capacity among both hospitals and physicians were important preconditions for competition. However, had it not been for the application of the antitrust laws, it is unlikely that market competition would have occurred.

Medical societies and state practice acts inhibited market competition by limiting advertising, fee splitting, corporate practice, and delegation of tasks. Blue Cross and Blue Shield maintained the principle of "free choice"; that is, their subscribers had no incentive to choose between providers on the basis of price. Blue Cross enrollees had a service benefit policy. Regardless of whether the participating hospital had high or low costs, Blue Cross paid 100 percent of their enrollees' hospital costs. Under Blue Shield, price comparisons by enrollees were also discouraged; Blue Shield reimbursed participating physicians according to their usual fees (up to a percentile limit).

In the 1930s, during the Depression, the same preconditions for market competition existed. Physicians and hospitals had excess capacity; patients and their insurance companies were concerned with the cost of healthcare. And yet market competition did not occur. For example, insurance companies in Oregon attempted to lower their insurance premiums so as to better compete for subscribers. The method used to reduce the cost of the insurance premium was to place restraints on physician utilization. Preauthorization of services and monitoring of claims were the methods used. Physicians accepted such constraints on their behavior because they did not have as many patients as a result of the Depression and were not sure of their ability to collect from those they did have. Consumers benefited from the lower insurance premiums.

The response by the medical societies in Oregon to a competitive market in medical care was twofold: first, the medical societies threatened to expel any physician who participated in these competitive insurance plans. Second, the medical societies started their own insurance plans, which did not use aggressive utilization methods. With the growth of their own insurance plans, physicians were encouraged to boycott other plans. The effect of these policies was to cause the other insurance plans to decline. To have physicians participate in their plans, the insurance companies had to drop their aggressive cost-containment efforts. The medical societies were thereby able to determine that the type of insurance programs offered to the public were also those in the physicians' economic interests.[21] Therefore, unless the antitrust laws were applicable to the health sector, physician and hospital boycotts and other anticompetitive behavior could have prevented market competition from occurring once again.

Up until 1975 it was believed that the antitrust laws did not apply to "learned professions," which included the health professions. In 1975 the U.S. Supreme Court decided the case of *Goldfarb v. Virginia State Bar.* The local bar association, believing that lawyers were not engaged in "trade or commerce," established a minimum fee schedule. The Supreme Court ruled against the bar association, thereby denying any sweeping exclusion of the learned professions from the antitrust laws.[22] In another important precedent, the Supreme Court in 1978 denied the use of anticompetitive behavior by the National Society of Professional Engineers even if it was to prevent a threat to either the profession's ethics or to public safety. Encouraged by these Supreme Court decisions, the Federal Trade Commission (FTC) began to vigorously enforce the antitrust laws in the health field. The FTC, in 1975, charged the AMA and its constituent medical societies with anticompetitive behavior. In a 1978 decision, the FTC prevailed. The AMA appealed the verdict to the Supreme Court, but was again unsuccessful.

The Supreme Court's decision, rendered in 1982, was a clear signal to health providers that they would now be subject to the antitrust laws.

The AMA led other professional associations in a lobbying effort in Congress to exempt state-regulated professions from the jurisdiction of the FTC. It was reported by one lobbyist that this was the AMA's most important fight since its battle against Medicare in 1965.[23]

The AMA was able to gather 219 cosponsors (a majority) to their bill in the House of Representatives, placing a moratorium on the FTC's jurisdiction. The AMA's stated position was, "The standards of quality established by the American Medical Association and other medical societies . . . are being undermined by a federal agency that possesses no medical qualifications."[24]

Reminiscent of the political influence of the truckers and Teamsters, the AMA was successful in having their self-interest legislation passed in the House. The AMA and its state societies contribute a great deal more to political campaigns than any other health association.[25]

Although the AMA attempted to portray the legislation as preventing the FTC from "meddling" in the quality of medical care, it was quickly viewed by others as being in the self-interest of its proponents. While lawyers would also have been one of the state-regulated professions exempted from FTC jurisdiction (and thereby able to prohibit advertising among lawyers and set minimum prices for legal services), the "American Bar Association's antitrust section urged lawyers to oppose exemption, calling it a special-interest ploy that would injure consumers."[26] Still others said that the AMA was more interested in placing "the economic health of its members above the nation's physical health."[27] The press also began to pick up the story. An analysis of campaign contributions by health political action committees prepared by Congress Watch stimulated new articles and editorials around the country, and a commentary by newsman Bill Moyers on the *CBS Evening News* (May 18, 1982). The opponents of the legislation were able to generate "the rarest of political weapons—public opinion."[28]

Other organizations also opposed the AMA and the bill's proponents. The Washington Businessman's Group on Health, which represents nearly 200 of the Fortune 500 companies, believed the FTC restrictions proposed by the AMA would increase the cost of employee health insurance. An incident affecting the practices of some of their members convinced the American Nurses Association that it needed the FTC's protection. Under the pressure of local medical societies, certain rural clinics, where nurse practitioners were working under the supervision of physicians, were closed when the insurance companies revoked the malpractice insurance of the participating physicians.[29] These and more than 30 other health and consumer organizations formed a coalition opposing the bill restricting the FTC. They stimulated grassroots support through TV programs, newspaper editorials, and articles on the op-ed pages.

Despite this publicity and grassroots pressure, the bill passed by a large margin in the House of Representatives, 245 to 155. Apparently, the representatives' continual needs for campaign contributions carried the day for the bill's proponents. The Senate, however, defeated the bill 59 to 37. The Senate's action was again similar to their rejection of restrictive trucking legislation. (The truckers and Teamsters were successful in the House but not in the Senate.) The Reagan administration also opposed the bill. The AMA and its allies were able to offer greater political support in the House so they were successful in that chamber. Once again, however, the Senate did not go along with the House. Perhaps the six-year terms of senators provided some insulation from the constant need for campaign contributions. Senators not up for reelection are more independent than members of the House. Alternatively, so much emphasis was placed on the AMA's contributions and the vote for and against the FTC by newspapers and the media that a number of senators became fearful that their vote would be used against them at election time.[30]

As a result of the Supreme Court's decision and their subsequent legislative defeat, professional associations could no longer inhibit competition. The FTC was able to bring suit to prevent physician and dentist boycotts against insurers (Michigan State Medical Society and the Indiana Federation of Dentists); prevent physicians from denying hospital privileges to physicians participating in prepaid health plans (Forbes Health System Medical Staff); enable advertising to be used (*FTC* v. *AMA*); oppose the per se rule against exclusive contracts (*Hyde* case); and enable PPOs and HMOs to compete.[31]

Implications of Market Competition in Medical Care

Implications to Health Professionals

The increased physician to population ratio created excess capacity among physicians. To increase their volume of patients, physicians were more willing to change their organizational affiliations as well as their practice patterns. As HMOs increased their share of the insurance market, they needed more physicians to care for their enrollees. More physicians were willing to work for HMOs than previously. As competition among HMOs and traditional insurers intensified, both types of insurers attempted to lower their enrollees' medical costs by decreasing hospital utilization. Physicians were required to follow utilization guidelines; they had to receive authorization to hospitalize patients, to extend their patients' length of stay, and to refer patients to specialists. HMOs and indemnity insurers also developed panels of physicians. Insured patients had a financial incentive to use these provider panels, if they did not then they had to pay higher out-of-pocket prices. To be included in these provider panels, physicians had to typically discount their fees to the insurers and not be "high" users of medical services.

As HMOs and insurers decreased hospital use rates and hospital excess capacity increased, hospitals had to compete on price, offering discounts to HMOs. To be price-competitive, hospitals had to increase their efficiency and become concerned with physician practices within the hospital. Hospitals were financially responsible for their physicians' practice styles. Competition provided insurers and hospitals with an incentive to monitor physician practice behavior.

To increase their own market power, physicians joined multispecialty medical groups to better negotiate fees and receive capitation from insurers and HMOs. To be competitive, these large medical groups had to have their own effective monitoring system to assure that their physicians were practicing quality and cost-effective medicine. To control use of services, these medical groups often require their physicians to refer to specialists associated with their medical group. Specialists that are not part of these medical groups or on insurer and HMO provider panels have experienced large decreases in their patient referrals. Their incomes are also decreasing.

These are only some of the consequences of market competition to health professionals. Physicians are finding that they must also learn marketing techniques and even consider advertising, a practice many physicians consider beneath the dignity of their profession. With the increased supply of physicians, the growth of HMOs, and closed-provider panels, more physicians are willing to become salaried employees. Physicians in different specialties have also come in conflict with one another. As physicians find themselves with extra time, they are trying to expand the services they offer by performing services previously performed by other specialties.

Health professionals are also engaged in intense political competition among themselves. Each health profession attempts to use the state practice acts to increase the tasks they are allowed to perform while preventing other professions from encroaching on their tasks. Thus optometrists are in competition with ophthalmologists, obstetricians with nurse-midwives, family practitioners with nurse practitioners, psychologists with psychiatrists, and podiatrists with orthopedic surgeons.

The economic returns to a career in medicine or other health profession have declined. Not only are the prospects for future income diminished but the costs of becoming a physician have increased. Tuition to medical and dental schools has been rising as federal and state support has declined.

Clearly, the increased supply of health professionals, the applicability of the antitrust laws, and the growth in market competition have had an adverse effect on the economic outlook and practice styles of physicians. It is therefore not surprising that health associations such as the AMA have been so opposed to market competition.

Changing Structure of the Medical Care Delivery System

The main determinant of the number and size of firms in a competitive industry is which size firm is most efficient. This relationship between cost and size is referred to as economies of scale and it differs for each industry. If there are no barriers to entering or exiting from an industry, then each firm will strive to take advantage of any economies of scale that may exist in order to maximize their income. If a firm cannot compete at the same price as a more efficient firm, then it will either merge so as to be a more efficient size or go out of business.

In the past, economies of scale played an insignificant role in determining the structure of the healthcare industry. Legal (or regulatory) and financing methods determined its structure. And many of these regulations negated the importance of economies of scale in the delivery of medical services. Of what use was a lower-cost delivery system, such as an HMO, if it was illegal?

The stated reasons for many of the legal restrictions were the enhancement of the quality of care and the protection of the public. Cynics, however, believed that the profession was better protected than the public. The effects of these restrictions were fewer providers, higher prices, and less innovation in the delivery of medical services.

As many of the legal restrictions have been swept away by the antitrust laws, and as methods of financing medical services have changed, economies of scale are becoming a more important determinant of the industry's market structure. Access to capital markets, lower interest costs on debt, volume discounts on supplies, advertising for all the specialties and services offered by an organization, lower data processing costs, and lower malpractice premiums are several economies that occur with increased size of a health organization.

Initially, hospitals of less than optimal size started taking advantage of economies of scale by forming loose affiliations with one another. As the competitiveness of the industry increased, hospitals began merging and forming large corporate chains. The next step was to go beyond horizontal mergers and vertically integrate. As the demand for hospital care declined, the number of financially viable hospitals also declined. Additional cost savings and increased revenue opportunities from continued horizontal integration became limited.

The federal government and private insurers, in their attempts to reduce expenditures, started providing insurance payment for less costly substitutes to hospitals. Hospitals facing a decrease in demand for their inpatient services became providers of these substitute services, for example, hospices, outpatient surgery centers, nursing homes, and home care. As both business and government became willing to pay for medical services according to an annual fee (capitation payment), hospitals became part of and started HMOs. To keep their facilities occupied, hospitals competed in the PPO market and affiliated with HMOs.

The product of this industry, medical services, is not a standard service. Consumers of medical care place different values on different aspects of that service. For example, some types of delivery systems are viewed by the patient as being more restrictive in their choice of provider. Patients are often willing to pay more to go to providers located nearby. Still other patients place a greater value on the manner in which the provider dispenses care (i.e., the concern expressed and the amount of time devoted to a visit). As long as nonmedical aspects of service, including location, choice of provider, and the manner in which service is delivered, are important to patients, many consumers will be willing to pay more for medical care or for health insurance, rather than accept the lowest-cost, most restrictive provider. As long as consumer tastes vary, a variety of delivery systems (and types of providers within each delivery system) can be expected to coexist in a competitive market.[32]

Consumers have different preferences as to how much they are willing to pay for choice of provider and other health plan attributes. It is therefore likely that health plans will offer enrollees several options. An organization can take advantage of economies of scale by expanding into related product lines. For example, a health plan could sell insurance for a fee-for-service delivery system, have an HMO, and also have a PPO option available to satisfy different consumers. Health plans are likely to try and segment the insurance market by offering different products to each segment. Health plans will also market an administrative services only option to those businesses that self-insure.

Insurance companies are forming and even purchasing their own delivery systems, such as HMOs and PPOs. The trend is toward increased vertical integration. It appears that the complementariness of products as well as economies of scale, particularly with respect to capital, may be the twin criteria of an optimally sized healthcare firm.

The structure of the market is moving in the direction of very large organizations that offer their services in different geographic markets. The healthcare corporation of the future is likely to be vertically integrated—offering the entire spectrum of care, from wellness centers to acute care centers to retirement centers. It will have sophisticated information systems to enable it to evaluate its providers, monitor the outcomes of its patient populations, and develop the actuarial data to compete on a capitation basis with other insurers.

Implications for the Public

The introduction of market competition has both positive and negative aspects.

On the positive side, the public now has greater choice of delivery systems. Those willing to limit their choice of provider, as with HMOs, can have lower out-of-pocket costs. There is also a great deal more innovation in methods of delivering medical services. Same-day outpatient surgery and home care are examples of alternative methods of providing care previously provided in the hospital. Providers have become more responsive to the public's preferences.

Insurance premiums in California, which has one of the most competitive medical environments in the United States, have increased at a lower rate than other, less competitive, states.[33] Increased concern by business over their employees' health costs and premium competition among insurers are resulting in greater efficiency in the provision of medical services. Hospitals must be efficient if they are to compete for HMO contracts. DRGs also provide hospitals with incentives to keep their costs down. The cost of duplicated facilities can no longer be passed on to third-party payers.

There has always been a concern that quality of care would suffer under a price-competitive system. There is the fear that some physicians might engage in unethical behavior to increase their incomes or that HMOs and other providers might have an incentive to provide fewer services, taking advantage of consumer ignorance. It is unlikely that with informed purchasers in a competitive market that quality could be lower than under the previous regulated market when the dissemination of information on quality was purposely prohibited and state licensing boards performed very poorly in monitoring and disciplining physicians.[34]

To the extent that HMOs and PPOs are enrolling employees directly at the workplace, unions and companies provide an oversight function. These alternative delivery systems must be approved either by the union or by the company. Further, there is increased sophistication today with computerized claims processing. Insurers, businesses themselves, and provider organizations are all using such systems to monitor costs and appropriateness of utilization and to detect poor quality. A greater emphasis on quality of care is likely for those providers that are part of larger groups or that participate in alternative delivery systems. (Poor quality is also likely to cost the HMO or PPO their business at that employer. Poor quality care does not make good business sense.)

Under pressure from their competitors, HMOs and managed care organizations are beginning to publish "report cards." These report cards include measures of their enrollees' health, the percent of their enrollees provided with preventive measures, and, eventually, outcomes of medical treatment. The quality of care provided and the health status of their enrolled population will become measures according to which health plans compete, in addition to their premiums. The pressure faced by health plans to also compete along this quality dimension provides benefits to enrollees that would not have occurred under a regulated system.

For a competitive market to benefit consumers, purchasers (consumers or those purchasing care on their behalf) must be well informed. Until report cards are developed and used by employers and their employees, health plans will compete just on price. The effect of just price competition, without any comparative measures of access, quality, and outcomes, will be to cause these other attributes of competition to be neglected. It is encouraging that large business coalitions are conducting employee health plan satisfaction surveys and pressuring health plans to develop report cards.

Under the previous cost-based system, many hospitals provided complex services because it was prestigious to do so, without too much concern about the costs. Some of these services, such as open heart surgery, require surgeons to perform a large number of procedures before they are sufficiently well experienced in the technique. Thus hospitals that performed few procedures not only had higher average costs, but also had a higher mortality rate. As insurers have become more price-competitive, they are negotiating contracts for transplant and other high-tech services with hospitals on the basis of both price and outcomes. Facilities performing few such complex procedures cannot compete, with a consequent reduction in the mortality rate.

The negative effects of price competition are typically found among individuals who have little information. It is more difficult for the individual to detect poor quality; as a consequence, the costs to the provider of providing less than optimal service are less. However, individuals who join the same managed care organizations as employee groups are often able to receive similar benefits. Performance measures of the managed care organization, as represented in their "report cards" would also include such individuals. Individuals, however, are often less successful than members of large employee groups in having the managed care firm respond to their dissatisfactions.

Medicare DRGs and the new Medicare physician payment system rely on regulated prices, determined by the government, and are not the result of a competitive market. As such, their consequences are quite different. Under Medicare DRGs, hospitals receive the same price regardless of how much service they provide. As government continues to reduce the DRG price relative to the costs of caring for Medicare patients, hospitals are likely to discharge patients early. As this occurs, some of the costs of care are being shifted to the patients and their families. Thus part of the apparent reduction in government expenditures from reducing DRG payments is merely a shift in costs. The same occurs when the government sets too low a Medicare price for primary care physicians. Medicare patients will increasingly find it more difficult to receive primary care services. Access problems for Medicare patients are not the result of a competitive market but of government regulated prices that are set below "market" prices.

Competition has, unfairly, been blamed for a decrease in care available to those unable to pay. As hospitals face strong competitive pressures, many have reduced the amount of charity services they provide. Exacerbating this problem is that Medicaid programs have been reducing the amount they pay hospitals for their care of the medically indigent. The decreased provision of charity care by hospitals and low Medicaid reimbursement rates have resulted in some hospitals trying to shift the indigent to other hospitals. This problem, referred to as "dumping," has received media attention.

Public hospitals, including those teaching hospitals operated by state governments, receive more of the patients refused at other hospitals. These hospitals find themselves disadvantaged if they are forced to compete while subsidizing the costs of patients refused by their competitors.

Inadequate care for the poor is not the result of a competitive system. It is instead the consequence of government unwillingness to fund medical care to the poor. Competition eliminates cross-subsidies. Unless government payments for the aged and medically indigent are sufficient to cover their costs of care, hospitals will be discharging these patients too soon or these patients will be shifted to other providers, namely the public hospitals. While one outcome of a competitive system is increased efficiency, another is that the manner in which the poor are financed and provided for becomes more obvious and requires society to make explicit choices on how we wish to provide for them.

Concluding Comments

As a result of the 1981 recession and severe import competition, industry became more concerned with costs and, in particular, with employees' health insurance premiums. As a result, industry developed a concentrated interest in lowering the rate of increase in its healthcare expenditures. One approach used by business was to self-insure. In this way, a firm could exercise greater control over its employees' utilization of medical services. Up until that time, health insurance companies had not been very aggressive in introducing utilization review programs or in monitoring health providers' charges. Consequently businesses found themselves paying successively higher premiums. The trend by business toward self-insurance and the increased emphasis on reducing health insurance premiums in turn stimulated price competition among insurers.

In response to industry demands for lower rates of increase in their health insurance premiums, insurance companies began to introduce cost-saving innovations in their benefit packages. By insuring low-cost substitutes to hospital care, increased cost sharing by employees, and the use of HMOs and PPOs, hospital admissions rates and lengths of stay were reduced.

HMOs, traditionally unable to attract sufficient numbers of physicians, now found it easier to do so as a result of the increased supply of physicians. HMOs also found it easier to market their services as companies offered their employees dual-choice options. In addition, insurance companies started to form prepaid plans and PPOs as HMOs became more successful and were able to offer employee groups lower premiums. Hospital occupancy rates declined as a result of the cost-saving measures of the private sector.

The federal government had in turn developed a concentrated interest in controlling the rise in medical expenditures as a result of rapidly rising Medicare and Medicaid expenditures. The options facing the federal government were increasing Social Security (or general income) taxes or reducing benefits to the aged. Neither option was politically acceptable. The only acceptable alternative, therefore, was to squeeze the providers. From the 1970s on, the federal government, through successive Democratic and Republican administrations, became more aggressive in opposing health trade associations, such as the AMA and hospital associations. It instituted the DRG program, which led to a decline in hospital occupancy rates. To survive, hospitals had to move away from their traditional role and had to compete for market share in a declining market. The effect was that hospitals had to join forces with PPOs and HMOs for fear of being excluded from these markets. They offered discounts to larger purchasers and started advertising. To secure new sources of revenue, hospitals became providers of substitute (to hospitals) services, such as outpatient surgery, home care, hospices, and so on. The existence of these services and insurance coverage for their payment served to further decrease the demand for inpatient care.

The excess capacity among physicians and hospitals and the change in business incentives and in government were important preconditions for market competition. However, it is unlikely that market competition would have begun had it not been for the applicability and enforcement of the antitrust laws. In a previous time, with similar preconditions, anticompetitive behavior by physician associations would have been able to prevent the emergence of market competition. In the 1930s excess capacity also existed among physicians, but prepaid plans and efforts by insurance companies to institute cost-control measures were thwarted by local medical societies.

The reasons for the emergence of market competition in healthcare were similar to those of other deregulated industries. Business and the federal government each developed a concentrated interest in holding down the rise in their medical expenditures. Low-cost substitutes to traditional providers developed, namely HMOs and outpatient surgery centers. These new delivery systems decreased hospital and physician revenues. The growing supply of physicians increased competitive pressures among physicians. Declining occupancy rates did the same for hospitals.

And the judicial system ensured that market competition would occur when the Supreme Court upheld the applicability of antitrust laws to the healthcare industry.

Study Questions for Chapter 6

1. What are examples of anticompetitive practices that existed in healthcare before price competition occurred?
2. What purchaser and supplier conditions changed during the 1970s and 1980s that made it likely that price-based competition would occur in healthcare?
3. Why was it necessary for the antitrust laws to apply to healthcare for price competition to occur?
4. Which federal health policies indirectly contributed to the conditions that enabled price competition to start?
5. Explain why employers and government (at both the state and federal level) developed a "concentrated" interest in limiting the rise in health expenditures.
6. Why are "Any Willing Provider" laws anti-competitive?
7. Contrast the predictions of the public interest and economic theories with regard to how effective Certificate of Need legislation was expected to be in reducing the rate of increase in hospital expenditures.

Notes

1. Karen Davis. 1975. "Equal Treatment and Unequal Benefits: The Medicare Program," *Milbank Memorial Fund Quarterly*. The Milbank Memorial Fund; and G. Wilensky, L. Rossiter, and L. Finney. 1983. "The Medicare Subsidy of Private Health Insurance," mimeo. National Health Care Expenditure Survey, National Center for Health Services Research. The above data are published in Paul J. Feldstein. 1993. *Health Care Economics*, 4th ed. New York: Delmar Publishing Co. 477–79.

2. Joseph P. Newhouse. 1978. *The Erosion of the Medical Marketplace*. Santa Monica, CA: RAND Corporation.

3. Katherine R. Levit, et al. 1994. "National Health Spending Trends, 1960–1993," *Health Affairs* 13 (5) 14–31.

4. Ibid.

5. David S. Salkever and Thomas W. Bice. 1979. *Hospital Certificate-of-Need Controls: Impact on Investment, Costs, and Use*. Washington, D.C.: American Enterprise Institute.

6. A 1981 update of the Congressional Budget Office's study of PSROs stated, "Although PSROs appear to reduce Medicare utilization, the program consumes more resources than it saves society as a whole." Congressional Budget Office, *The Impact of PSROs on Health Care Costs: Update of CBO's 1979 Evaluation*. Washington D.C.: The Congress of the United States, January 1981.

7. Paul J. Feldstein and Glenn Melnick. 1984. "Congressional Voting Behavior on Hospital Legislation: An Exploratory Study," *Journal of Health Politics, Policy and Law* 8 (4) 686–701.

8. W. Wendling and J. Werner. 1980. "Nonprofit Firms and the Economic Theory of Regulation," *Quarterly Review of Economics and Business* 20 (3) 6–18.

9. David H. Hitt. "Reimbursement System Must Recognize Real Costs," *Hospitals* Part I, January 1, 1977; Part II, January 16, 1977.

10. Feldstein, *Health Care Economics*, 355–59.

11. "Health Professions Educational Assistance Amendments of 1965," *Hearing Before the Subcommittee on Health of the Committee on Labor and Public Welfare,* United States Senate, 89th Congress, 1st Session, September 8, 1965, 39–40.

12. Feldstein, *Health Care Economics*, Table 13–3, 358.

13. The physician assignment rate on Medicare claims was 51.8 percent in 1975 and remained constant until 1980 (51.5 percent) at which time it started increasing and reached 68.5 percent in 1985. Alma McMillan, James Lubitz, and Marilyn Newton. 1985. "Trends in Physician Assignment Rates for Medicare Services, 1968–1985," *Health Care Financing Review* 7 (2) Table 2, 59–75. For evidence on changes in the geographic distribution of physicians, see William B. Schwartz, Joseph P. Newhouse, Bruce W. Bennett, and Albert P. Williams. 1980. "The Changing Geographic Distribution of Board-Certified Physicians," *New England Journal of Medicine* 303 (October 30) 1032–38.

14. S. E. Berki and Marie L. F. Ashcraft. 1980. "HMO Enrollment: Who Joins What and Why: A Review of the Literature," *Milbank Memorial Fund Quarterly* 58 (4) 588–632. For a complete discussion of the background of the HMO legislation, see Lawrence D. Brown. 1983. *Politics and Health Care Organization: HMOs as Federal Policy.* Washington D.C.: The Brookings Institution.

15. For a complete discussion of CON and its legislative changes, see Clark C. Havighurst. 1982. *Deregulating the Health Care Industry: Planning for Competition.* Cambridge, MA: Ballinger Publishing.

16. Ibid.

17. Alain C. Enthoven. 1980. *Health Plan.* Reading, MA: Addison-Wesley Publishing Co.

18. Prospective Payment Commission. 1995. *Report and Recommendations to the Congress March 1, 1995.* Washington, D.C. 16.

19. Prospective Payment Commission. 1995. *Medicare and the American Health Care System, Report to the U.S. Congress.* Washington, D.C. 69.

20. Ibid., 49

21. Lawrence G. Goldberg and Warren Greenberg. "The Emergence of Physician-Sponsored Health Insurance: A Historical Perspective," in Warren Greenberg, ed., *Competition in the Health Care Sector.* Germantown, MD: Aspens Systems Corporation; Reuben Kessel. 1958. "Price Discrimination in Medicine," *The Journal of Law and Economics* 1 (October); Reuben Kessel. 1970. "The AMA and the Supply of Physicians," *Law and Contemporary Problems.* Chapel Hill, NC: Duke University Press; and Elton Rayack. 1967. *Professional Power and American Medicine: The Economics of the American Medical Association.* New York: The World Publishing Co.

22. *Goldfarb v. Virginia State Bar in United States Reports, v. 423 October Term* 1975, 886.

23. *Congressional Quarterly* 42 (7 January 1984) 15.

24. William Rial. 1982. "Should the FTC Regulate American Medicine?" *National Journal* 14 (37) 1576–77.

25. Paul J. Feldstein and Glenn Melnick. 1982. "Political Contributions by Health Pacs to the 96th Congress," *Inquiry* 19 (Winter) 283–294.

26. *National Journal* 14 (18 September 1982) 1590.

27. *Congressional Quarterly* 42 (7 January 1984) 15.

28. *National Journal* 14 (18 September 1982) 1590.

29. Ibid., 1592.

30. *Congressional Quarterly* 42 (7 January 1984) 19.

31. For a review of antitrust actions in the health field, see Arthur N. Lerner. 1984. "Federal Trade Commission Anti-Trust Activities in the Health Care Services Field," *The Antitrust Bulletin* 29 (2) 205–224. Several recent articles of interest are: Kathryn Fenton and Barry Harris. 1994. "Vertical Integration and Antitrust in Health Care Markets," *The Antitrust Bulletin* 39 (2) 333–362, and Dennis Yao, Michael Riordan, and Thomas Dahdouh. 1994. "Antitrust and Managed Competition for Health Care," *The Antitrust Bulletin* 39 (2) 301–331.

32. In the period before deregulation of the medical care industry, the industry was characterized by fee-for-service payment with many independent providers. If this system was the result of a competitive market, it would suggest that consumers had relatively similar tastes. In a country as large and as diverse as the United States, this would be highly unlikely. Instead, the delivery and payment system that existed was indicative of a noncompetitive market that prevented the exercise of differences in consumer tastes.

33. Katherine Levit, Helen Lazenby, Cathy Cowan, and Suzanne Letsch. 1993. "Health Spending by State: New Estimates for Policy Making," *Health Affairs* 12 (3) 7–26.

34. For references on this issue, see Chapter 4.

THE CONTROL OF EXTERNALITIES: MEDICAL RESEARCH, EPIDEMICS, AND THE ENVIRONMENT

Political Support Maximization as a Basis for Government
  Intervention When There Are Externalities
Federal Support for Medical Research
Public Crises as a Cause for Government Intervention
    Drug Legislation
    The Swine Flu Epidemic (That Never Arrived)
    AIDS
    Environmental Protection
Concluding Comments

I t is generally accepted by economists that the government should intervene in the private sector when externalities exist. Externalities are side effects that can occur when goods are produced or consumed. A business only considers its production costs and the selling price in determining how much to produce. Similarly, an individual considers only the price they must pay and the benefits they expect to receive in determining how much of a particular good to purchase. However, as a result of these private decisions other persons and businesses, not directly involved in the production or purchase of that good, may be affected. These external effects can be either beneficial or harmful. The following are examples of externalities.

In producing its product, a chemical company may also produce chemical waste, which it then dumps in a nearby lake. The lake may then no longer be usable for fishing or recreational purposes. The chemical company has imposed a harmful externality, referred to as an external cost, on all who use that lake. In calculating its costs of production, the chemical company does not include these external costs. The purchasers of those chemicals pay a price that is lower than if all costs, including external costs, were included. The result is that more chemicals are sold than if the selling price reflected both the firm's costs of production and the external costs imposed on others.

Medical research is an example of external benefits being provided to others. If a company undertakes research and discovers a cure for AIDS, many people, other than those purchasing the company's drug, would also benefit. The company calculates the costs of conducting research, their probability of success, and the monetary return of success in deciding whether or not to undertake the research. The individuals purchasing the drug do so based on calculations of their costs and benefits. The external benefits to those who have a lessened chance of contracting the disease are not included in either the producers' or purchasers' calculations. If these external benefits were included in the company's calculations, then the profitability of the research would be increased and it would be worthwhile for the firm to spend additional funds on research.

There are many other examples of externalities, such as a neighbor playing loud music late at night, that may be trivial in terms of public policy (but not to the enraged neighbor), to cases where the external costs and benefits are sufficiently widespread and significant to warrant government intervention.

Both the purchasers and producers of a good only consider their own benefits and costs when deciding how much to buy or produce. Since external costs or benefits are not part of their calculations, the outcome is that there is either too much (in the case of external costs) or too little (external benefits) produced. This result is referred to by economists as an *inefficient* allocation of resources. Technically, an *efficient* allocation of resources occurs when the marginal benefits (both private and external) are equal to the marginal costs (again, both private and external) of producing the product. As long as the value (marginal benefits) of the output exceeds its costs of production, then an increase in output would be worthwhile; the output will result in greater benefits than costs. Alternatively, when the costs of the last units exceed the benefits derived from those units, then those resources should be moved into other uses where they can produce output with a higher value.

The appropriate role of government in cases of externalities is to assess the magnitude of these external costs and benefits and to have them included as part of the private decision-making process. For example, in the case of pollution the government should determine the external costs and place a tax on the amount of pollution produced. The production costs and the selling price of the good produced would then include all of the relevant costs. In the case of external benefits, the government should calculate the size of the benefits and provide a subsidy to their producers.[1]

A great many difficulties are involved in determining the external costs and benefits of different activities. What are the harmful health effects of air pollution? How should one assess the lost recreational use of polluted lakes? How much weight should be assigned to these external costs so that they may be translated into monetary amounts?

Determining external benefits is also fraught with difficulties. For example, everyone benefits from having the government defend this country, even though the size of the defense budget and the nature of foreign threats may be subject to dispute. No one can be excluded from enjoying the benefits of a secure national defense. However, it is rational for any one individual not to voluntarily contribute, since each will receive the same benefit whether or not a contribution is made. The individuals hope to receive a free ride, i.e., to enjoy the benefits without having to pay. If too many individuals become free riders, then an activity with external benefits will not be undertaken or would be smaller than if all the benefits were included. (Asking people how much the external benefit is worth to them is likely to lead to their understating its value so as to reduce their contribution.)

Unless the government is able to determine the external costs and benefits of various activities, either too much or too little of that activity will be undertaken.

The involvement of government in cases of externalities is generally accepted to be within its proper role. And government legislation dealing with pollution and medical research is observed. Is this therefore evidence that at least in this legislative area the Self-Interest Paradigm is not applicable? Unless a theory can explain a wide range of applications, it becomes necessary to explain why a theory is applicable in some cases but not others. The bases of the theory would have to be reexamined.

This chapter provides an explanation of government intervention when externalities arise based on the self-interest of concentrated interests and of legislators, namely maximization of their political support.

Political Support Maximization as a Basis for Government Intervention When There Are Externalities

According to the concept of political support maximization, elected officials also undertake a cost-benefit analysis when deciding which programs to support or oppose. The definition of costs and benefits to the elected official, however, are not related to issues of external costs and benefits. The only relevant costs and benefits for a legislator are the political support gained from taking an action (the benefits) as compared to the political support lost (the costs) of that same action. When the benefits exceed the costs, then the legislators will gain more from their positions on an issue than they will lose.

Given the divergence in definitions of costs and benefits used by the legislator and those used by economists to determine the appropriate role of government when there are externalities, it is not surprising that the outcomes are not similar.

From a legislator's perspective, they must perceive the existence of political support before they enact legislation. In nonhealth areas, such as national defense and space exploration, political support from narrow constituencies as well as from the public at large is essential before Congress will appropriate funds. The debate over the size of the defense budget represents differences of opinion between legislators whose constituencies differ on this issue. National defense is very visible and unless legislators represent their constituents' views, they are likely to lose political support and face opposition at the next election. And they are loath to generate opposition to their own reelection.

Separate components of the military budget are also visible, and various constituencies have strong feelings as to its appropriate size. Legislators have not favored closing military bases nor eliminating military contracts in their own districts, even though such changes might result in a more efficient defense budget. In fact, there are numerous cases where the military has favored closing some bases or shutting down the production of some plants (e.g., an outdated plane factory in Texas), but has been opposed by the district's legislators. What is in the public interest must not be contrary to their constituents' interest or a legislator will not vote in favor of it.

When President Kennedy announced in 1961 that the United States would place a man on the moon by the end of the decade, he was responding to the public's desire not to be second to the Russians in space exploration. President Kennedy was also demonstrating leadership on a popular issue. From a political perspective, the space program had all the ingredients for legislative success; the public favored it and there was limited opposition; the political benefits exceeded the political cost of the action.

Government intervention on issues that involve externalities are based on the degree of political support for those issues. Analyses of what should be done and the optimal amount to spend on such programs are of secondary, if any, importance. The size and composition of the defense budget is for the most part a political determination. The military establishment may attempt to develop a budget based on a calculation of the equipment and personnel required to meet various strategic objectives; however, the military also considers its own needs (the size of military pensions) as well as the likely response of Congress. It is no secret nor coincidence that military expenditures and military bases are concentrated in those congressional districts where the legislators have the greatest control over the military budget.

When externalities exist, government intervention occurs only when there is a net gain in political support from the government's action. If there is widespread public support, as evidenced by public opinion polls and organized environmental groups, then those programs that have little or no opposition will be passed quickly. The only controversy will be over which politician can take credit for the legislation. The legislation may even result in a serious attempt to resolve the concern in a meaningful manner.

When there is a likelihood that the legislation will address harmful externalities by imposing costs on some group, such as requiring certain industries to invest in equipment or causing a reduction in the labor force of an industry, then for legislation to be enacted there must be a net gain in political support by satisfying, if possible, two competing political constituencies. The public concerned with these issues, if it is not well-informed, is likely to be satisfied by passage of symbolic legislation. The affected industry and union are likely to be appeased by having the regulations written in such a manner so they will not be harmed (or they will be compensated for any harm). The concerned public provides the political support necessary to have the legislation passed, while those likely to be directly affected provide political support to ensure that they are not harmed. Since the public does not have information on the details of the legislation, it is unaware of the methods used to achieve the legislation's objectives. It is for this reason that the stated goals of the legislation are so often at odds with its effects.

The following examples of externalities in the health field serve to illustrate these principles.

Federal Support for Medical Research

Prior to 1940, most medical research was funded by nonfederal sources. The drug companies undertook research in those areas in which they hoped to earn a profit. Most medical research, however, was funded by private foundations through gifts to medical schools and medical research institutes. These private foundations were started by wealthy businessmen who "hoped for recognition in this world or the next."[2] There were also several private groups that raised funds for research. For example, the National Tuberculosis Association was very successful in their sales of Christmas seals, which provided the funds for tuberculosis research.[3]

Support for medical research from these private sources was usually given for research on specific diseases, such as cancer and syphilis, since the public was more apt to contribute the greater their fear of the disease.[4]

Of all federal research during this period, approximately one-third was undertaken by the Department of Agriculture. Early on farmers recognized the economic value of medical research.

> Federal aid was extended in this period to studies on the health of farm animals, while almost no funds were available for direct work on the diseases of man. . . . This was partly because of the nature of medical science . . . and partly because human welfare brought no direct financial return. Hogs did.[5]

The Bureau of Agricultural Economics, which was created in 1922, brought together some of the country's best social scientists. Their goal was to apply their talents to problems of "profitability and productivity" in agriculture.[6]

Federal support of medical research received its impetus from World War II. The prestige of scientists increased with the application of scientific knowledge to the war effort—the atomic bomb being the most notable example. Another example is the development of penicillin in 1941. Although penicillin had been discovered earlier, it took a coordinated effort by scientists to make it usable for American troops. As the war ended, there was a belief that science could do a great deal to alleviate human suffering.

Mary Lasker and Florence Mahoney, who had access to great wealth and a newspaper chain, are given a good deal of credit for the growth in federal support for medical research in the post-World War II period. While they were certainly influential in the early stages, it is naive to believe that Lasker and Mahoney were the primary reason for the vast funding of the National Institutes of Health (NIH). These two women were also very much in favor of national health insurance during that same time period. And yet despite all their efforts in that regard, they were unsuccessful. To understand why they were so successful in securing federal support for medical research and so unsuccessful in their other endeavors, it is necessary to take a closer look at the differences in political support for these different federal programs.

President Truman's proposal for national health insurance generated strong opposition, and the American Medical Association (AMA) mounted a national campaign to defeat it. The AMA also demonstrated that they could defeat representatives who opposed them on this issue. The AMA's political influence during this period, the late 1940s through the 1950s, was at its peak.

Medical research was not controversial. In fact, once Lasker and Mahoney were able to enlist the help of certain representatives and senators, who then saw it in their own political interest to support medical research, these legislators made a career out of doing so. Lasker and Mahoney had the foresight to see the political, as well as the societal, advantages for supporting medical research.

Lasker and Mahoney were initially able to convince Sen. Claude Pepper (as the chairman of the appropriate Senate committee) to hold hearings on medical research and to be a proponent of their cause. Senator Pepper was in turn rewarded with contributions and newspaper endorsements in his reelection campaign.[7] When the Republicans gained control of the Senate in the late 1940s, Sen. Styles Bridges became chairman of the Senate subcommittee. Bridges was similarly persuaded by Lasker and Mahoney to take up the cause of medical research.[8]

Senator Bridges, as had Senator Pepper before him, realized that support for medical research brought favorable newspaper coverage and visibility as a compassionate legislator. When the Democrats regained control of the Senate, Sen. Lister Hill realized the political advantages of continued support for medical research. Such support made Senator Hill a national figure. Previously known primarily as a southerner opposed to civil rights legislation, he was able to gain tremendous prestige (and reelection numerous times) for his support of medical research.[9]

Lasker and Mahoney were equally successful in the House of Representatives in convincing the appropriate subcommittee chairs of the benefits of supporting medical research. In the late 1940s, Frank Keefe, the Republican chairman of the Labor-Federal Security Subcommittee, told Mahoney " . . . that he had only one speech on the campaign trail, and that it was on health and what the federal government must do to advance it. That speech got him elected to five consecutive terms in Congress."[10] When the subcommittee chairs changed as the Democrats took control of the House, support for medical research became a bipartisan issue.[11] Rep. John Fogarty was quick to realize the political benefits of supporting medical research and was an ardent proponent until his death in 1964.

The 1971 Cancer Act was motivated by the public's fears about cancer. Public opinion polls indicated that "the American people fear cancer more than any other disease and they want something done about it."[12] According to informed observers, "Senator Yarborough's interest in the matter [cancer] was genuine, but he also hoped his sponsorship of the committee would meet with widespread approval and help him secure reelection."[13] Sen. Edward Kennedy subsequently proposed a new large-scale research effort on cancer. Not to be outdone, President Nixon proposed his own plan to find a cure in his State of the Union Address in January 1971. The public's fears "prompted politicians to compete for the role of the most compassionate and determined public trustees, by launching a new war against the dread disease."[14]

The AMA's opposition to legislation affecting the financing of personal health services left Congress with few alternative approaches to demonstrate to their constituents that they were compassionate individuals deserving of their support. Members of Congress clearly believed that they were responding to the public's desire for increased medical research. Newspaper polls showed that the public was willing to spend more on cancer research even if they had to pay increased taxes. An indication of the public interest in health was by the very high readership of newspaper articles on health.[15]

When Congress perceived a political advantage in supporting medical research, they responded with a vengeance. Congressional committees appropriated more than was requested by the administration or even by the research agencies. A favorite tactic was for the committee chair to ask the agency director what they could do if they had a few more million dollars. When President Eisenhower budgeted $126 million for medical research in fiscal year 1957, Congress appropriated $183 million. The next year the administration proposed $190 million; Congress responded with $211 million. For fiscal year 1961 the Kennedy administration proposed $400 million and Congress provided $547 million.[16]

There was a concern by some that the research institutes were receiving more funds than could reasonably be spent. A number of times the NIH had to return funds to the Treasury. The NIH went along with congressional wishes and appropriations because they feared that if they did not, Congress would start a competing agency. This in fact was one of the major contentions of the 1971 Cancer Act.

The interest by Congress in medical research did not stop with providing excess research support. Congress also directed the research institutes on the diseases to be investigated, based on public interest. For the public to appreciate what it was doing on their behalf, Congress wanted research conducted on specific diseases and not for basic medical research.[17] Congress created additional research institutes, each named for a specific disease. In 1955, for example, the Microbiology Institute became known as the National Institute of Allergy and Infectious Diseases. After all, as one congressman commented, "Whoever died of microbiology?"[18]

Increased funding for medical research also served the economic interests of the medical schools. In the late 1940s, medical schools claimed that they were in financial difficulty and needed federal support. The AMA was concerned that if the federal government provided institutional support as the medical schools requested, the government would then require that medical schools increase their enrollment. (At this time there were claims of a physician shortage.) The AMA therefore opposed federal support.

The tremendous increase in federal support for medical research served as a substitute for direct federal support of medical education. Approximately 200 universities and medical schools received 90 percent of all federal research funds from NIH in 1960.[19] The proportion of medical schools' operating budgets that was supported by federal medical research and research training reached 45 percent in 1965. In the 15-year period from 1951 to 1966, the number of full-time medical school faculty members increased from approximately 3,500 to more than 17,000.[20] This increase was largely the result of federal medical research and training expenditures. (During this same time period the rate of increase in U.S. medical graduates was virtually unchanged.)[21]

A new and powerful lobby group, the Association of American Medical Colleges (AAMC), now had a vested interest in ensuring that federal support to medical schools be continued. In the debate over a new cancer agency in 1971, the AAMC opposed the creation of a new agency because it feared " . . . that the medical colleges it represents—which perform 30 percent of the basic cancer research funded by NIH—would suffer a loss of funds as the federal government adopts a more narrowly targeted approach to attacking disease."[22]

The dramatic increases in federal support for medical research began to level off in the mid-1960s. Competing budgetary demands for other federal programs made it difficult to fund medical research at the previous rate. Expenditures for the space program were increasing. The Vietnam War was beginning to escalate, and President Johnson did not want to seek a tax increase for these competing demands. Medicare and Medicaid were finally approved in 1965, and expenditures under these programs rapidly exceeded their initial projections.

Overcoming the opposition of the AMA, Congress was now able to show its compassion for health by supporting other health programs (whose constituencies, e.g., unions, the aged, and the middle class, offered greater political support than did the AMA). Congress also passed the Health Professions Educational Assistance Act in 1963, which provided institutional support for medical schools to enable more middle-class children to have access to a medical education. As Congress was able to receive political support from these other groups, it began providing financing for different types of personal health service programs. Legislators now faced a budget constraint. The administration was reluctant to seek an increase in taxes, which would have cost it political support. Legislators therefore had to make choices among different health programs. As a result, medical research funding suffered; although the funds continued to increase, their growth rate declined.

Medical research was a bipartisan issue. With visible public support and no opposition, Congress recognized a good political issue. The only competition was over who would be viewed as the most compassionate legislator to overcome the public's fear of disease. Even the AMA did not oppose federal support for medical research; in fact, new discoveries would increase physicians' productivity. Physicians could now do more for their patients.

In their support for medical research, Congress was responding to the public's fears and their belief in science. This is entirely appropriate. However, Congress went too far. In catering to the public, Congress provided more funds than could reasonably be used; it appropriated more funds than requested by the research institutes, as evidenced by the fact that institutes returned funds to the Treasury at the end of the fiscal year, a rare action. Congress also directed research strategy. Many scientists favored increased funding for basic research. However, Congress required that the funds be spent on disease-specific programs (such programs were more "saleable") so that the public could better understand what their legislators were doing for them. Further, Congress was often too directive, even providing research guidelines for the scientists to follow.

If the provision by government for externalities rests on the amount of political support for such programs, then it is unlikely that the optimal funding for these programs will be forthcoming over a sustained period of time. As explained previously, it is an appropriate function of government to calculate the size of external benefits received by the population and provide sufficient funding so that an efficient allocation of resources for medical research occurs. Instead, the participants in the decision-making process, namely Congress and the producers of medical research (primarily the medical schools), use a different set of costs and benefits for determining medical research appropriations. Congress views the benefits in terms of the immediate political support they might receive from the interested voting public. There are no costs involved in Congress' decision since it is unlikely that they would lose political support by appropriating too much. The outcome is therefore excessive funding, in the short run. Those seeking research funds are also likely to place a greater weight than would others on the benefits of medical research. Although the researcher's perspective has a longer time horizon than does Congress, they too are unlikely to consider the costs of such programs, since they do not bear them. (The real costs of medical research are the other uses to which the funds could be applied.)

Public Crises as a Cause for Government Intervention

Crises have been an important stimulant to the passage of health legislation. Media attention is focused on the event, and the public wants leadership from its elected representatives. Legislators or a president portrayed by the media as being the public's protector can expect to be rewarded with favorable publicity and reelection. The following examples illustrate the importance of health crises to the passage of health legislation; each case involves the issue of externalities.

Drug Legislation

The first drug legislation was part of the Pure Food Act of 1906.[23] The supporters of this act were primarily concerned with the quality of food, rather than with drugs. Pure food acts had been submitted to Congress at least ten years before one was finally passed. The impetus to pass an act came from a great deal of publicity generated by newspapers, magazine articles, and Upton Sinclair's *The Jungle*,[24] with its graphic descriptions of what was being included in the foods the public was eating. The result was public outrage, to which Congress responded by passing the 1906 Pure Food Act.[25]

The act also required drug companies to provide accurate labeling information, including whether the drug was addictive. Further, if a drug was labeled (the manufacturer did not have to do so), then the manufacturer had to disclose its ingredients. The government could then verify the accuracy of the drug's contents. The drug-related portion of the act was quite limited and was modeled by the public's concern with the contents of food.

In the 1930s, the modern drug era began. As drugs were introduced, a tragedy occurred providing the impetus for new legislation. A company seeking to make a liquid form of sulfanilamide for children dissolved it in ethylene glycol (antifreeze). The company was unaware of the toxic effects. As result, more than 100 children died.[26] Responding to the public outcry, Congress passed the Food, Drug, and Cosmetic Act in 1938. The 1938 law was intended to protect the public from unsafe, potentially harmful drugs. A company had to seek approval from the Food and Drug Administration (FDA) before they could market a new product. At this time it was left up to the drug company to determine the necessary amount and type of premarket testing before stating that the drug was safe for its intended use. The requirements for testing drugs were not changed until the thalidomide crisis.

In the late 1950s, Sen. Estes Kefauver, while running for the Democratic nomination for president, held hearings on the drug industry. He was concerned that drug prices were too high and that drug companies undertook unnecessary and wasteful advertising expenditures.[27]

Following the introduction of thalidomide in Europe, an American drug company introduced it to the United States on an experimental basis. The 1938 FDA amendments permitted such limited distribution to qualified experts as long as the drug was labeled as being under investigation. As soon as reports began to appear in Europe that deformed babies were born to mothers who had taken the drug during pregnancy, the American company withdrew the drug. Congress responded to the public's fears over drug safety and passed the 1962 drug act amendments.

The 1962 amendments have been very controversial. The FDA now requires a great deal more information before a drug is given approval. The type of premarket testing is specified. These amendments were passed in spite of the fact that the 1938 legislation was effective in keeping thalidomide off the market. Further, had the new amendments been in effect at the time of thalidomide, they "would not have prevented a thalidomide-type tragedy."[28]

The consequence of the new amendments was that the cost and time required to introduce new drugs was greatly increased. With higher development costs, the profitability of new drug research decreased along with the decline in the number of new drugs. Further, a large time lag developed between when drugs were available for use in other countries and when they could be used in the United States. For example, drugs proven effective for the treatment of heart disease and hypertension were used in Great Britain as early as 1965, but it was 1976 before they were fully approved for use in the United States.[29]

One analyst examining the new amendments concluded that they made the public worse off.[30] Sam Peltzman attempted to quantify the benefits of the new amendments by estimating the effect of the new regulations on keeping ineffective and dangerous drugs off the market (of which there were very few before 1962) as compared to the lost benefits of having fewer new drugs, higher prices for existing drugs (since there is less competition from new drugs), and the reduced availability of drugs due to the time lag. The decline in the development of new drugs was the greatest disadvantage of the amendments and this factor alone, according to Peltzman, made the costs of the new amendments greatly in excess of its potential benefits.

The response by legislators to the drug crisis resulted in a much greater emphasis on the short-term benefits of their action, which are more visible to the media and to the public, than to the longer-term consequences. The media publicizes the effects of a drug that has unfortunate side effects. Victims' names are given and photographs printed. The media do not publicize all the nameless people that may have died because a new drug was not allowed to develop or was slow in receiving approval. For example, the higher cost of developing new drugs has made it unprofitable for "orphan" drugs, i.e., drugs that would benefit small population groups, to be developed. (Special legislation had to be enacted to provide drug companies with a financial incentive to develop drugs for small population groups.) The benefits to legislators (and to the FDA) of protecting the public by favoring more stringent safety requirements are obvious. Less obvious but also very important are the enormous costs of decreased availability of new drugs to relieve pain and suffering.

The Swine Flu Epidemic (That Never Arrived)

An example of the government's response to a possible public health crisis is found in the anticipated swine flu epidemic of 1976. The administrative and congressional actions were typical responses to public health problems, such as epidemics.

In February 1976 an army recruit stationed at Fort Dix, New Jersey, died from pneumonia of possible influenza origin. A number of other army recruits were also ill from influenza. The influenza specimens were sent to the New Jersey Public Health Laboratory for analysis. Most of the influenza strains were determined to be a common variety. Several strains, however, could not be identified. They were then sent to the federal laboratory at the Centers for Disease Control (CDC) in Atlanta for further analysis.[31]

Further tests revealed that the unidentified strains were similar to the swine flu virus that was believed to have been responsible for the great flu epidemic in 1918–19. This virus had not been seen for 50 years. The CDC, which is responsible for administering a variety of federal programs in preventive medicine and disease control in collaboration with state and local health officials, was alarmed. The 1918–19 epidemic caused the deaths of 450,000 people, 400 out of every 100,000 Americans. In contrast, in an average year, influenza causes about 17,000 deaths, or 9 per 100,000 population. The most susceptible population groups to swine flu would be those under 50 years of age. If a swine flu epidemic were to occur in late 1976, approximately one million Americans could die.

Unfortunately, the scientists at CDC did not know how likely it would be that such an epidemic would actually occur, given the discovery of these swine flu strains. They were by no means certain that these new strains foretold the start of a new epidemic. But given the magnitude of the tragedy that had occurred in 1918–19, the CDC proposed that a government immunization program be initiated before the next flu season. CDC stated, "Better to have an immunization program without an epidemic, than an epidemic without an immunization program."[32]

To vaccinate 200 million Americans by the fall of 1976 would be a vast undertaking. Government funds would have to be appropriated, private drug companies would have to develop a sufficient quantity of the new vaccines, and states and localities would have to be mobilized. It would be the first time this country undertook such a large program in such a short period of time.

Once the information about the swine flu strain was released, there was a great deal of publicity. The horrors of the 1918–19 epidemic were reviewed. The media interest and the public concern necessitated a response by our country's representatives.

President Ford was provided with a set of options on how to respond to the public's fears about a possible repeat of the 1918–19 epidemic. The president faced several choices. If the president took no action and the feared epidemic did not occur, then the government would save $134 million, the cost of the vaccination program. However, the media, Congress, and the American people expected some kind of leadership. It was believed by President Ford's advisers that the public would prefer to have the money wasted rather than not have the vaccine if truly needed. Further, if the president did not act, then the Democratic Congress would step forward as the party concerned about the nation's health and pass a mass vaccination program.

Any legislator knows that in choosing between spending money or risking American lives the public would prefer that the money be spent. A politician could not go to the electorate later and say that he was just trying to save money because the epidemic had such a small probability of occurring. If he was wrong, the electorate would never forgive him.

In addition, 1976 was an election year. President Ford was having a difficult time against Ronald Reagan in the primaries and the Democrats continually characterized him as being weak and indecisive. What would happen to his reelection prospects if he appeared to be more interested in balancing the budget when the epidemic arrived in the fall, just in time for the election? President Ford consulted with a large number of prominent scientists, received their unanimous approval, and decided to go ahead with the mass vaccination campaign.

The Democrats in Congress were upstaged by a conservative president on an issue—health—they believed belonged to them. Congress, however, had to respond positively to the president's request for an additional appropriation for the vaccination campaign, because "a presidential charge of congressional irresponsibility in the face of a health emergency would be politically unbearable."[33] However, the immediacy of the president's request was also seen by Congress as an opportunity to do something for its members. After attaching additional funds for temporary jobs ($1.2 billion), water pollution control ($300 million), comprehensive manpower assistance ($528 million), and community service for older Americans ($55.9 million), Congress passed President Ford's emergency appropriation of $135 million. Congress was sure that the president would not veto his own program.

The swine flu program ran into a number of obstacles. One drug company produced the wrong vaccine, thereby setting back the date at which immunizations could start. The drug companies had earlier warned that unless Congress relieved them of the insurance liability of people getting ill from the vaccine, they would not proceed with production. Congress delayed. Then doubt began to spread in the media that there would be an epidemic in the fall. All of a sudden a new fearful disease, Legionnaires' disease, broke out in Pennsylvania. At first it was believed to be connected to swine flu. Media attention and the public became concerned again with the possibility of an epidemic. President Ford used his office to castigate Congress for not moving on legislation to waive immunity for the drug companies.

According to a member of Senator Kennedy's Senate Health Subcommittee:

> This was greater heat than the members of Congress could bear. Here was President Ford, apparently willing to go before the Republican convention and into the presidential campaign with accusations that the opposition party cared so little for the health and safety of the American people that they would let this important immunization program die. This would be unbearable during a normal year, but doubly so during an election year.[34]

Once the vaccination program finally began, there was the discovery that people being vaccinated were at higher risk of contracting a rare disease, Guillain-Barré Syndrome. This finding finally ended the ill-fated vaccination program. By then the election was over and no epidemic appeared. The vaccination program was not renewed.

Much has been written on the swine flu affair.[35] While situations always become clearer with hindsight, it is not clear that the country is any more ready now to deal with the threat of another killer epidemic. The federal bureaucracy, the CDC, is unlikely to favor saving a very small amount of government funds only to be blamed if an epidemic occurs and people die. It is similarly unlikely that any president would want to be accused of sacrificing lives for dollars. Given the media attention concerning a possible epidemic, Congress would seek a leading role on the issue if the president hesitated. The political costs and benefits have not changed. Congress, however, has still not resolved the issue of insurance liability if an emergency situation were to arise. With the media coverage of the swine flu situation gone, Congress lost interest in immunization programs.

AIDS

It is instructive to contrast the political response to the swine flu epidemic with that of the most recent epidemic, AIDS. Although the first reported AIDS cases appeared in March 1981, the Reagan administration did not acknowledge a need for funds to combat this disease until May 1983.[36] After being relatively unresponsive, the government increased AIDS funding.

The reasons behind the initial and subsequent government responses involved a perceived change in political support. The swine flu epidemic was expected to affect everyone. The media had made the public fearful of the recurrence of such an epidemic. The public demanded action, and legislators and the administration competed with one another over who would be perceived as being more responsive.

The AIDS epidemic differed from swine flu in three important respects. First, there is no known cure for the disease. Second, a vaccine was not available and therefore other, more complex, policies had to be pursued. Third, and most important, AIDS differed from other contagious diseases with regard to the methods of transmission and the population groups affected. The victims of AIDS and those at high risk were believed to be homosexuals and intravenous drug users, two groups considered by many as not deserving of sympathy and compassion. In fact, one political spokesperson suggested that AIDS was nature's revenge on homosexuality.[37] Members of the religious right, who were politically influential, were opposed to homosexuality and not inclined to offer political support for homosexuals' concerns. Those at high risk to the disease were unable to offer much political support of their own to persuade legislators to take on the cause. It was only in those communities where high-risk groups were politically influential that treatment programs for AIDS victims were developed. The political appeal of legislating increased funding for AIDS patients was further limited by the fact that there were only a few geographic areas that would benefit, basically San Francisco and New York.

Three types of public policies are appropriate with regard to AIDS: funding for research to discover a cure and a vaccine against the disease, public education on methods to prevent the spread of the disease, and expenditures to pay for the care required by its generally impoverished victims. The publicity over AIDS occurred at a time when the federal government was attempting to reduce the budget deficit, and the administration was reluctant to increase expenditures for a population group that offered little political support. Different constituencies were competing for portions of the federal budget; initial funding for AIDS, when it came, was achieved by reducing the allocations of other programs rather than by appropriating new dollars.

Public education to prevent the spread of the disease required public information on "safe" sex. Fundamentalist religious groups and social conservatives opposed government programs, such as the distribution of condoms and needle exchange programs (to intravenous drug users) on the grounds that such programs might be viewed by the young as condoning behavior that these groups opposed. Because of this political opposition, funding for such programs was limited.

The victims of AIDS often become impoverished once they contract the disease; the debilitating effects require them to give up their jobs, lose their work-related health insurance, use up their savings, and rely on Medicaid. Insurers attempted to limit their financial risk by requiring an AIDS test before selling individuals and the self-employed health insurance. The financial burden of caring for AIDS victims has fallen on Medicaid and on hospitals providing uncompensated care.[38] These hospitals have become advocates for increased funding for AIDS treatment.

It was only when it was believed that the disease would spread to the heterosexual middle class and that all congressional districts would be affected that federal expenditures increased. Adding to the change in the public's perception of AIDS was the story of a boy from Indiana, Ryan White, who had AIDS and had to endure discrimination because of it. The publicity surrounding this case led to the Ryan White Act in 1990, which made treatment funds available (over $600 million in 1995). In addition, the AIDS community developed a small, but very well organized, lobby group that became very active in the political process. The result was special treatment for AIDS-related programs. Even though the death rate from AIDS is very small relative to heart disease (3.1 percent) and cancer (4.4 percent), federal appropriations for AIDS research has grown much more rapidly. New drugs for AIDS patients have also been able to receive an exception to the FDA's lengthy approval process, unlike comparable life-saving drugs for heart disease and cancer patients. From its initial slow start, political support for AIDS programs and government expenditures has grown very rapidly.

AIDS was viewed as a social issue, not as a public health problem. Part of the blame for the political response belonged to "politicians who pander to unreasonable public fears."[39] The initial political response would have been different if a broad constituency had been affected over a wider geographical area, if the victims had been viewed more sympathetically, and if the preventive measures had not been disturbing to politically influential population groups. The initial response by legislators, when it developed, reflected the concerns of their constituencies, namely, to test and exclude those suspected of having the disease. That early response would have been quite different if the disease affected the middle class at large and was transmitted in a different manner.

Environmental Protection

As public interest in medical research began to wane, the late 1960s saw an increase in the public's interest in the environment. "As a political issue, the country seemed unequivocally behind it. Local bond issues for environmental improvement passed handily. Much attention was given to environmental matters by the press. The Congress responded by producing a wealth of legislative proposals for budgeting expenditures, for administrative reorganization, and for further regulation."[40]

As important an issue as the environment was, it did not change the congressional response nor approach from what one would expect, based on a political support model.

The federal government did not become engaged in pollution control until pollution became a visible public issue. Instead of Congress establishing federal agencies to perform the functions described earlier when externalities occur, Congress (and various administrations) did not act until several pollution crises occurred and the public became concerned with their environment. *Although pollution was a health issue, it first had to become a political issue before Congress would respond.*

Early federal efforts at pollution control (in 1899) were concerned with the dumping of debris in navigable waterways. The intent of the law, however, was to ensure navigable waterways rather than clean water.[41] Federal policies during the 1930s and 1940s mainly involved grants to the states for construction of waste treatment facilities. These federal programs were also public works projects and were popular pork barrel legislation.[42]

It was not until the mid-1960s that more serious efforts to control water pollution began. The Water Quality Act of 1965 stressed water quality standards to be set by the states as well as increased federal funding for waste treatment facilities. The states, however, were reluctant to set too stringent standards for fear of losing industry. When the administration attempted to create regional agencies to be responsible for pollution control, Congress was more "enthusiastic" about public works programs and "suspicious of regional approaches which might undermine the political base of senators and representatives . . . [and] was also reluctant to tamper with the state allocation formula contained in the existing act."[43]

The 1966 act contained a provision, inserted by the representative from Texas, an oil-producing state, that precluded any enforcement against oil pollution.[44] It wasn't until the oil tanker *Torrey Canyon* sank off the coast of England, resulting in extensive oil pollution and media publicity, that Congress passed stronger oil pollution legislation. Further legislative refinements against oil polluters occurred as additional oil disasters received widespread media attention. In 1969, an oil rig off the coast of Santa Barbara suffered a "blowout," sending hundreds of thousands of gallons of oil onto the California beaches. The media attention lasted weeks, as did the oil spill. Congress was "forced" to act.

During this period, Rachel Carson's *Silent Spring*[45] was published. This book pointed out the dangers of pesticides. It also raised the public's consciousness about pollution in the environment and increased their desire to have Congress do something about the issue.

By 1970, pollution was so politically visible that President Nixon sent a special message on the environment to Congress, thereby raising the political stakes of environmental issues. In the 1972 presidential election, Sen. Edmund Muskie, known for his environmental initiatives, was viewed as the front runner for the Democratic nomination. In April of that year, the first annual Earth Day was held, an indication of the public's interest and awareness of environmental issues. Further, studies began to be published that were critical of federal pollution control efforts. The pork barrel nature of water pollution control programs was criticized. The Nader group issued a report that was very critical of Senator Muskie's efforts. In response, Senator Muskie attempted to regain the initiative as the protector of the environment.[46]

When Congress finally passed a new water pollution bill in 1972, instead of embracing it, President Nixon vetoed it. Congress had appropriated federal expenditures greatly in excess of what the President requested. Responding to the perceived support by their constituencies in an election year, Congress overrode the veto.[47] The main aspects of the 1972 act were the creation of standards in granting permits to individual dischargers and a greatly enlarged public works program to build municipal treatment plants.

The 1972 Act, and subsequent amendments to that act, set unrealistic deadlines and guidelines. The Environmental Protection Agency

(EPA) has indicated the "ineffectiveness and unenforceability of its regulations."[48] Deadlines and goals have come and gone. While the specification of too stringent standards and unrealistic deadlines may demonstrate to the public that Congress was against pollution, they took an unrealistic approach. Given the complexity of the problem, pollution control must be a continuing effort, unlikely to result in the total elimination of pollution in the short term. "In fact, the principal lessons to be learned from the experience of the 1970s are that the problems are far more difficult, will be with us far longer, and will require far more patience and continuous management than the [Congress] imagined."[49]

In addition to setting unworkable, rigid standards and deadlines, Congress has also favored an expensive nonregulatory approach to water pollution control: funding for waste treatment plants. These expenditures have grown over time and are considered by analysts to be politically popular pork barrel programs for congressional districts all over the country. However, since municipal governments are the cause of approximately two-thirds of all water pollution, such large federal programs should have had some positive environmental effects. (However, it is not clear that it is appropriate for the federal government to fund projects where the benefits and costs are so localized.)

Most pre-World War II legislation dealing with air pollution involved local laws against smoke. Enforcement of these laws varied greatly. The first real effort to control air pollution began in the late 1940s in Los Angeles when the public objected to odors from wartime plants and to eye-irritating smog. Then in 1951, automobile emissions were pinpointed as the major contributor to air pollution in Los Angeles. Other events increased the public's awareness of the dangers of air pollution. In 1948, 6,000 people became ill in Domora, Pennsylvania, from industrial smog. Fears about radioactivity arose from publicity on nuclear testing.[50]

Early federal legislation on air pollution (1955), aided by the event in Domora, Pennsylvania, called for a temporary program of research, training, and demonstrations.[51] Subsequent legislation was strengthened as little was done to control air pollution. Until the mid-1960s, these acts were generally believed to be "seriously defective."[52] Increased pressure was placed on Congress to act when in 1966 an air pollution problem in New York City "was estimated to have caused the death of eighty persons."[53] Late in the 1960s and early 1970s, federal pollution legislation mandated deadlines to meet certain controls on automobile emissions. (The automobile industry, while against emission standards, was not strongly opposed to this legislation; the companies were concerned that it would be more costly to them if each state imposed its own standards on emissions. A federal standard was preferable to 50 different state standards.[54])

Much credit is given to Senator Muskie for the stringent air pollution standards established in the 1970 legislation. These same sources, however, emphasize his presidential ambitions at that time and point out he was sharply criticized for his performance in protecting the environment by a Ralph Nader organization.[55]

Again, the tough standards and deadlines established in the 1970 legislation were not met. The automobile industry and their union, the United Auto Workers (UAW), successfully lobbied Congress to weaken and delay the emissions standards.[56] The oil crisis in the early 1970s was an opportunity for industry groups to lobby for relaxation of the standards so as to conserve costly fuel oil. And in many cases, EPA did not have the staff nor resources to monitor all the sources of air pollution. When large firms, such as the steel industry, were found not to be in compliance with the air quality standards, officials "were reluctant to force large industries with marginal profits to invest large sums in pollution control."[57]

An interesting example of congressional environmental policy is the 1977 Amendments to the Clean Air Act.

In the fall of 1973, OPEC raised the price of oil dramatically. Many electric utilities that had previously used oil switched to coal. Environmentalists were concerned that the switch to coal would increase the amount of sulfur oxides in the air and worsen air quality. The region that would suffer the most in terms of deterioration of air quality would be the Midwest, which is both more industrialized and more heavily populated.[58]

Coal produced in the United States varies in sulfur content according to its origin. Western coal is low in sulfur and cheaper to mine, and is therefore a competitive threat to eastern coal interests.

When Congress looked for an environmental policy that would reduce the amount of sulfur discharged into the air as utilities increased their use of coal, it was faced with a series of options. The simplest approach, and the one that would have made the most sense, would have been for Congress to set a tax on or a limit to the amount of sulfur oxide emissions by electric utilities, or both. This requirement would have left it up to the utilities to determine how they might best meet that limit (or the cheapest method of paying the emissions tax). However, what would have been the most efficient approach and good for air quality is not necessarily good politics. And politics always takes precedence.

Faced with a limit on the amount of sulfur emissions, utilities would be expected to achieve that limit in the least costly manner. Given the lower cost and lower sulfur content of western coal, midwestern and eastern utilities would find it profitable to pay higher transportation charges and increase their purchases of western coal. Such a market response would have had adverse consequences on the owners and employees of midwestern and eastern coal mines. Eastern coal mines are heavily unionized by the United Mine Workers, while western mines are not. It was estimated that between 10,000 and 20,000 jobs would have been lost. Joining with the coal producers, the United Mine Workers lobbied the Carter administration to use a different approach for reducing sulfur emissions. The Carter administration was also interested in saving jobs in Appalachia (Robert Byrd, the Senate Majority Leader was from West Virginia) and in the Midwest.[59]

The approach selected by Congress was to emphasize the *process* of meeting the air quality goal rather than the desired outcome. Congress mandated specific technology be used. New sources of sulfur emissions, whether by industry or utilities, would have to install and use expensive "scrubbers." As long as the mandated technology was used, any type of coal could be burned.

The effect of mandating scrubbers was to decrease the incentive to use low-sulfur western coal. Why should a utility pay higher transport cost for low-sulfur coal when they have to install scrubbers anyway? The incentive facing the utility was to seek out the cheapest coal, even though it may have the highest sulfur content.

The effect of the congressional approach toward improving air quality may in fact have had the opposite effect.

> [The] EPA accepted evidence that scrubbers can remove as much as 90 percent of (Sulfur Oxides) from stack gases when operating efficiently, but it ignored the fact that it has neither the technology nor the resources to assure compliance with the (Sulfur Oxides) emissions limits. . . . Stack-gas scrubbers require enormous amounts of maintenance, which utilities are unlikely to provide in a diligent manner if environmental authorities do not monitor their results carefully. . . . [A] scrubber failure can lead to enormous increases in emissions. The burning of low-sulfur coal carries no such risks. Therefore, it is possible that full . . . scrubbing increases cost and emissions concurrently—hardly the result an environmental policymaker would wish.[60]

Earlier, in 1971, different air quality standards had been set for existing and new sources of air pollution. If existing sources of air pollution, primarily electric utilities, had to meet tighter air quality standards, they would have passed these higher costs onto the public in the form of higher utility rates. Legislators from the heavily industrialized Midwest, whose utilities emit much of the pollution that returns to earth as acid rain, were concerned with having their utilities bear the economic burden of reducing air pollution. The utility customers would then have become upset with Congress over their higher utility bills. Further, the concern by environmentalists was that air quality not deteriorate. To resolve both of these concerns, Congress exempted existing sources of air pollution and imposed the technology requirements only on new sources of air pollution.

The policy of applying more stringent requirements on new sources and mandating the use of scrubbers was harder on the western and southwestern regions of the country. Since population is growing more rapidly in these regions, these regions were more likely to be required to use scrubbers. Further, even though these regions have vast amounts of low-sulfur coal, and they could meet the air quality standard in a less costly manner, all new sources of pollution had to use scrubbers.

Had flexibility in reducing pollution from acid rain been incorporated into the 1977 Clean Air Act, less costly methods would have been adopted. However, by forcing the use of scrubbers, absurd situations occurred. In the West where low-sulfur coal is used, engineers had to actually add sulfur to the scrubber to make it work.[61]

A flexible approach to reducing air pollution was, however unlikely, " . . . because the congressional committee that dominates the EPA's acid rain agenda is dominated by coal, the EPA's own acid rain approach tends to be dominated by coal; . . ."[62]. Higher utility bills and loss of jobs in the coal industry determined the approach to be used for reducing air pollution from high sulfur coal.

Applying the more expensive technology only to new pollution sources also provided utilities with an incentive to postpone replacing their high pollution plants. "In short, the new rule does very little to improve air quality in those areas that have the biggest problems while imposing very large emissions-reduction burdens upon the growing western and southwestern portions of the country."[63]

In 1990, Congress amended the Clean Air Act placing new controls on auto emissions and mandating the increased use of an alternative fuel, ethanol. To understand these regulatory strategies for reducing air pollution, one must know the interests involved rather than simply determining the most cost-effective approach for reducing air pollution.

Given the great deal of money at stake in reducing air pollution, each group attempts to minimize its costs while penalizing their competitors. The EPA became a focal point for lobbyists. For example, ethanol, which is made from corn, is a more costly fuel than gasoline. However, by having the EPA force refineries to produce ethanol, farmers and distillers benefit, even though it increases the price of gasoline by 20 cents a gallon. The ethanol proponents (supported by Sen. Robert Dole, the Senate's Minority leader) were the Archer Daniels Midland Co. (the largest domestic producer of ethanol), the National Corn Growers Association, environmentalists, and other alternative fuel interests. Although opposed by the oil and auto industries, the EPA created a vast new market for ethanol.[64]

The attempt to reduce auto emissions pitted the oil and auto industries against each other. Automakers lobbied to force service stations to install new $3,000 pump nozzles, while the gasoline industry lobbied to force the auto industry to install $80 fume catching cannisters on all new cars.[65] As a result of the 1990 amendments, automakers will be forced to market more expensive, less practical, electric cars. Starting in 1999, electic cars will be introduced in California and by the year 2003, 10 percent of all new cars sold in California will have to be electric cars. These cars, which will be more expensive to buy, will result in people keeping their older (greater polluting) cars longer.

Congressional politics results in types of regulation that serves the interests of some firm, industry, or region. It is for this reason that technology mandates are imposed rather than providing incentives for the private sector to improve the environment. If the EPA decided upon an emission level for autos instead of mandating technology to meet that standard, the level of emissions could be achieved in a less costly manner. For example, an emission tax could be imposed on cars by model type and year according to their smog emissions. Alternatively, since 10 percent of the cars are responsible for about 50 percent of smog-forming emissions, it would be more effective to target these cars than impose costs on all car owners. Remote sensing devices could be used along highways to determine each vehicle's emissions and fines levied on their owners until the cars are repaired. Each community can decide on their own fee schedule for polluting cars. Each of these approaches is a more efficient and equitable method for reducing auto pollution.

Concluding Comments

When externalities exist, as in the case of medical research, prevention of epidemics, control of pollution, and so on, it is an appropriate function of government to implement policy to match the costs and benefits in each of these areas. The public's interests would be served when external costs and benefits are included in the decision-making process that determines the level of production. Not all government policy in situations of externalities must necessarily be undertaken by the federal government. The geographic scope of the problem should determine the level of jurisdiction. Municipalities should be responsible for local pollution problems. When problems cross state boundaries, regional agencies, established by state coordination, may be the appropriate agency. Other types of problems require federal intervention.

The brief description provided of federal intervention in these issues suggests the following. Congress also considers the benefits and costs of their actions; they may at times act in the public interest when they perceive gains to themselves (or a loss if they do not). However, Congress is unlikely to act in the public interest when there are no net gains from doing so. (Legislators could be spending their time on activities that would provide them with political support.) Only when an issue gains high visibility and the public is perceived as wanting Congress to act, will Congress act. The type of action, however, will differ according to the opposition to their actions.

In the case of medical research, there was no opposition. Congress could not spend enough on this popular issue. (Congress bore no costs and saw large potential benefits to themselves.) In doing so, Congress became very directive on how those funds were to be spent, so as to maximize public awareness of their actions. Congress also appropriated too much, more than could have been well spent, as evidenced by agencies returning research funds to the Treasury.

With respect to a possible swine flu epidemic, no political leader would have chosen to save money at the possible expense of losing lives, no matter how remote that possibility might be. This strategy makes sense in terms of a legislator's costs and benefits. The cost is the government's money while the benefit is the legislator's political future.

The lack of an initial federal response to the AIDS epidemic was a result of the lack of political support by those at greatest risk for contracting the disease. Once the middle class became concerned that they were also at risk and the geographic areas affected expanded beyond New York and San Francisco, the political support materialized for legislators and the administration to take greater action. The preferences of politically important population groups, however, affected the types of prevention and educational programs. Government support for AIDS programs, such as AIDS research and treatment expenditures and fast-tracking AIDS-related drugs for FDA approval, has increased sharply. A well-organized AIDS lobby group has been very politically effective.

Eliminating pollution is politically attractive. Public awareness is very high and opinion polls indicate that public concern is also very high. Environmental groups initially were established to lobby the federal government to protect and enlarge wilderness areas and parks. The constituency of environmental groups—largely middle class—grew during the 1960s and 1970s when concern over air and water pollution increased. By placing restrictions on "growth," however, environmental groups favored the status quo; limits on industrial growth favor the "haves" over the "have-nots." Labor unions have, therefore, been major opponents of environmental restrictions on industry. Racial minorities considered environmental issues a luxury and not relevant to their constituency.[66] By regulating growth, environmentalists preserve their quality of life as well as their relative wealth.

The political influence of environmental groups is also indicated by the large number of interest groups (approximately 5,000) that are concerned with protection of the environment in their local areas. These groups are active in lobbying for a cleaner environment, bringing lawsuits against the EPA to ensure that it enforces strict compliance standards, publicizing legislators' votes on environmental issues, and endorsing candidates at election time. Politicians compete with one another to show the public who is most concerned over the environment.

The most popular response by Congress to these issues has been to appropriate funds for municipal waste treatment plants. A legislator can thereby be pro-environment, as well as provide projects for their home districts. There is no opposition to this approach. In fact, various associations of mayors, cities, and counties actively lobby for such funds. This is the ideal environmental policy for legislators.

When it comes to air pollution, however, it is difficult for Congress to find a comparable response. Costs must be imposed on business, and ultimately on consumers, if air pollution is to be reduced. Congress is thus forced to make choices. One person's pollution is another person's job. Initially, Congress would prefer to delay or even pass symbolic legislation, two alternatives effective when the public has little information. With a pollution crisis, there is a great deal of media attention, and Congress cannot delay any longer. To demonstrate their concern for the public and pressured by environmental groups, Congress establishes strict and unrealistic deadlines to achieve environmental goals. The short-term political benefits to Congress of this aggressive action in time of crisis is high. Once the crisis and media attention have passed, Congress can gain greater political support from companies and unions by delaying deadlines and requirements that may adversely affect company profits and jobs.

The EPA, the governmental agency responsible for carrying out congressional mandates, is unable to force compliance on recalcitrant large industries. This is another way for Congress to lessen the impact of its stringent requirements on industry. An industry will often use the excuse of loss of jobs in an area if they are forced to undertake heavy expenditures. This occurred with the steel and automobile industries. Compromises are then worked out between the industry and the EPA.

Often the penalties for noncompliance are so severe they cannot be imposed, e.g., stopping Chrysler Corporation's auto production.[67]

The experience of one EPA administrator, Anne Burford, and one of her deputies, Rita Lavelle, administrator of the Superfund (to clean up toxic wastes), is instructive. The large degree of discretion permitted by the EPA in administering environmental guidelines led to a public scandal. The EPA was more concerned with minimizing the consequences of their guidelines on industry than in carrying out their mandate. Protection of the environment was an important value held by the public. The loss of public support on a popular issue became too great a political liability for the Reagan administration to bear. The two administrators were fired.

Economists focus on the use of taxes, emission fees, and pollution credits to limit air pollution. Legislators and regulators have generally favored mandating the use of specific technology, limits on total pollution, and differential standards for new and old firms. The reason for these inefficient approaches and differential treatment is to benefit existing firms over new competitors. Restrictions on the total amount of pollution prevent increases in output, thereby enabling firms to raise their prices; the consequence is the same as when firms form cartels. For this policy to be successful, the costs associated with mandated technology (when this policy is used) must not exceed the increase in the firm's price and, second, entry into the industry must be restricted.[68] Requiring their competitors to meet more costly standards is an example of this approach. The use of catalytic converters to control auto emissions, the method chosen by U.S. automobile companies, is a high-cost method; it reduces gas mileage and adds equipment to the car. They can be, and are, easily tampered with. These pollution control requirements are more costly for foreign-made cars thereby providing a competitive cost advantage to U.S. automakers.[69] Requiring scrubbers, rather than direct limits on sulfur oxide emissions, imposed large costs on western utilities, while protecting midwestern and eastern coal mines and workers from their competitors—low-sulfur western coal producers. New sources of pollution are subject to greater pollution costs than existing sources, thereby providing a competitive cost advantage to existing firms.

Some legislators, such as Senator Muskie in the 1960s, were able to anticipate the public's interest in the environment, however, little meaningful legislation was able to pass Congress at that time. Only when the public's awareness was heightened by a series of crises and by media attention did Congress respond.

The initial response was to spend federal dollars. There is no reason, other than political, why municipalities should not have been required to spend their own funds to clean up their own wastes. However, Congress was able to provide a benefit to their districts without having to be accountable for the costs. When Congress perceived political support from the public by imposing more stringent pollution standards, it chose inefficient methods (specifying equipment), rather than establishing effluent charges. Establishing pollution charges would eliminate much of the discretion that the EPA has in enforcing industry and government compliance. It would encourage industry to innovate, since new methods would save pollution charges, and it would not place new firms at a competitive disadvantage. Such a market-oriented approach, however, would lessen the role of Congress in policymaking and limit industry and local governmental input in the regulatory process, two important political constituencies at the local congressional level.

Currently, there is concern that environmental protection is being taken too far; regulators are demanding unreasonably large reductions in pollution. The EPA refuses to undertake cost/benefit analyses of these pollution standards, thereby overemphasizing the benefits to the neglect of the costs involved. Further, the EPA no longer just focuses on a few major air and water pollutants, but is attempting to control hundreds of pollutants, many of them at trace levels that pose no real risk to human health. Given the public's general interest in the environment, the cost of regulations and mandated technologies to achieve more stringent pollution levels is not visible in terms of lower incomes, higher prices, and lost jobs.

The benefits of further improvements in air quality could be achieved at lower cost if greater flexibility were permitted in achieving specified targets. However, public policy to resolve problems concerning externalities is unlikely to adopt the most efficient solution as long as the costs and benefits of the decision makers are different from the costs and benefits required for an efficient solution.

Study Questions for Chapter 7

1. Explain why an "externality" can be used to justify government intervention in the marketplace.
2. Explain how congressional funding for medical research accommodated both producer interests and the public's political support for such funding.
3. Contrast the political response to the swine flu epidemic with that of another epidemic, AIDS.
4. Using the public interest and economic theory, provide separate explanations for the congressional approach of mandating "scrubbers" to reduce air pollution.

5. Explain how the conflict over environmental policy between producers and those favoring less pollution evolved over time.

Notes

1. Taxes and subsidies are not the only approach that can be used to deal with externalities. For example, rights to produce pollution may be sold by the government once the appropriate level of pollution is determined. Government regulations that every child attending school be vaccinated do not require taxes or subsidies to achieve the efficient number of vaccinations.

2. Richard H. Shryock. 1947. *American Medical Research* New York: Commonwealth Fund. 99.

3. Ibid., 111.

4. Ibid., 111.

5. Ibid., 44.

6. Edward J. Burger, Jr. 1980. *Science at the White House*. Baltimore, MD: The Johns Hopkins University Press. 21.

7. Stephen P. Strickland. 1972. *Politics, Science, and Dread Disease*. Cambridge, MA: Harvard University Press. 34.

8. Ibid., 54.

9. Senator Hill was also the coauthor of the Hill-Burton Act. This legislation was considered to be very popular. It provided federal support for hospital construction based on a formula that gave each state a share of the funds. Thus this legislation had all the ingredients of a successful bill; senators and representatives could all show what they did for their constituents.

10. Ibid., 79.

11. Congressional subcommittees were the main determinant of legislation and the level of appropriations. When there was unanimity among subcommittee members, the subcommittee's recommendations were generally accepted by the full committee and subsequently by the House itself. The bipartisan approach to medical research led to unanimous recommendations by the subcommittee; thus these subcommittees had a great deal of power.

12. Stephen P. Strickland. 1972. "Medical Research: Public Policy and Power Politics," in Douglass Cater and Philip R. Lee, *Politics of Health*. New York: MEDCOM Press. 75.

13. Stephen P. Strickland. 1978. *Research and the Health of Americans*. Lexington, MA: Lexington Books. 17.

14. Ibid.

15. Strickland, "Medical Research," 126.

16. Ibid., 127.

17. Under the able leadership of Dr. Shannon, NIH continued its basic research while following the guidelines set down by the congressional subcommittees.

18. Strickland, "Medical Research," 192.

19. Ibid., 170.

20. Ibid., 249.

21. Paul J. Feldstein. 1993. *Health Care Economics* 4th ed. Albany, New York: Delmar Publishing Inc. 358.

22. Strickland, "Medical Research," 95.

23. Peter Temin. 1980. *Taking Your Medicine: Drug Regulation in the United States.* Cambridge, MA: Harvard University Press. 27–31.

24. Upton Sinclair. 1906. *The Jungle.* New York: Doubleday.

25. The Pure Food Act also presented an opportunity for firms to use it to gain a competitive advantage over their rivals. For example, the dairy industry was able to restrict the sale of oleomargarine. Ibid., 30.

26. William M. Wardell. 1979. "The History of Drug Discovery, Development, and Regulation," in Robert Chien, *Issues in Pharmaceutical Economics.* Lexington, MA: Lexington Books. 8.

27. For a history of the 1962 FDA Amendments see Richard Harris. 1964. *The Real Voice.* New York: Macmillan Co.

28. William M. Wardell and Louis Lasagna. 1975. *Regulation and Drug Development.* Washington, D.C.: American Enterprise Institute. 1.

29. William M. Wardell. "The Impact of Regulation on New Drug Development," in Chien, *Issues in Pharmaceutical Economics.* 147.

30. Sam Peltzman. 1974. *Regulation of Pharmaceutical Innovation.* Washington, D.C.: American Enterprise Institute.

31. The following account of the 1976 swine flu episode is based on Arthur M. Silverstein. 1981. *Pure Politics and Impure Science.* Baltimore, MD: The Johns Hopkins University Press. The author is a Professor of Ophthalmic Immunology at The Johns Hopkins University School of Medicine. The book was based on the author's year as a congressional science fellow on the staff of Senator Kennedy's Senate Health Subcommittee at the time of the swine flu episode. In the preface to his book, the author states, "I was quickly disabused of the notion that this was a question [swine flu] on which Science would triumph. As the months passed and Congress dealt with the swine flu issue in its various forms, it soon became apparent that the course of events was being decided more by political and occasionally economic considerations than by scientific ones. For the first time, I witnessed in great detail the sometimes subtle, sometimes not so subtle, influences that affect the course of events in government. The swine flu issue brought into play the frictions that exist between a Republican presidency and a Democratic Congress, the frictions and differences of style between the Senate and the House of Representatives, and the frictions between congressional committees vying to protect their own jurisdictional rights. Finally and not least, there were the political consequences of all of this happening in a presidential election year."

32. Arthur J. Viseltear. 1977. "A Short Political History of the 1976 Swine Influenza Legislation," in June E. Osborn, *Influenza in America 1918–1976.* New York: PRODIST. 49.

33. Silverstein, *Pure Politics and Impure Science,* 67.

34. Ibid., 102.

35. After President Carter took office, HEW Secretary Califano asked two distinguished scholars to conduct a study to determine what went wrong. Richard E. Neustadt and Harvey Fineberg. 1983. *The Epidemic That Never Was.* New York: Vintage Books.

36. Philip R. Lee and Peter S. Arno. 1987. "AIDS and Health Policy," in John Griggs, *AIDS: Public Policy Dimensions*. New York: United Hospital Fund of New York. Also see Randy Shilts. 1988. *And the Band Played On*. New York: Penguin Books.

37. Patrick Buchanan. "AIDS Disease: It's Nature Striking Back," *New York Post,* May 24, 1983.

38. John K. Iglehart. 1987. "Financing the Struggle Against AIDS," *New England Journal of Medicine* 317 (3) 183.

39. Julie Kosterlitz. 1987. "The AIDS Schism," *National Journal* 19 (27) 1756.

40. Burger, *Science at the White House*, 75.

41. J. Clarence Davies and Barbara S. Davies. 1975. *The Politics of Pollution*, 2nd ed. Indianapolis, IN: Pegasus. 27.

42. Kenneth J. Meier. 1985. *Regulation: Politics, Bureaucracy, and Economics*. New York: St. Martin's Press 142.

43. Davies and Davies, *The Politics of Pollution*. 35.

44. Ibid., 36.

45. Rachel Carson. 1962. *Silent Spring*. Boston: Houghton Mifflin.

46. Meier, *Regulation: Politics, Bureaucracy, and Economics*, 144.

47. Davies and Davies, *The Politics of Pollution*, 40–43. President Nixon proposed $1 billion for each of four years; the cost of the congressional bill was $24 billion over three years.

48. Larry E. Ruff. 1981. "Federal Environmental Regulation," in Leonard W. Weiss and Michael W. Klass, *Case Studies in Regulation: Revolution and Reform*. Boston: Little, Brown and Company. 235–61.

49. Ibid., 259.

50. Davies and Davies, *The Politics of Pollution*, 19.

51. Burger, *Science at the White House*, 86.

52. Ruff, "Federal Environmental Regulation," in *Case Studies in Regulation: Revolution and Reform*, 240.

53. Davies and Davies, *The Politics of Pollution*, 49.

54. Ibid., 48.

55. Ibid., 54–56.

56. Meier, *Regulation: Politics, Bureaucracy, and Economics*, 149–50. When GM faced a $386 million government fine for failing to meet federal fuel economy standards on its 1987 and 1988 model cars, GM threatened to close some plants and lay off workers if the Department of Transportation (DOT) did not ease its standards. DOT received 12,000 letters from GM workers, dealers, and shareholders, as well as 100 letters from representatives in support of GM's position. The rules were relaxed by DOT because, as they explained, they did not want to be accused of causing the loss of tens of thousands of jobs and worsening the trade deficit as more auto production is shifted overseas. *The Wall Street Journal*, October 2, 1986, 56.

57. Meier, *Regulation: Politics, Bureaucracy, and Economics*, 153.

58. This discussion is based on Robert W. Crandall. 1983. "Air Pollution, Environmentalists, and the Coal Lobby," in *The Political Economy of Deregulation*, edited by Roger G. Noll and Bruce M. Owen. Washington, D.C.: American Enterprise Institute 84–96. Also see, Bruce A. Ackerman and William T. Hassler.

1981. *Clean Coal/Dirty Air: Or How the Clean Air Act Became a Multibillion-Dollar Bail-Out for High Sulfur Coal Producers and What Should Be Done about It.* New Haven, CT: Yale University Press.

59. Ibid., 87.

60. Ibid., 91–92.

61. C. Boyden Gray. 1988. *The Fettered Presidency: Legal Constraints on the Executive Branch.* American Enterprise Institute: Washington, D.C.

62. Ibid., 216.

63. Crandall, "Air Pollution, Environmentalists and the Coal Lobby," in *The Political Economy of Deregulation*, 93.

64. Fred L. Smith Jr. 1995. "Markets and the Environment: A Critical Reappraisal," *Contempory Economic Policy* 13 (1) 62–73. Also see the following articles in the same issue, W. Michael Hanemann, "Improving Environmental Policy: Are Markets the Solution?" 74–79, and Robert W. Crandall, "Is There Progress in Environmental Policy?" 80–83.

65. "Breathing Easier: Clean-Air Legislation Will Cost Americans $21.5 Billion a Year," *The Wall Street Journal*, March 3, 1990, 1.

66. Rochelle L. Stanfield. "Environmental Focus," *National Journal* January 31, 1987, 292. Further, through the use of zoning restrictions to "protect nature," environmental concerns were also used by the middle-income and high-income groups to limit growth in their surrounding areas, thereby increasing its value.

67. Ibid., 207. "Former EPA Administrator Ruckelshaus, when he announced his decision on the 1975 auto standards, stated, 'The issue of good faith as it relates to Chrysler Corporation has been particularly troublesome for me in these proceedings. . . . If Congress provided me with some sanctions short of the nuclear deterrent of in effect closing down that major corporation, my finding on good faith may have been otherwise.' Solutions to this problem, such as a tax on emissions, are possible, but the industry is undoubtedly happier with an unrealistic 'nuclear deterrent.' "

68. Michael T. Maloney and Robert E. McCormick. 1982. "A Positive Theory of Environmental Quality Regulation," *The Journal of Law and Economics* 25 (April) 99–123.

69. Meier, *Regulation: Politics, Bureaucracy, and Economics*, 150.

REDISTRIBUTIVE PROGRAMS

Medicare and Medicaid, which started in 1966, were broad redistributive programs. The intended beneficiaries were population groups: the aged (Medicare) and the poor (Medicaid).
While health providers also benefited from these programs, Medicare and
Medicaid were clearly different from producer-type regulations (which
are also redistributive). Medicare and Medicaid were "visible" forms of
redistribution, the legislative debates were publicized, and the intended
beneficiaries were specific population groups.

Examples of broad redistributive programs outside the health field
are welfare, Social Security, food stamps, farm subsidies, and subsidized
higher education. To understand the development of Medicare and Medicaid, as well as these other broad redistributive programs, it is necessary

to view such programs within the context of the political-support theory of legislation.

The underlying assumptions of the Self-Interest Paradigm are that individuals and groups, as well as legislators, act according to their self-interests and that legislation is a means of transferring wealth to those with political power from those without. Such a theory is more readily understood when it is applied to producer-type legislation. The previous chapter was an application of the theory to explain the legislative response in the face of externalities. Another generally acknowledged function of government is an explicit redistribution of wealth, for instance, to the poor. In this chapter, the Self-Interest Paradigm provides an explanation as to why Congress passes broad redistributive legislation and to the design of that legislation.

Chapter 9 uses the concepts developed in this chapter to explore why Medicare and Medicaid were passed. Why were two redistributive health programs enacted rather than one? Why were these programs structured so that rapid increases in medical prices were inevitable? Why are the solutions to the current financial problems of these two programs likely to be both less equitable and less efficient than need be? In fact, why was the original Medicare program deliberately designed to be both inequitable and inefficient?

The equity of a program is defined by those who receive the benefits and those who bear the costs. In nonredistributive programs, such as city garbage collection, the government provides a service in return for a user fee. Those who receive the benefits also pay the cost. No explicit redistribution of wealth occurs, nor is it intended.[1] With explicit redistributive programs, however, beneficiaries (presumably those with lower incomes) are expected to receive benefits in excess of their costs, that is, the taxes they pay to finance those programs. The "losers" under redistribution programs are expected to be those with higher incomes; the taxes they pay to support such programs are expected to be greater than the benefits they receive. A "normative" approach to redistribution implies that redistribution *should* be from higher-income to lower-income groups. A self-interest analysis of such policies hypothesizes that redistribution will be toward those who are able to provide political support, regardless of their "need" for wealth transfers. In the latter case, the redistribution is likely to be inequitable; lower-income groups are likely to bear costs in excess of their benefits.

Efficiency is defined in terms of the cost for producing a given level of output or service. A more efficient program will be able to achieve a greater output for the same cost than an inefficient program.

A Theory of Broad Redistributive Programs

Broad redistributive programs can be classified into two types: charitable and universal. Charitable (or welfare) programs have as their beneficiaries people with low incomes. Universal programs do not use income as a basis for determining beneficiary status. Universal programs either provide benefits to everyone or to a particular class, such as to all the aged. Since the motivations underlying these two types of programs differ, it is important to be able to distinguish between them.

Charitable redistributive programs are specifically designed to assist the poor. Program eligibility is based on income, and program financing comes from general taxes. According to these criteria, the program's benefits go to those with low incomes, and the costs of these programs are borne by those with higher incomes who carry the tax burden. Charitable programs redistribute income from those with higher incomes to those with lower incomes.

Universal programs, on the other hand, do not require an income-related means test for eligibility for the program's benefits. Instead, everyone in the appropriate category is eligible, regardless of income. The financing of universal programs often, although not always, comes from excise taxes that are applied to all, regardless of income (for example, a payroll tax, which is an excise tax on labor).

Charitable Redistributive Programs

Charitable programs are based on a desire of society to help the less fortunate. While some individuals contribute to private charities (or organizations whose goals they share), taxes can also be used to provide for charity. In fact, some persons may prefer that the government be the mechanism to provide the charity since everyone would contribute (according to the taxes they pay). Otherwise, if only some persons donate to private charity, others who benefit from seeing the poor cared for do so without having to contribute. They have a "free ride." Having the government provide the charity is a way of overcoming this free rider problem.[2]

The poor are typically not able to offer a great deal of political support to legislators. Therefore the political support for welfare programs must come from other groups, those with middle and high incomes who finance welfare programs through their tax payments. The middle-income and high-income groups are also politically more powerful than the poor; they are more numerous and more likely to vote, and they provide campaign contributions and volunteer their time. Unless the middle-income and high-income groups favor the welfare programs, they are unwilling to support them. They are the ones whose political demands for welfare must be listened to by Congress.[3]

If the only objective of charity programs were to improve the condition of the poor, then, according to economic theory, the most efficient way to do so would be to provide the poor with cash.[4] Instead, most of the benefits provided to the poor are for specific services (referred to as "in-kind" benefits), such as food stamps, housing, medical care, and so on. If the poor could have the cash equivalent of the in-kind benefits, they would be better off. They could spend the cash on those goods and services they believe they need most.

Welfare programs, however, are designed not just to aid the poor, but, perhaps more importantly, to match the preferences of the two powerful groups supporting welfare legislation. Welfare programs must accommodate both the donors' (middle-income and high-income groups) and the producers' desires rather than those of the poor. It is for this reason that welfare programs provide specific services rather than cash.

The middle class may prefer to provide in-kind subsidies because they may distrust the ability of the poor to make the "right" choices. Further, the donors may favor subsidies to the poor only if the poor buy those services that the donors believe they need.

Welfare programs are often provided under conditions that differentiate these programs from those that the rest of society are able to purchase. It is unlikely that the middle class, particularly the lower middle class (the working near-poor), would favor providing services to the poor that are more generous than they themselves could afford. And, if the same services are provided to the poor, then those services should be provided in a differentiated manner. After all, the recipients of charity should not fare better than the donors. For this reason, means-tested programs have, in the past, been administered using obvious and embarrassing methods. Requiring persons on welfare to work is also based on donor preferences.[5]

The second group that promotes subsidies to the poor are those industries that would benefit from an increase in demand by the poor. Producers, whether in agriculture or in medical care, have a concentrated interest in increasing the demand for their industry's output. Whether originated by the industry or by those with a redistributive motive, welfare programs are provided in accordance with producer interests. The legislature thus responds not only to the public's demand for charity but also serves the industries having an interest in the services being provided.

Thus redistributive programs motivated by charity reflect the charitable desires of the middle-income and upper-income groups—and the economic interests of the suppliers of those services—rather than the political power of the poor.[6]

Political support by the middle class for welfare programs is also high when the beneficiaries are viewed as being "deserving." Typically, *deserving* means that the beneficiaries are similar to those of the middle class but, because of unfortunate or temporary circumstances, find themselves in need of charity. Examples of "deserving" groups are those who are temporarily unemployed, the aged, children, and widows. Welfare programs that do not have these groups as their beneficiaries rapidly lose political support.

Universal Redistributive Programs

Universal redistributive programs do not have the same underlying motivation as charitable programs, although they are often promoted on the grounds that they will benefit the poor. Proponents of universal programs claim that by eliminating means tests for determining eligibility, the poor can be treated the same as others. The actual effect of universal programs, however, is that they are more likely to provide net benefits to groups other than the poor. Universal programs are hypothesized to have as their prime motivation economic self-interest rather than charity. In fact, as will be discussed, universal programs may leave the poor worse off than a means-tested program.

Proponents of universal programs are more likely to favor expanding population eligibility than increasing the benefits to just those who are poor. However, to include a greater number of eligible persons requires a greater cost. An increased cost can be promoted only by including politically powerful groups as part of the eligible population. The cost of the expanded program is consequently shifted to those who are less politically powerful, generally those with low incomes.

Regardless of the initial motivation for universal programs, whether it is based on a sincere desire by some to abolish means-tested programs for the poor, or a desire by some to expand the opportunities of the program to everyone (including themselves), the analysis of such programs can best be explained within the framework of self-interest. While it is difficult to know what someone's intentions really are, inferring a selfish interest on the part of the group that benefits provides a fairly good explanation of the effects of universal programs.

Universal redistributive programs are designed to benefit persons belonging to either certain income or age groups, which are categories related to tax and expenditure policies of government. Income and age groups therefore provide a basis for the formation of political interests and voting coalitions. When universal programs are instituted regardless of income, then the prime beneficiaries will be the middle-income groups. The losers will be those in either the lowest-income or highest-income groups, most likely the lower, since more money can be raised from a diffuse regressive tax than from a highly visible increase in income taxes. When universal programs are designed according to age groupings, then the beneficiaries will be the aged (i.e., those 65 years and older), who also have the political support of the near-aged and their children. The costs of universal programs based on age will be borne by the young.

Universal programs that provide subsidies for particular services will, as in the case of welfare programs, be designed according to producer preferences.

Income groups in society may be classified into any number of categories: for example, the nonworking poor, the working near-poor, middle-income groups, upper middle-income, and so on. For simplicity, three income groups are used: the poor or low income, the middle class, and the rich.

Each of these three income groups may be viewed as a special interest group; through their votes and political power they would like to use the government to transfer wealth to themselves by imposing the cost on another group. Different voting coalitions are possible among these three groups. All that is required is for a particular group to be part of the majority. The majority can then impose its will on the minority.

Generally, the middle class is likely to be able to form a coalition with either the rich or poor against the other. After all, the median voters are the middle class; under majority voting the median voter and the median political view receive a disproportionate share of influence. To receive a majority of the votes and hence be reelected, a legislator moves to the position favored by the median voter. Political competition enhances the political influence of the median voter. The median voter holds the key to the formation of majorities, hence political power.[7] Further, because the middle class is the determining factor in any majority coalition, the middle class is able to extract a higher price than their coalition partners and to be favored by any explicit redistributive programs.

Economist Gordon Tullock claims that majority voting coalitions between the rich and the poor have been unsuccessful largely because of the miscalculations of the poor. A redistributive program based on a means test would transfer funds from the high-income to the low-income group. By excluding transfers to the middle class, the poor could receive more than if they were in a coalition with the middle class. The wealthy would benefit since such a redistribution would cost them less than if they also had to subsidize the middle class. Tullock says, "The poor realize that the interests of the wealthy are clearly not congruent with their interests, but they do not realize that the interests of people between the 20th and the 51st percentile of the income distribution are also not identical with theirs. They therefore tend to favour a coalition with the second group (the middle class) rather than the former (the wealthy)."[8]

In the past, various majority voting coalitions, by income level, have been formed to receive economic benefits by imposing the costs on the minority income groups. A coalition between the middle class and the rich against the poor would require only that a small diffuse tax be imposed on those with low incomes. A coalition against those with high incomes would require very large taxes on the wealthy since there are fewer persons with high incomes and a great many persons with middle and low incomes. Faced with a large, more obvious tax, the rich would be expected to offer greater opposition than would the poor; the voting participation rates of the rich are higher and they can provide more funds to legislators than can the poor.[9]

Given that the middle class is likely to hold the majority of power in any coalition, the objective of universal redistributive programs is assumed to be to provide the middle class with benefits in excess of their costs.

Examples of Charitable Redistributive Programs

The major means-tested programs are those providing subsidies for housing, food, medical care, and cash payments under the category of Aid to Families with Dependent Children (AFDC). Medical care for the medically indigent (Medicaid) will be discussed along with Medicare in the next chapter. The following examples illustrate the application of the Self-Interest Paradigm to welfare redistribution programs.

Food Subsidies

In 1946 the National School Lunch Act was enacted. The objective of the program was to provide assistance to states to establish, maintain, operate, and expand school lunch programs.[10] In 1954 a school milk program was passed, and in 1965 Congress added a breakfast program to schools located in poor areas. Although the legislation received widespread support from educators, women's groups, and labor unions, the legislation was originated in the House Agriculture Committee, whose primary purpose was to benefit farmers. In its report, the House Committee on Agriculture stated,

> The Federal Government has always had an active interest in providing markets for agricultural production and for maintaining agricultural production at a high

level. Any measure that will expand the domestic production of agricultural products, both immediately and in the future, and assume a larger share of the national income to farmers, should receive support. With an established school lunch program, a means of disposal of surplus products is likewise available. It has been demonstrated time and time again that price-destroying surpluses, even though of relatively small amount compared with the total production, must be disposed of if a fair price is to be maintained by the farmer.[11]

The origin of the 1954 school milk program was "an Act to provide for greater stability in agriculture . . . and for other purposes." Further, "it is the policy of Congress to assure a stabilized annual production of adequate supplies of milk and dairy products."[12]

By 1965, food product surpluses were smaller and the Johnson administration wanted to reduce its expenditures for farm subsidies. The administration therefore proposed that the lunch and milk programs be reduced by redirecting them from areas that could afford to pay for these programs to poor school districts. Congress rejected that proposal and instead authorized a new program to provide breakfasts to schools located in poor areas, while retaining the earlier school lunch and milk programs.[13] Congress gave the Department of Agriculture the authority to oversee the school lunch, milk, and breakfast programs.

These programs were primarily passed because Congress wanted to serve a powerful constituency, the farmer. The legislation did not visibly impose costs on the public (although they paid for the programs through increased taxes and higher food prices). Congress could thereby do good while serving their farm constituents.

The original intent of the legislation became clearer when subsequent legislation was proposed to achieve its more "public" goals directly. It was suggested that the milk program be incorporated as part of the school lunch program and as part of child nutrition programs. Sen. William Proxmire, from the dairy state of Wisconsin, objected on grounds that "it would be far easier to sharply slash school milk programs that were an unidentified part of a general nutrition effort."[14] The school milk program was not incorporated into these other programs, even though a study had shown that it was not directed to the needs of the poor. Only $7 million of the $104 million went to needy children.[15]

Food stamps to low-income persons help remove agricultural surpluses from the market. The food stamp program replaced an earlier food distribution program, under which the federal government gave surplus food to the states to distribute to their needy. Under the food stamp program, the recipients would have to buy the food stamps (a requirement since dropped), which could then be used to purchase food at a retail store. Imported food products could not be purchased with food stamps. When the permanent food stamp legislation was signed by President Johnson in 1964, he stated that it was "one of our most valuable weapons for the war on poverty . . . [and a step toward] the fuller and wiser use of our agricultural abundance."[16]

Housing Programs to Benefit the Poor

Federal involvement in housing construction started during World War I, when it was feared that there was insufficient housing for shipyard and defense industry workers.[17] But it was not until the New Deal that a major federal commitment to housing was initiated. It would be a mistake to believe that the Wagner-Steagall Act of 1937 was solely concerned with helping the poor. There were two main reasons for the new housing initiative. One was the large number of unemployed, the new poor, those who had lost their jobs because of the Depression. These people were considered the deserving poor. The other reason was the government's desire to create jobs.

Private housing construction had fallen from 900,000 units in 1925 to 60,000 units in 1934. Yet, with the decrease in new construction, there was no housing shortage; rents were low, there were vacancies. But people lived in "Hoovervilles" and shanties. A federal program to increase the supply of housing could, however, have adverse effects on the private housing market. Federal housing legislation therefore required that existing dwellings be destroyed in number equal to the number of new units being built. This policy eliminated potential opposition from landlords and the housing industry. At the same time, the policy was appealing to those who favored elimination of slums for the submerged middle class, the new poor, and to those who favored increased jobs. The building trades unions lobbied vigorously for the public housing act. The original public housing projects were row houses built mostly in the suburbs.

At the end of World War II, there was a large demand for housing by returning veterans and the rising middle class. Federal housing policy provided tax breaks and mortgage insurance for veterans and also had the effect of stimulating the construction industry: the government was concerned that the country not return to a depression. Public housing lost its initial clientele as the middle class moved out and suburban sites were taken over for veterans' subdivisions. Public housing became confined to the inner city. The new middle class did not want the poor, no longer the submerged middle class, in their neighborhoods. And as land for public housing in the city became expensive, the size of the buildings increased. As the inhabitants of public housing began to change, fewer from a middle-class background and a greater proportion of blacks, the political support for public housing declined.

By the 1960s, public housing was in disrepute. The only public housing that has any political constituency is for the elderly. Communities that have traditionally been hostile to public housing have welcomed housing for the elderly, who are predominantly middle class, white, and not vandals. Subsidized housing for the elderly also helps the middle class find a place for their parents to live.

Other federal housing programs were also enacted, such as urban renewal.[18] Rather than benefiting them, however, the urban poor were, on net, displaced. Urban renewal destroyed more units than were built, thereby decreasing the available supply of housing. According to the 1949 Act, federal funds were available if slums were torn down. However, the slums could be, and were, replaced by nonresidential projects.[19] Urban renewal was used to revitalize a city by eliminating urban slums, but there was little concern for the displaced urban poor. Cities built coliseums and civic centers. The beneficiaries were downtown businessmen, construction workers and firms, and those who wanted a revitalized city. Middle-income and high-income groups were attracted back to the city to live in newly constructed housing.

Two other federal housing programs of interest are the rent-supplement and leased-housing programs. In 1965, a rent-supplement provision was added to the Housing and Urban Development Act. By providing supplements to low-income people, the government would avoid owning public housing. Initially, the rent supplement was to be used in new projects or in projects requiring major rehabilitation, thereby assisting the building unions. A number of the groups that took advantage of this program were churches and nonprofit organizations. (The landlords were able to select their tenants.) Thus these organizations could serve the housing needs of their needy members.[20]

The leased-housing program (1965) authorized local authorities to lease private apartments and homes (with the landlord's approval). This program was welcomed by landlords since it helped eliminate vacancies in areas with high vacancy rates and guaranteed government rent payments. The leasing program was to "take full advantage of vacancies or potential vacancies in the private housing market."[21] There were also incentives for buildings to be rehabilitated. To avoid increasing rents to the middle class, the lease program could not leave the area with too few vacancies.[22]

Both the rent-supplement and leased-housing programs benefited landlords, the elderly (who were often the recipients), and others from the submerged middle class.

Aid to Families with Dependent Children

The AFDC program differs from all other welfare programs in that it provides cash to the recipient, rather than in-kind services, such as food, housing, and medical care. It is therefore of interest to determine why a cash subsidy, which does not benefit any specific producer group, is provided. Subsequently, a producer group was created—welfare employees to administer the program, who developed a concentrated interest in its continuance.

AFDC had its roots in the "mothers' pension" movement. In the early 1900s, there was concern that children not be denied the benefits of a home life because of poverty.[23] If a mother became a widow, her children might have to be cared for in an institution. The social reformers of the day wanted to establish a program that would provide financial assistance to children in their own homes.

The states started their own programs to aid needy children; however, they were not meant to aid all needy children. The rules the states promulgated were quite explicit about who the beneficiaries should be. The children had to have parents of "worthy" character, parents who had suffered from temporary misfortune. Further, the mother had to be able to provide a "suitable" home.

To determine "fit" mothers, the state focused attention on two issues; the first was the father's status. Was the father dead or was he imprisoned, divorced, or unmarried? The second criterion was the mother's fitness to have children. The local determining agencies established the criteria known as "gilt-edged widows." The father was dead, and the mother was white and came from a middle-class background. Blacks and unmarried mothers were excluded. Caseworkers were also encouraged to visit the mothers after their grants had been approved to assure that a suitable home continued to be maintained.

Thus the AFDC program was not meant to provide for all the poor. It was instead meant to aid those who were from the same middle-class background as the donors. During the Depression, many states' funds became depleted as more workers were temporarily unemployed. Additional funding was required to assist the states. After the passage of the Social Security Act in 1935, both the federal and state governments became involved in the financing of the AFDC program. Basic control over the program, however, was to the states. There were many variations among them in their eligibility determinations, although blacks were widely discriminated against in general.

During the 1950s and 1960s, the program changed because of demographics and economics. As more of the recipients were black mothers, public support for the program began to fade. Instances of welfare fraud occurred, and the program was blamed for causing an increase in illegitimacy. AFDC came under permanent attack. The middle-class constituency that had initially favored the program now withdrew its support. The desire to impose conditions, such as "workfare," is an indication of this change. Another indication of the lack of public political support is that Congress has not tied AFDC benefits to the consumer price index, as has been done for many middle-class entitlement programs.

The Nixon and Carter administrations tried to change the welfare system; both failed. The objective of these welfare reform proposals was to eliminate the various in-kind subsidies currently being provided to the poor and instead provide the poor with cash. However, the political constituencies favoring continuance of the multiple-program approach were too powerful. They argued that the special needs of the poor can best be met by in-kind subsidies—which incidentally benefit powerful producer groups—rather than a single, simple, integrated cash system. Cash would obviously be preferable to the poor. However, the poor do not have a strong political constituency. Author Henry Aaron writes

> Welfare reform has no natural political constituency. Although the poor can play on the national conscience successfully at times, they do not organize themselves or vote to the extent that other groups do; in any event, there aren't enough of them to wield a lot of political power.[24]

One might think that the welfare workers would represent the interests of the poor. Unfortunately, that is not necessarily the case. There are more than 100,000 employees involved in the administration of various welfare programs. These state bureaucracies have themselves become an important political constituency.[25] As George Shultz observed,

> It was . . . instructive . . . to observe the opposition of social workers to the family assistance program [President Nixon's welfare reform proposal] under which federal dollars would have been channeled directly to the poor to permit each poor family to decide for itself how best to spend its allotment. We should not be surprised that many social workers supported the retention of the existing system, under which a large portion of those dollars go to social workers, a middle-income group, in return for supervising the allocation of in-kind benefits and the expenditure of funds by the poor.[26]

In his discussion of why President Nixon's Family Assistance Program was not enacted, Sen. Daniel Moynihan speaks harshly of the role played by the leadership of middle-class welfare professionals, who wanted to ensure that welfare workers would benefit (or at least not be harmed) by any new poverty program. "The de facto strategy of social-welfare groups was to seek to kill the program, . . . by insisting on benefit levels that no Congress would pass and no president would approve."[27] "A proposal to put an end to poverty, or the largest share thereof, through direct cash payments was by definition a threat to an agency proceeding at the same task by indirect means."[28] Instead of the Family Assistance Program, directors of community action agencies, funded by the federal government, wanted a program of block grants to their own agencies. They wanted to ensure that their own federally paid antipoverty workers would participate in the funding.[29] Jerry Wurf, head of the American Federation of State, County and Municipal Employees, the largest public employee union in the United States (approximately 30,000 members), testified in his opposition to the Family Assistance Program before the Senate Finance Committee, "This legislation threatens to eliminate the jobs of our people."[30]

Examples of Universal Redistributive Programs

Universal redistributive programs do not use a means test to determine beneficiaries. The users or beneficiaries of the service receive the same subsidy regardless of income level. Such programs appear to be egalitarian. However, the effect of universal redistributive programs, as will be shown by the following examples, is that the middle-class and even high-income groups receive most of the subsidies. The methods by which the subsidies are provided are according to the producer's preferences.

Higher Education

State and federal subsidies are provided to institutions of higher learning. Higher education, including undergraduate, graduate, and professional schools (such as medical schools), are all examples where the majority of the benefits are received by students from the middle-income and upper-income groups. Typical of other state-supported educational institutions is the California system of higher education. Hansen and Weisbrod found that family incomes of students who attended the state-supported universities were on average higher than families whose children did not attend the state university system. Further, the annual amount of state subsidy (the difference between tuition and cost of education) per student who attended the state university system exceeded, on average, their family's yearly payment of state taxes.[31] Thus families who sent their children to the state universities, predominantly the middle-income and upper-income groups, received a net subsidy from the state. Even after considering the additional state taxes the students paid once they started working (assuming they remained in California), the state subsidy still exceeded the additional taxes paid, on a present-value basis. Since the annual state subsidy exceeded the annual amount of state taxes paid by families with children in the state system, the subsidies for the state university system had to be paid by those families whose children did not attend the university and whose incomes were, on average, lower. This system of subsidies to middle-income and upper-income families for their children's higher education exists in all states that have publicly supported state universities.

The reason often stated for such education subsidies is that without them students from low-income families would not have the opportunity to attend college. While this would appear to be a charitable motivation, why is it necessary to subsidize in an equal manner all students who attend, particularly those from the highest income groups? The true motivation for such programs can again be questioned when it is realized that most of the students are not from low-income families, but middle-income and upper-income families. Thus one important characteristic of universal programs is that the subsidized services are used predominantly by those with middle and higher incomes.

A second characteristic of universal redistribution programs is that the subsidies are provided in a manner in accordance with the producers' preferences. State subsidies for college education could be provided to state universities, as they are now, or they could be provided to students to be used at the college of their choice. If the state provided the student with a "voucher" (i.e., a fixed-dollar subsidy for education to be mailed to the university selected by the student), then the state university would have to compete with other universities for that subsidy. It is more in the state university's interest that the subsidy be given directly to the state university. Thus the student who wished to be subsidized would have to go to the state university. The state university receives a competitive advantage over other, nonstate-supported universities; its price of education is lowered.

It is not surprising, therefore, that the state universities are the major lobbyists for state subsidies to higher education. After all, the members of the university community have a concentrated interest in the size and method of distributing those subsidies.

Medical Education

A more obvious case in which the net benefits accrue primarily to those in the middle-income and higher-income groups is that of medical education. (The same analysis would apply to all professional education except that the size of the subsidies per student are so much greater for medical education.) Public medical schools are primarily subsidized by the state, although in the past the federal government has also provided large subsidies. Currently, government subsidies are estimated to be greater than $100,000 per student for a four-year medical education.[32] These subsidies are in addition to those received during the student's four years of undergraduate education.

How are these subsidies in medical education distributed with regard to family incomes? In 1967, 42 percent of the families of medical students had incomes greater than $15,000, while only 12 percent of the families in the population had comparable incomes. In 1975, three times as many families of medical students had incomes greater than $25,000 than did families in the population at large.[33] And once these medical students graduate, they enter the top 10 percent of the income distribution in society.

A charitable motivation is again used as the justification for extensive medical education subsidies; without subsidies, low-income and minority students would be unable to afford a medical education. Only the children of the rich would be able to become physicians. However, if the motivation were truly to aid low-income persons, then it would be more efficient to provide the subsidies according to the family incomes of the medical students. A smaller state subsidy would be required if only low-income students qualified (or if the subsidy was graduated according to family income). A medical education subsidy is a universal redistribution program: all students, regardless of family income, receive the benefits. Since the large majority of medical students come from the middle-income and upper-income groups, the subsidies go predominantly to these groups. Low-income groups pay state taxes, which are used for such subsidies, but the benefits they receive from these programs are less than their costs.

The method by which these subsidies are provided is again based on producers' (the medical schools) preferences. The subsidies go to the schools, which enables them to lower tuition rates. In this way, students are subsidized only if they attend a state medical school. Given the higher tuition at private medical schools, state-subsidized medical schools have a large price advantage when competing in the market for medical students.

Based on the distribution of education benefits, both undergraduate and professional, particularly medical education, the most likely reason for such subsidies is not altruism but the economic self-interest of the middle-income and upper-income groups and the subsidized medical schools. These beneficiaries are aware of the program's economic benefits and are likely to oppose any attempts to make the program either more efficient or more equitable.[34]

Farm Policy

Another example of a large universal redistributive program has been this country's farm policy. In 1929 the Federal Farm Board was established with the mission of "stabilizing" (raising) prices for farmers' crops. President Hoover and then President Roosevelt (and succeeding presidents) also urged plowing under crops. The stated intent of these programs was to assist the family farmer. However, rather than being a means-tested program, which would supplement family farmers' incomes, the farm program treats all farmers alike. The approach used to subsidize farmers is to raise the price of their crops above what they would be otherwise. The methods used to raise farm prices above market level have varied over time, from guaranteed farm prices to restrictions of farmers' output.

The main beneficiaries of this universal subsidy program have been the larger, well-to-do farmers. Approximately 2 percent of the recipients receive 25 percent of the subsidies. When the price of farm products is artificially increased, those who benefit the most are those who are the most productive. Thus most of the subsidies do not go to those small farmers who most need assistance. Approximately $10 billion was used to subsidize farmers in 1995, and yet large numbers of small family farmers are still being forced into bankruptcy.[35] A government study showed that almost two-thirds of direct federal farm subsidies go to farmers with generally strong financial positions and few, if any, financial difficulties. Most of the financially distressed farmers own the small-sized and medium-sized farms; they have been getting far smaller federal subsidies than large farmers, despite their worsening condition.[36]

The cost of the farm program is borne by the public in two ways: as consumers of farm products they have to pay a higher price; as taxpayers they must pay to enable the government to purchase and store the farm produce that cannot be sold at the higher prices. The higher price to consumers is similar to an excise tax, which is a regressive tax; all consumers of food pay higher prices regardless of differences in their incomes. Thus those with low incomes pay a greater proportion of their incomes for higher-priced farm products.

At the end of 1985 the administration estimated that the recently enacted farm bill would cost taxpayers $50 billion over the next three years. Independent analysts claim that the cost could reach upward of $75 billion.[37] This farm bill did not include any new aid for the nation's most troubled farmers. In fact, it was estimated that the losers under this farm legislation, the most costly ever, will be those farmers who are the most distressed. The taxpayers are also considered to be the losers, since they will be paying for these huge subsidies. According to one analysis of the legislation, "Grain-exporting companies will benefit. . . . Wealthy farmers are winners, too. They escaped a proposed lowering of the $50,000 ceiling on direct federal payments to individual farm operators, signaling a continuing improvement in their status relative to financially troubled farmers."[38]

An extreme example of farm subsidy programs is dairy price supports, which in 1982 resulted in $10,000 in public support, on average, for each dairy farmer in the United States.[39] The dairy industry, however, does not consist solely of small farmers trying to eke out a living. Instead, milk is a modernized, $35 billion industry, dominated by large milk cooperatives. Two such cooperatives are among this country's 50 largest diversified businesses.[40] The reason for the success of the dairy industry in securing subsidies worth billions of dollars a year is that the industry is very well organized. The fees that dairy cooperatives charge farmers include an amount for political activities, and the highly focused political activity by the cooperatives is the maintenance of high milk price supports.[41]

The inequities of the farm program—low-income consumers subsidizing wealthy farmers and large corporate farms—has been brought to the attention of Congress numerous times. Congress has for some time also been aware of the inefficiencies of this subsidy system—greater subsidies could be received by the low-income farmers if a means-tested rather than a universal program based on price supports were used. Thus the continued existence both of the farm problem (low-income family farmers) and of farm policy (universal price supports) cannot be attributed to altruism. Economic self-interest on the part of the majority of well-to-do farmers is a more accurate explanation.[42]

Social Security

The last example of a universal program, whose underlying motivation can best be explained by economic self-interest rather than altruism or charity, is the current Social Security program. Since Medicare is more directly related to this type of universal program, a more extensive discussion of Social Security is provided.

Since its beginning, the Social Security program has provided benefits to the aged in excess of their contributions.[43] Congress has increased these benefits over time. The beneficiaries of this subsidy are the aged regardless of their income, while those who bear the cost of these subsidies are the working young. Both the size of the tax and the base on which it is levied have increased over time. The Social Security system is not based on insurance principles; the benefits are not related to the amount a worker has invested in the system. Rather, it is a "pay-as-you-go" method of financing. The benefits are paid from current tax contributions made by employees and employers.

Each time Social Security benefits are increased, those who receive the greatest benefit are the oldest, since they pay less of the additional tax needed to finance the new benefits. Thus those 65 years of age would be expected to favor increased Social Security benefits because they would be the immediate beneficiary of the benefits without having had to finance them. Those 55 years of age would also receive benefits in excess of their costs since they would not have to pay the full costs of the additional benefits. If those in older age groups receive a higher rate of return when benefits are increased, then those who have the longest to work must receive a lower rate of return on their contributions. The benefits are not proportionate to taxes paid, but are inversely related to the taxes.[44]

One study that compared the value of benefits relative to the taxes paid by typical workers who were 25, 40, and 55 years of age found that there is a substantial drop in the expected net benefits for younger generations. In fact, it is estimated that many younger workers will receive benefits lower than the amount they will have paid into the system in payroll taxes.[45]

Further, if the working young receive fewer Social Security benefits when they retire than do the current elderly, then their burden will be even greater. The number of persons in the different age cohorts are not equal. In 1940, there were 10.9 elderly persons for every 100 working persons. By 1990, this ratio had increased to 20.6 aged per 100 working persons. This ratio is expected to continue increasing over time, reaching 29 per 100 by the year 2020 and is expected to increase rapidly to 37 per 100 by 2030.[46] (This support ratio is important in economic terms because the working population can be thought of as supporting nonworking age groups.) Since Social Security is on a "pay-as-you-go" financing system, to provide the same set of benefits to the current working young would require future generations to pay even greater Social Security taxes. Thus, by providing additional benefits to the current aged, Congress shifts the burden of financing those benefits to those currently working as well as to future generations and raises doubts that future generations will receive the same benefits as the current aged.

Various comparisons have been made of the economic status of the aged and non-aged. When such comparisons are made, it is important to adjust for differences in family size, in-kind benefits received by the aged, and their different tax advantages. One of the conclusions from these studies is that the economic status of the elderly has sharply improved over time. In 1966, 28.5 percent of the aged were at or below the poverty rate while for non-aged adults the poverty rate was 10.6 percent. By the late 1980s, the poverty rates for both groups were much closer, 12.4 percent for the aged and 10.8 percent for non-aged adults.[47] These figures, however, mask wide differences in income among the aged. Minority aged, women, and those over 75 are more likely to be impoverished. It is clearly inequitable when the burden of financing increased benefits for all aged, including high-income aged, is placed on low-income workers.

Social Security is financed by a tax on earnings, not on income from all sources. The amount of the employee's earnings (the base) subject to this payroll tax, as well as the size of the payroll tax, has been increased in recent years. The tax is paid equally by both the employee and the employer. However, regardless of whether the entire tax is placed on the employee, or on the employer, or is shared, as is currently done, the effect of who bears the tax burden is the same. Brittain's findings indicate that the worker generally bears all the tax.[48] Although the legislation divides the tax between the employee and the employer, this appears to be more of a device for diminishing the visibility and the employee's awareness of the size of the tax than for sharing its burden. Employees are misled into believing that they bear only one-half of their actual Social Security tax when in reality they are paying all or most of it.

The Social Security tax is a flat percentage on earnings up to a certain earnings base. Each worker who earns up to that limit pays the same dollar amount of tax. Thus low-income workers pay a greater proportion of their earnings in Social Security taxes than higher-income workers.[49] The burden of financing the Social Security system falls on those who were younger each time benefits for the current retired are increased.[50] And those who die early—most frequently those who are poor and black—do not collect much of their benefits. This finding led the 1971 White House Conference on Aging to recommend, "The minimum age-eligibility requirement for primary beneficiaries of [Social Security benefits] should be reduced by eight years for black males so as to reduce existing racial inequities."[51]

Despite the expansion of benefits in the Social Security system over time, many aged are still poor and for these aged persons, as well as for the blind and disabled, a separate cash assistance program, Supplemental Security Income, is provided. This is a federal program that is financed from general tax revenues. Eligibility is based on a strict means and asset test. Since the "pay-as-you-go" financing system that places the greatest burden upon the working poor is not sufficient to provide a minimum income (above the poverty level) to all the aged, a separate means-tested program is required.

Social Security is an inequitable method of helping those who are less well off. The proponents of Social Security, however, have never called it a welfare program, even though it is a massive redistributive program. If the current Social Security system is not based on providing for low-income aged, then what is the motivation for continually expanding the benefits to all aged, regardless of their incomes, and placing increased burdens on future generations? The only credible explanation is one based on economic self-interest of the aged and their supporters.

Political Power of the Elderly

Since the changes in the Social Security system are hypothesized to be based on economic self-interest, it is necessary to examine whether the aged have sufficient political power to achieve their economic goals. Those population groups favoring wealth transfers to the elderly at the expense of other population groups are: the elderly themselves, those members of the working population who view Social Security as a substitute for the family support they themselves may have to provide their parents, and those of working age who are voting on behalf of themselves for when they reach old age.

At whose expense are these benefits transferred to the elderly? If the redistribution of wealth is determined by the political process, then the financial burdens must be imposed on those who have less political power. The natural groups to bear these burdens are the young and future generations.

The young and children don't vote. Historically, the young working-age population has relatively low voting participation rates. The lowest voting participation rates are those 18–19 years of age. In presidential election years their voting participation rates are in the low 30s; for congressional elections it falls to less than 20 percent. Those in the 20–24 age group have a slightly higher voting rate (about 40 percent and mid-20 percent, respectively). The voting participation rate then increases with age with the highest participation rates being those in the 55–74 age groups at about 70 percent for presidential elections and mid-60 percent for congressional elections. Typically, one-third of those voting are 55 or older.[52]

The rewards to be gained from the political process have provided the aged with the incentive to become more politically aware, and their increasing political power can be seen from examining other statistics. The elderly are the fastest growing proportion of the population. And more of the aged can name their Congressional representative than any other age group.

Policies favoring the aged also have the political support of the non-aged. The percent of households with children present are decreasing. Only 38 percent of voters live with a child.[53] Further, the voting participation rate of households with children under six was only 38 percent, while households with no children under 18 years of age, i.e., older couples, voted at a 60 percent rate in the 1982 elections.[54] For couples with children, that is, a 40-year-old couple, their average number of children equaled their number of living parents. Given demographic trends, the number of living parents per couple with children are likely to exceed the number of children per couple.[55] The potential financial and social burden of caring for a greater number of elderly parents exceeds the costs of caring for their declining number of children. Therefore, even couples with children have an economic self-interest in shifting concern with their parent's economic well-being away from themselves.

The above facts, however, are of interest only if people vote according to their economic interests. It is important, therefore, to determine whether this in fact occurs.

There are few empirical studies to enable one to distinguish between contrasting studies of voting behavior. Economist Donald Parsons examined welfare payments to the aged by states in two periods: 1934, before the Social Security Act of 1935, and again in 1940. In this latter period, states were provided with federal matching funds. The purpose of Parsons's study was to determine whether "the increased voting power of the aged in states with relatively more older individuals offset[s] the effect of the increased tax burden on the working population."[56]

After controlling for other factors affecting public generosity, such as per capita incomes and proportion of the population that is white, Parsons concludes that benefit levels in states with a disproportionate number of aged are not significantly reduced; this "would suggest that the increased welfare burden on the younger voters of more aged dependents is approximately offset by the increased voting power of the aged."[57] The results of a study based on a period 50 years ago may not be applicable to today's situation. However, Parsons suggests that as the proportion of the elderly increases, the intensity of the debate over transfer payments to the elderly will become greater, but that aged benefit levels are unlikely to be altered.

Additional information is also instructive in this regard. A 1983 Gallup survey on attitudes toward public schools asked whether people would vote for increased school taxes. Acting according to their self-interest, the aged would be expected to oppose these increases. For those over the age of 50, opponents of increased school taxes easily defeated proponents, 62 to 28 percent.[58] With regard to the question of how the Social Security crisis can best be resolved, a 1982 survey found that the elderly were in favor of increased contributions by the working age population, and also a delay in the retirement age for the nonelderly.[59]

Still another example of the political power of the aged was congressional passage of the Age Discrimination Act of 1975. In an analysis of that act, Peter Schuck describes the source of the aged's political power.

> A number of ingredients combined in the case of the ADA (Age Discrimination Act of 1975) to yield a formidable, indeed irresistible, political offering. It promised benefits to a visible, politically influential group that all Americans hoped someday to join; its sponsors argued that it could confer these benefits at no additional cost; its redistributional implications were not clear, or at least were not noticed; and it was a small and inconspicuous part of a large omnibus bill that both Congress and the Administration supported. Perhaps most important, it drew strength from the moral legitimacy and rhetorical force of the civil rights movement of the 1960s and early 1970s, a provenance that is critical to understanding how Congress conceptualized and responded to the problem of age discrimination.[60]

Further,

> If the elderly constituted a powerful political force simply by virtue of their numbers (and their marked propensity to register and vote), their real strength had additional sources including, among others, the absence of any consistent opposition to their agenda, their ability to form political alliances, and a strong public image of legitimacy stemming from their status and broad distribution throughout all strata of society. As Peter Drucker has observed, "[I]n sharp contrast to every other minority group, the older population has a very large constituency outside its own ranks."[61]

The results of this political power are, Schuck concludes,

> The elderly translated their political power into a series of formidable legislative achievements. By 1975, their successes included Medicare and Medicaid, which together pay for over two-thirds of the healthcare costs of the elderly; rapidly rising Social Security benefits indexed against inflation; the Supplementary Security Income program, which established a minimum federal income for the elderly, blind, and disabled and also is indexed against inflation; special housing programs; pension reform; the Age Discrimination in Employment Act of 1967; and preferential tax treatment. Another example of the political effectiveness of the elderly is the extraordinary growth in appropriations under the Older Americans Act of 1965. The Act, which authorizes a pastiche of grant programs for services, planning, research, and training, was implemented by appropriations that mushroomed from $7.5 million in 1966 . . . to . . . $696.4 million (in 1978). As one observer recently noted, "the aging have proved a difficult group for officials to ignore or 'buy off' with purely symbolic concessions."[62]

And finally,

> Although the most important effects of the ADA, as of any social reform, may well be those that cannot now be anticipated, several predictions may nevertheless be ventured. First, the ADA is likely to increase the proportion

of total program resources allocated to the elderly. If Congress may be said to have had any single coherent expectations in enacting the ADA, it was that the elderly would receive a larger share of program benefits in a world free of "ageism." But if resource levels remain unchanged, increases for the elderly will be at the expense of members of every other age group.[63]

An important indication of the rewards of political activity is the allocation of the federal budget. In 1960, less than 15 percent of a $93 billion federal budget went to the elderly (in the form of cash or in-kind benefits). By the late 1980s, the elderly received more than 25 percent of a much larger federal budget.[64]

A further display of the aged's political power (and perhaps later generalizability to Medicare's problems) was the approach agreed upon by Congress to solve the Social Security crisis in the early 1980s. Changes were made to Social Security in 1983 to enhance its financial viability. These changes, however, had minimal effect upon current (or soon-to-be) beneficiaries. The age of eligibility was increased to age 67, but this was to be phased in after the year 2000. In addition, beginning in 1984, a portion of Social Security benefits were included in taxable income. Aged couples whose adjusted gross income, including 50 percent of their Social Security benefits, was $32,000 would be subject to taxes on one-half of their Social Security income. The proportion of the current aged affected by this provision, however, was very small. In 1980, only 3 percent of the elderly had cash incomes greater than $35,000.[65] Future generations, however, will have greater private pensions and Individual Retirement Accounts (IRAs). Together with inflation-induced increases in incomes (the earnings base is not adjusted for inflation), this 1983 legislation will cause many future retirees to lose part of their Social Security payments to income taxes.

Congress then voted to increase both Social Security taxes and the earnings base on which those taxes apply. Thus the approach used for saving the Social Security system was to impose increased taxes on the working population. The major loss to the current beneficiaries of ensuring the viability of the Social Security system was a six-month delay in their cost-of-living adjustments (COLA).

Since 1981, there have been numerous reductions in federal programs in an attempt to reduce the federal budget deficit. Examining which constituencies have had the largest program cuts once again provides an indication of the relative political influence of the aged. A study of these budget reductions found that "elderly households face much smaller reductions in benefits than do younger households. Benefit reductions since 1981 have, in general, fallen more heavily on means-tested programs than on social insurance programs on which the elderly are more likely to rely. . . . In contrast, programs serving the non-elderly have had larger reductions. For example, . . . the child nutrition programs were cut by about 28%."[66] A conclusion of this study was that "households with elderly members have been less severely affected by benefit reductions, relative to the share of benefits they receive, than have any other population group."[67]

Before 1972, Congress continually voted for increases in Social Security benefits during election years. Fiscal conservatives were alarmed at this attempt to buy the vote of those on Social Security. To halt this practice, Social Security benefits were indexed for inflation. If inflation was below 3 percent then there would be no cost-of-living adjustment that year. However, if the cumulative rise in inflation in the following year reached 3 percent, then the aged would receive their COLA. Thus if a COLA is not received in one year it would be received the next; it would not be lost, merely delayed.

Because of the low rate of inflation in 1986, an election year, the aged were not due to receive their COLA increase. The statistics that determine the COLA are published two weeks before the November elections. Both Congress and the administration came out in favor of giving the aged an increase in benefits even though inflation was less than 3 percent. As John Rother of the American Association of Retired Persons said, "I don't think we have to do anything to preserve the COLA. It's an election year."[68]

One final example of the use of age as a basis of redistribution is the issue of the federal budget deficit. By spending in excess of revenues, the administration and Congress are able to provide benefits in excess of costs to current taxpayers. To bring the budget into balance, it would be necessary for Congress to either reduce spending or to increase taxes. In either case, some groups of current taxpayers or beneficiaries would be adversely affected. Maintaining current expenditures with a deficit, therefore, requires that the revenues that will have to be made up (i.e., increased taxes), are shifted to future generations. The effect is the same as an intergenerational transfer of resources from the young to current taxpayers. The political support for this transfer comes from those who vote who are also the current taxpayers.

Although there is currently a great deal of political interest in achieving a balanced federal budget sometime in the next seven to ten years, it is far from certain that this goal will be achieved. Even if a balanced budget resolution (or even a constitutional amendment) is enacted by Congress, the work of actually carrying it out will be very difficult. Whether a budget is balanced in future years depends on the accuracy of assumptions on interest rates, inflation, and the economy's growth rate.

The Congress that enacts a balanced budget resolution would receive the political support for such a goal, but it will be up to future Congresses to bear the cost of reducing expenditures on politically popular programs. The actual attainment of a balanced budget will be difficult, if not impossible, since when it comes to implementing it short-term interests are likely to dominate long-term general interests.

Concluding Comments

The Self-Interest Paradigm provides a rationale why both producer and nonproducer groups receive legislative benefits. Population groups are large and have high costs of organization. However, certain population groups, measured either by income level or age, are able to use their political support to transfer wealth to themselves by imposing the cost of programs on those unable to provide much political support. These programs are referred to as redistributive programs. The motivation underlying both producer and redistributive legislation are the same: economic self-interest. Producer groups as well as population groups attempt to use the political process to enrich themselves at the expense of those with little political influence.

An important distinction between producer legislation and redistributive legislation is visibility. Producers are provided with their benefits in an indirect manner. And the public is generally unaware of the consequences of producer-type legislation. They therefore offer little opposition. Redistributive legislation has to be very visible, otherwise the beneficiaries of such legislation would not offer their political support.[69]

When redistributive legislation provides services regardless of income level, then the prime beneficiaries are the middle class, which represents the median voter. The middle class holds the key to the formation of coalitions; it is likely to form a coalition with either the high-income or low-income groups. Since high-income persons are fewer in number and more capable of political action, the low-income groups are more likely to bear the burden of redistributive programs. The least obvious method of imposing a tax on those with low incomes is to finance the service through an excise tax, either on property, products, or labor. In this manner low-income workers or consumers pay a cost greater than the benefits they receive.

When age is the criterion for providing redistributive benefits, then the aged are likely to be the beneficiaries. The aged participate more in the political process than do the young, particularly those too young to vote. The aged also have a great many supporters—their children, who are relieved of a financial responsibility, and the near-aged.

Empirical support for the distinction between charitable and universal redistributive programs is provided in the federal budget. According to the Congressional Budget Office, $177 billion was spent on means-tested programs in 1994. (These programs included Medicaid, food stamps, Supplemental Security Income, and the Earned Income tax credit.) In that same year, $612 billion was spent on non-means-tested programs, the largest ones being Social Security and Medicare. The non-means-tested programs were also expected to have a much larger absolute increase over time.[70]

Producer groups are often strong supporters of redistributive policies. The rules and regulations implementing such policies are complex and not very visible to the public. By serving producer interests, Congress is able to garner political support from the major participants affecting redistributive legislation.

The motivations underlying charitable redistributive programs are also in accordance with the Self-Interest Paradigm. The legislative process is used to implement the preferences of the middle class, the median voters. Based upon the examples cited, the middle class, which provides the political support for charitable redistribution, prefers to provide such charity to the "deserving" poor; that is, those who come from the middle class. This was the basis for the AFDC program (white widows who could provide a suitable home for their children) and for federal housing subsidies (the unemployed during the Depression and returning veterans from World War II). Once these programs lost their middle-class recipients, the political support for them declined.

Charitable redistributive programs are based on a means test. Since the benefits to the recipients are intended to outweigh their costs, the financing for such programs is based on general tax revenues, to which the poor contribute less than other income groups.

The self-interest role of producers (and labor unions) in promoting charitable redistributive programs cannot be underestimated. Producers may often be the ones who initiate such programs (housing; school lunch, milk, and breakfast programs; food stamps).[71] Their motivation is the same as for other forms of producer-type legislation. Producers are interested in legislation that increases the demand for their services when they have excess capacity. Such legislation is rarely proposed when producers are at capacity. Charitable redistribution is primarily in the form of in-kind subsidies because it benefits the producers and reflects the values of the middle class. The donors who provide the public support for such legislation want to help the recipients according to what the donors believe is necessary, not according to what recipients believe is most needed.

This self-interest view of redistribution describes the principles underlying redistributive programs. These same self-interest principles form the basis of producer-type legislation. The next chapter applies these principles to the main redistributive programs in the health field, Medicare and Medicaid.

Study Questions for Chapter 8

1. Using the economic theory, contrast the two types of broad redistributive programs (charitable and universal) in terms of their motivations, the basis of their political support, the intended beneficiaries, and the methods of financing.
2. Economists claim that "in-kind" redistributive programs, whereby the recipient receives goods and services such as food stamps or housing, are less efficient than providing the recipient with just cash, which enables them to purchase those goods and services they need most. Why is it unlikely, therefore, that cash will be used instead of in-kind services?
3. Evaluate subsidies to medical schools (which enable public medical schools to reduce their tuition to all students) in terms of whether this approach is the most equitable and efficient method for enabling low-income students to attend medical school.
4. Social Security is referred to as a "pay-as-you-go" financing method. Describe how this approach works. Also discuss the redistributive effects inherent in a "pay-as-you-go" system.
5. Social Security is financed by a payroll tax that is a flat percentage of earnings up to a maximum wage base. Evaluate this method of financing as contrasted to one where there is no maximum wage base. Similarly, what would be the redistributive effects of having this flat tax apply to income from all sources or from just earned income?
6. Why are the aged considered to be politically powerful?

Notes

1. Actually, government programs, such as garbage collection, do involve redistribution. These government employees are likely to receive higher wages and benefits than if these services were provided competitively. These higher costs are financed by higher costs to the users of such services.
2. Once the government provides charity, determining the appropriate amount and method of providing it is not an easy task. Voters are unlikely to disclose their true preferences on the amount of government charity to be provided. Voters both favoring and opposing greater amounts of government charity will exaggerate their preferences expecting to offset their opponent's exaggerated preferences.
3. There is also another hypothesis why charity or welfare is provided. Piven and Cloward hypothesize that welfare is provided by society to achieve two objectives: to maintain civil order and to enforce work. To forestall revolution or property losses, such as was feared would occur during the Great Depression of the 1930s or the civil unrest during the 1960s, the welfare system was expanded. In stable periods,

welfare was provided in such a manner as to ensure that those who were able to work would do so. Frances F. Piven and Richard A. Cloward. 1971. *Regulating the Poor: The Functions of Public Welfare*. New York: Pantheon Books.

Whether the motives underlying charity differ (i.e., altruism or to control labor) is not essential to the argument presented, since both hypotheses assume that it is the political power of the non-poor that decides the amount and conditions by which welfare is provided to the poor. The acceptance of higher taxes to pay for welfare, either for purposes of altruism or the desire to control the poor, is based on the self-interest of the non-poor.

4. Rather than lowering the price of specific goods and services, a cash subsidy would lower the price of all goods and services. B. Peter Pashigian. 1995. *Price Theory and Applications*. New York: McGraw Hill. 78–81.

5. Rather than basing welfare spending on a charitable motivation, Overbye claims such programs are consistent with the self-interest of the median voter, based on a demand for insurance among different risk categories in the electorate. Even though the beneficiaries may, at any time, be those with low incomes, the demand for such insurance programs results from market failure and has majority backing. For example, everyone runs the risk of growing old, not having a pension, nor funds to pay for their medical care. Unemployment can also occur to everyone during their working life. Market failures may make it too costly to purchase private insurance against such events and those who perceive themselves to be of higher risk in these categories want to shift their insurance costs toward lower risks. Einar Overbye. 1995. "Explaining Welfare Spending," *Public Choice* 83 (3–4) 313–35.

6. A prediction of the above theory could be made with respect to the suggestion by then Secretary of Education William Bennett, in the Bush administration. At that time, the federal government was spending $3.6 billion a year for remedial aid. These funds were distributed directly to the school districts and were in addition to the large support provided by each state to its own school systems. Bennett's proposal was to take an average of $600 per student from the federal monies and, instead of giving it to the school district, give it directly to the parents of educationally disadvantaged children in the form of a voucher, which could only be used for education. The voucher could then be used at either a public school in that district or at another school outside that district. Thus, if a school in a ghetto area is not adequately serving its children, the parents could use that voucher to secure a better education for their children at another school.

Bennett's proposal was opposed by the New York City Board of Education, among others. A voucher system permits parents of disadvantaged children greater choice in finding a school that would best serve the children's educational needs. However, a voucher threatens the monopoly position of the schools that do a poor job in serving disadvantaged children. Producer (teacher's union) interests have prevailed over those of low-income families regarding the education of their children.

7. Anthony Downs. 1957. *An Economic Theory of Democracy*. New York: Harper & Row. 198–201; George J. Stigler. 1970. "Director's Law of Public Income Redistribution," *The Journal of Law and Economics* (April) 1–10; and Dennis C. Mueller. 1979. *Public Choice*. Cambridge, MA: Cambridge University Press. Also see, Gordon Tullock. 1983. *Economics of Income Redistribution*. Boston: Kluwer Nijhoff Publishing Co.

The median voter model is similar to the consumer choice model in the private market for explaining demand for goods and services and the supplier response to those demands. Utility maximization by consumers and profit maximization by firms lead those firms to produce goods and services according to consumer preferences. Consumer demands are expected to vary according to relative prices and their incomes. Utility maximization by voters and legislators, and political competition among legislators, is similarly expected to result in policies that reflect the interests of the median voters, who are assumed to be those families with median income. Comparable to the outcomes expected in the private sector, the output of the public sector, namely tax and expenditure policies, is expected to be consistent with the demands of the median voter. The use of a "taxpayer choice" model suggests that governments are hypothesized to act as if they were attempting to maximize the well-being of those with median family incomes.

8. Gordon Tullock. 1986. *The Economics of Wealth and Poverty*. New York: New York University Press. 59.

9. Bruno S. Frey. 1971. "Why Do High Income People Participate More in Politics?" *Public Choice* 11 (Fall) 101–5.

10. Robert H. Bremer, ed. 1971. *Children and Youth in America*, Vol. II, Parts 7 and 8. Cambridge, MA: Harvard University Press. 1438.

11. Ibid.

12. Ibid., 1442.

13. Ibid., 1443.

14. *Congressional Quarterly Almanac*, 1969, 843.

15. Ibid. When one congressman questioned "why the small taxpayers should be asked to subsidize a milk program for the children of . . . private schools which obtain students from very wealthy families," the sponsor of the legislation (Representative Poage, Chairman of the House Agriculture Committee) responded, "A child from the wealthiest home is just as subject to malnutrition as is a child from some other home."

16. Congressional Quarterly. 1965. *Congress and the Nation*, 1945–64 ed. Washington, D.C. 740–41.

17. Lawrence M. Friedman. 1968. *Government and Slum Housing: A Century of Frustration*. Chicago: Rand McNally and Company. 95.

18. Housing policy generally consists of two parts; the first is establishing and enforcing housing codes. The second is providing subsidies for housing construction and/or rehabilitation. The above discussion on redistributive housing programs is concerned with federal subsidies, which have been the major federal approach. Housing codes have primarily been state and local government functions. Early tenement laws were directed at containing epidemics (cholera) and fires, each of which threatened the rest of the city, not just the slum areas. Later housing codes, whose effect was greatest in slum areas, were initiated by social reformers around the turn of the century. Although the slum landlords opposed these measures, they were not an effective political force. They were small landlords, generally living in the slums themselves (33). Through the magazines and newspapers they had been portrayed as venal persons. The publicity generated by the social reformers resulted in the passage of housing codes. The enforcement of these codes, however, varied. Once these laws were passed, the reformers believed that they had achieved their

goal. They had little concern with the administration and enforcement of the codes. Modern housing codes were a prerequisite for cities to qualify for federal urban renewal subsidies.

Housing code policy imposes costs on landlords to upgrade their buildings. Since there are no excess profits in slum housing (otherwise there would be a rush to invest in slums, rather than to abandon them), an increase in costs results in a decrease in supply of such housing. While such a policy will result in halting the deterioration of housing in an area (if enforced) and thereby benefiting the rest of the community, it will also result in eliminating slum housing. Unless subsidies are provided to house the displaced, they may then be worse off.

19. Ibid., 147–72.

20. James E. Krier. 1967. "The Rent Supplement Program of 1965: Out of the Ghetto, Into the . . . ?" *Stanford Law Review* 19 (February) 563.

21. Lawrence M. Friedman and James E. Krier. 1968. "A New Lease On Life: Section 23 Housing and the Poor," *Pennsylvania Law Review* 116, 612.

22. Ibid., 633.

23. This discussion is based on Winifred Bell. 1965. *Aid to Dependent Children*. New York: Columbia University Press.

24. Henry Aaron. 1980. *On Social Welfare*. Cambridge, MA: Abt Books. 72.

25. Ibid., 62.

26. George P. Shultz. 1976. "Reflections on Political Economy," in Ryan C. Amacher, Robert D. Tollison, and Thomas D. Willett, eds., *The Economic Approach to Public Policy*. Ithaca, NY: Cornell University Press. 486.

27. Daniel P. Moynihan. 1973. *The Politics of a Guaranteed Income*. New York: Random House. 306.

28. Ibid., 311.

29. Ibid., 312.

30. Ibid., 325.

31. W. Lee Hansen and Burton A. Weisbrod. 1969. *Benefits, Costs, and Finance of Public Higher Education*. Chicago: Markham Publishing Co. 76.

32. Paul J. Feldstein. 1993. *Health Care Economics*, 4th ed. Albany, New York: Delmar Publishing Co. 388.

33. Ibid., 390–391.

34. It is not difficult to think of other universal programs that have middle-income rather than low-income groups as their prime beneficiaries. For example, the interest deduction for home mortgages on the federal income tax benefits middle-income and higher-income families rather than those with low incomes. Persons with higher incomes are more likely to itemize and the deduction is worth more to someone in a higher income tax bracket. The military draft was another universal program. Many children from middle-class and high-income families were able to avoid being drafted during the Vietnam War since they were able to take advantage of college deferments. Opposition to the war might well have started much earlier had these deferments been unavailable to the middle class.

35. Congressional Budget Office. 1985. *The Economic and Budget Outlook: Fiscal Years 1986–1990*, A Report to the Senate and House Committees on the Budget—Part 1, Washington, D.C.: Congress of the United States. 61.

36. "Richer Farmers Get Most U.S. Aid, GAO Study Finds," *The Wall Street Journal,* April 18, 1986, 40.

37. "New Farm Program Isn't Likely to Ease Crisis," *The Wall Street Journal,* December 20, 1985, 6.

38. Ibid.

39. John D. Donahue. 1983. "The Political Economy of Milk," *The Atlantic Monthly.* 252 (4) 59–68.

40. Ibid., 60.

41. Ibid., 63. While price supports are the overriding concern of dairy farmers, Donahue states, "[It is] too dull and confusing an issue for most voters to know or care much about it. Opposing the system would be likely to lose votes without winning any. Finally, pressing the matter means declaring war on powerful colleagues who have made political careers out of protecting price supports."

42. In 1995 the congressional Republicans promised to balance the federal budget in seven years without increasing taxes. The Republican leadership in Congress believed that failure to keep this promise would cost them a great deal of political support among voters. However, to be able to keep this promise required the Republicans to make reductions in many programs previously considered sacrosanct to various interest groups. The overriding concern with being able to balance the budget is likely to result in changes in the farm program that would not otherwise have occurred.

43. James H. Schulz. 1995. *The Economics of Aging,* 6th ed. Westport, CT: Auburn House, Chapter 2.

44. Edgar K. Browning. 1975. "Why the Social Insurance Budget Is Too Large in a Democracy," *Economic Inquiry* 13 (September) 373–88.

45. James H. Schulz, *Economics of Aging,* 179. Also see Robert Moffitt. 1984. "Trends in Social Security Wealth by Cohort," in Marilyn Moon, ed., *Economic Transfers in the United States.* Chicago: University of Chicago Press. 327–58.

46. Special Committee On Aging, United States Senate. *Aging America: Trends and Projections,* 1987–88 ed. Washington, D.C.: U.S. Government Printing Office. 21–22.

47. Ibid., 57.

48. John A. Brittain. 1992. *The Payroll Tax For Social Security.* Washington, D.C.: The Brookings Institution.

49. The earnings base on which the Social Security tax is applied was increased in recent years, thereby increasing its progressivity. The maximum wage taxable for Social Security was $60,600 in 1995.

50. One analysis of the Social Security system method of financing concluded, "The regressivity and other inequities of the payroll tax, rather than its stabilization and allocative-efficiency effects, are the grounds for considering it inferior to the personal income tax. The major differences that exist between the two taxes—the exemptions, the personal deductions, and the broader income concept under the personal income tax—argue in favor of the personal income tax rather than the payroll tax. The payroll tax bears too heavily on low-income persons and on those with heavy family responsibilities." Joseph A. Pechman, Henry J. Aaron, and Michael K. Taussig. 1968. *Social Security: Perspectives For Reform.* Washington, D.C.: The Brookings Institution. 188.

51. James H. Schulz, *Economics of Aging*, 182.

52. *Aging America: Trends and Projections*, 147.

53. Samuel H. Preston. 1984. "Children and the Elderly: Divergent Paths for America's Dependents," *Demography* 21 (4) 452.

54. Ibid., 447.

55. Ibid., 446.

56. Donald O. Parsons. 1982. "Demographic Effects on Public Charity to the Aged," *The Journal of Human Resources* 17 (1) 144–51.

57. Preston, "Children and the Elderly," 447.

58. Ibid.

59. Ibid.

60. Peter H. Schuck. 1980. "The Graying of Civil Rights Laws," *The Public Interest* 60 (Summer) 69–93. This article is based on a larger article by the same author, 1979. "The Graying of Civil Rights Law: The Age Discrimination Act of 1975," *The Yale Law Review* 89 (1) 27–93.

61. Schuck, "The Graying of Civil Rights Laws," 76–77.

62. Ibid., 90.

63. Ibid., 90.

64. *Aging America: Trends and Projections*, 154.

65. U.S. Special Committee on Aging, United States Senate. *Developments on Aging*. Washington, D.C.: U.S. Government Printing Office.

66. Patricia Ruggles and Marilyn Moon. 1985. "The Impact of Recent Legislative Changes in Benefit Programs for the Elderly," *The Gerontologist* 25 (2) 156.

67. Ibid., 159.

68. "Political Pressures Build to Assure Social Security Increases," *The Wall Street Journal*, March 28, 1986, 1.

    Under pressure to balance the budget and to limit cutbacks in projected expenditures for Medicare, congressional Republicans and Democrats in 1995 were considering changing the formula by which the aged receive COLAs. Congressional testimony by a group of economists stated that the CPI overstates the amount of inflation in the economy. Therefore limiting the COLA update to the CPI minus 1 percent would save several hundred billions, which would then require smaller reductions from projected Medicare spending. The Senate Majority Leader, Robert Dole (R, Kansas) said that this approach was acceptable, if both political parties agreed to it.

69. Rent control can also be analyzed as a universal program. Rent control was legislated in a number of cities and was ostensibly started to prevent sharp increases in rents from occurring when there has been a rapid increase in demand. The immediate beneficiaries of this legislation are renters, regardless of their incomes. The losers are landlords. Sharply increased rents represent a large increase in an obvious cost to renters. It is thus in the renters' economic interests to prevent this cost from being imposed. The key issue is whether renters can organize to effectively present their case to legislators. If renters can organize themselves then they represent, in terms of votes, more political support than landlords.

    The longer-term effects of rent control, however, are a deterioration in the stock of housing and the elimination of rent controls on new housing. With the decrease over time in the number of rent-controlled housing units, the overall supply of housing is less than what it would otherwise have been and the overall rental price is greater. There is less old housing available, a greater increase in new housing (since it is decontrolled), with consequently higher rents. One additional result is that with a decline in the supply of rent-controlled housing over time, those with lowest incomes are either forced out of the area or must pay higher prices for housing.

70. Unpublished data from the Congressional Budget Office, Washington, D.C. 1995

71. Not all legislators need receive political support from each interest group desiring a particular legislative benefit. Through the process of logrolling, legislators receive backing for their own special interest bills by voting for other legislators' special interest legislation.

MEDICARE

Medicare and Medicaid were enacted into law in 1965. Medicare is a universal program providing the same benefits to all the aged who contributed to the Social Security system (the eligibility requirements have been relaxed since 1965). There are two parts to Medicare: Part A is predominantly for hospital care, while Part B covers physician services. Part A is financed by an increase in the Social Security tax; Part B is a voluntary program in which the participants pay part of the premium and federal tax revenues subsidize the rest. Both Parts A and B have deductibles and cost-sharing requirements. Medicaid is a means-tested program for the medically indigent of all ages that is administered by the states. While the federal government contributes to the cost of the program, the states establish the eligibility criteria and the benefits. Medicaid is financed from general taxes at both the federal and state levels.

Alternative hypotheses have been put forth about the passage and design of Medicare. One explanation involves the altruistic desire to help the elderly. There were (and still are) many poor elderly whose needs for medical care exceed those of the rest of the population.

Viewing Medicare as a charitable redistribution program does not satisfactorily answer certain questions. First, why was it necessary to enact two separate programs, Medicare and Medicaid, each with different and distinct financing mechanisms, to provide for the medical needs of the aged on the one hand and the poor on the other? Second, how could the poor elderly be expected to pay the deductible and coinsurance requirements of Medicare, or to purchase the subsidized physician coverage (Part B)? Third, why should Medicare, in theory a redistributive program to aid a disadvantaged population, be financed by a regressive tax?

The case for Medicare as a charitable redistribution program might be made along the following lines: First, legislators may have lacked information on the effect of various provisions of the legislation. Second, the legislation may have been unduly influenced by certain powerful legislators to reflect their own preferences. And third, there may have been certain "political realities" that had to be accommodated. However, an explanation based on altruism and charity but relying on a number of explanations specific to that legislation is not as useful (nor generalizable to other redistributive programs) as an alternative, simpler, self-interest hypothesis. Further, how well can an assumption of altruism, modified by knowledge of the particular participants involved, be able to predict likely legislative changes in Medicare?

The Self-Interest Paradigm of legislation provides an alternative explanation for the development of Medicare. It also provides alternative predictions about the likely outcome of legislative changes to ensure the viability of Medicare.

The assumption of charity serves as a good explanation for the Medicaid program, over which there was little controversy. Medicaid is an in-kind subsidy (i.e., medical services rather than cash), to the recipients who are defined as low-income persons of all ages who meet a strict means test. Medicaid was a continuation of previous welfare programs to provide medical services to the poor. Before Medicaid there was the Kerr-Mills legislation (1960), and before that a system of federally subsidized payments to providers. These medical assistance programs for the poor engendered little debate in Congress.[1]

The motivations for the Medicaid and Medicare programs are thus different. Any income-related program, in which a means test is required, can be reasonably explained by the assumption of charity on the part of the middle class and producers lobbying for legislation to increase the demand for their services. The purpose of income-related programs is to help those who are less fortunate. These welfare programs are financed more equitably, namely through general taxes rather than through excise taxes (i.e., a specific tax on either goods and services or on labor). The poor are the principal beneficiaries of income-related programs. The generosity of the benefits and the method used to implement the means test are reflections of the society that bestows these programs.

Programs such as Medicare and Social Security, however, do not have as their primary purpose an altruistic motivation. These programs are "universal"; all persons within a particular group are eligible regardless of income. Universal redistributive programs are based on motivations similar to those of special interest groups. The political process is used to transfer wealth from one group to another. It is within this framework that the legislative struggle over Medicare is examined.

The Passage of Medicare

The legislative fight over Medicare was emotional and lasted many years before being resolved in 1965. The legislation that emerged was the result of a number of compromises and differed from what was initially proposed.[2] Two parts of the Medicare legislation that were not changed, and which were the basis for much of the conflict, were that eligibility be based on age and that the program be financed through Social Security taxes. These two aspects were in fact related. If a person paid into Social Security, then upon retirement they would be entitled to the program's benefits; it would be an "earned right." If, as the bill's opponents preferred, eligibility was based on a means test, then the appropriate financing mechanism would have been from general tax revenues.

Attempts at compromise in the years before the passage of Medicare involved the structure of benefits; its proponents were even willing to endorse a catastrophic program. But a comprehensive catastrophic plan that was means tested, proposed by Sen. Russell Long, was defeated.[3] The one element for which there could be no compromise was with the method of financing; it had to be financed by Social Security taxes. At one point, the opponents of Medicare proposed an increase in Social Security cash payments to retirees. Medicare proponents opposed this because they believed that the increase in Social Security taxes to fund the cash payment would prevent later passage of Medicare, which would also have necessitated a similar tax increase.[4]

To understand the reasons for the conflict, why it lasted so long, and the final form of the legislation, one must know who the major interest groups were and how they perceived their economic interests to be affected by the proposed legislation. The battle over Medicare was a battle over economic self-interests.

Economic Interests

The major protagonists were health providers, spearheaded by the American Medical Association (AMA), and AFL-CIO unions. Organizations representing the elderly also became active, stimulated by the AFL-CIO. There were many important participants, particularly Sen. Wilbur Mills, chairman of the House Ways and Means Committee, and Sen. Robert Kerr, who, until his death in late 1962, was a strong opponent of Medicare. And finally, the Democratic landslide when President Johnson was elected in 1964 changed the composition of Congress, thereby increasing the prospects for passage of Medicare.

Unions

The unions were in the forefront of the battle for Medicare. Leading the offensive was the AFL-CIO, which resolved to use its vast power and influence to ensure passage of the legislation.

> The executive committee of the AFL-CIO had decided early in 1957 to commit the 14 million-member labor federation to an all-out battle for Government health insurance. In contrast with earlier rounds, the AFL-CIO took on a leadership role. Government health insurance was pressed as labor's number one legislative priority, and organized labor became the rallying point for all those who favored the measure.[5]

Further, labor's influence extended into the race for the presidency of the United States.

> Partly at the urging of labor leaders, all the major contenders for the Democratic Presidential nomination (1960) lent their endorsements to the social security approach.[6]

Still another indication of the leadership and influence of the unions on the shape of the Medicare legislation is provided in the following discussion of the confusion among Medicare's supporters to an amendment proposed by Senator Long.

> During the debate, several liberal senators who were uncertain about which way they should vote were told that the AFL-CIO was behind the amendment. When the story reached (Wilbur) Cohen, who was on hand outside the chamber, he rushed to a telephone and called Cruikshank (Director of the AFL-CIO's Department of Social Security) to ask if it was true. Cruikshank said it wasn't, and hurried over to the Capitol, where he found Douglas and Gore trying to rally the Medicare forces, and told them where the unions stood. Douglas and Gore passed the word around.[7]

The AFL-CIO's interest in this legislation was in the ability to increase the wages of their working members. The unions of the AFL-CIO, such as the United Auto Workers (UAW), generally have the highest-paid employees with the most generous employer-paid health benefits. Retirees' health costs were paid by the employer and represented a growing labor cost to the firm. Covering union retirees with Medicare would mean a decrease in employer payments. The legislation substituted government financing of healthcare for the employers' health insurance payments. Reducing such employers' payments would lower the cost of labor to the firm. The released funds could then be used to increase workers' wages. After Medicare coverage of their retirees, the union was interested in having the government cover the health costs of their employees under a comprehensive national health insurance system. If the firm no longer had to pay health benefits for employees, labor could receive potentially higher wages.[8]

The insistence by the unions on the use of the Social Security mechanism for financing Medicare can be explained within the context of union self-interest. Although union members may have favored Social Security financing for noneconomic reasons, it is unlikely that this approach would have received such strong union support unless it was also consistent with the union's economic self-interest. Social Security financing would have determined eligibility for Medicare. Union retirees would therefore be eligible.

Basing eligibility on a means test would have excluded large numbers of union retirees from those unions that composed the AFL-CIO. From the unions' perspective, even though Social Security is a regressive tax with the heaviest burden falling on low-income workers, the unions' retirees would, at no additional cost, immediately become eligible to receive the benefits, as would the rest of the unions' workers when they retired.[9]

While the unions insisted upon Social Security financing for Part A of Medicare (hospital services), they were not opposed to the use of general federal taxes for financing Part B (physician services). The likely reason for this inconsistency is that eligibility for Part B was already determined by Part A. Therefore the unions' members would have been eligible.

Increased Social Security taxes on union employees to pay for Medicare (or for a comprehensive national health insurance program, such as desired by the UAW) would have cost the unionized employee less than the amount the employer was paying for health insurance on behalf of UAW members. There would thus be a subsidy from low wage/low health users in other industries to high wage/high health users, such as UAW employees. This type of cross-subsidy, which is clearly inequitable, has in fact occurred under "community rating" by Blue Cross in Michigan to UAW employees.[10]

The Aged

To pressure Congress into enacting Medicare, it was necessary for the AFL-CIO unions, the bill's proponents, to generate mass public support for Medicare among the aged and their supporters. Thus the strategy used by the unions was to publicize Medicare's advantages to the aged and to organize the elderly into an effective political force. Senator Cohen had realized the immense political potential of this group. Referring to a 1952 Medicare bill of which he was coauthor, he said:

> At the time there were between twelve and thirteen million people over sixty-five, and every day there were a thousand more, almost all of whom were eligible to vote, and most of whom did. That's a massive political bloc. Generally speaking, older people are conservatives, but not when it comes to Social Security increases or government participation in healthcare.[11]

Self-interest transcends political beliefs. As the proposed beneficiaries of Medicare, the aged realized early the benefits to themselves. However, since the public debate over Medicare was in broad terms, the proponents of Medicare became concerned that the aged believed the bill was more comprehensive than it really was.[12]

The unions were instrumental in organizing the aged.

> A third project, aided by the [Democratic] White House and the Democratic National Committee as well, involved an effort to mobilize elderly people themselves in behalf of Medicare. . . . Starting with a nucleus of union retiree organizations . . . comprising several hundred thousand pensioners, the organizers of the National Council [of Senior Citizens] were able within a few months to build a loose confederation of senior-citizen groups (mostly union, golden-age, senior-center, and church groups) numbering about one million persons. Not only did the National Council establish itself as a spokesman for the elderly, but it was able to stimulate local political action through its various member organizations.[13]

It was ironic that Medicare's proponents favored limiting eligibility to only those aged already receiving Social Security, proposing limited benefits, and financing the program by a regressive tax. The opponents had countered with a more comprehensive set of benefits, to just the medically needy, proposing that the method of financing be based on general tax revenues, which is a more progressive form of taxation. Thus self-interest was a more important determinant of the design of Medicare than altruism.[14]

Medicare became a very visible issue, in contrast to most congressional legislation. Representatives' votes and their positions on Medicare became known to their constituents. In each of the several congressional elections leading up to the landslide presidential election of 1964, it was believed that the aged and their supporters voted based on their representatives' positions on Medicare.

> President Kennedy was also impressed by the analysis of the election returns, and . . . decided to make a push for passage of the Medicare bill in 1962. "With a pivotal congressional election coming up this fall, [reported the New York Times] it was patent the Democrats hoped to claim a major achievement if the bill passed, or a campaign issue with real bite if it failed."[15]

In the congressional elections of 1962, for example, the Democrats did much better than expected. They did not lose any congressional seats by candidates who campaigned for Medicare.[16]

American Medical Association

The passage of Medicare was viewed as a defeat for a powerful interest group, the AMA. Although other health groups such as the American Hospital Association (AHA) were also opposed to Medicare, the opposition was spearheaded by the AMA, which had had earlier success in defeating President Truman's proposal for national health insurance. The AMA tried very hard to defeat Medicare; it hired public relations firms and spent large sums of money in support of its position and to publicize its viewpoint to the public. The support of its physician members around the country was galvanized to present the AMA's viewpoint to legislators, patients, and local organizations.

The political power of the AMA was also based on legislators' fear that physicians would withhold their services if legislation adversely affecting physician interests was passed. In 1962, 44 physicians at a hospital in New Jersey signed a petition stating that they would "refuse to participate in the care of patients under the King-Anderson bill or similar legislation."[17] (King-Anderson was an earlier version of Medicare.) Other physician groups around the country stated their support for the New Jersey physicians. Shortly thereafter, a provincial medical society in Canada refused to provide care in other than designated emergency centers after the provincial government imposed a medical plan that the physicians had opposed.[18] The fear that physicians would not participate in any Medicare legislation was real. As an interest group, the AMA was correctly viewed as being politically very powerful.

And yet, in retrospect, after Medicare was passed over the opposition of the AMA, physicians were among the greatest beneficiaries.

The AMA believed its economic interests were threatened in two ways: first, that the government would set fees for physicians, and second, that the Medicare legislation would, over time, be extended to cover other nonneedy population groups. The AMA was not opposed to having subsidies provided on behalf of those who could not afford to pay for medical care. As an alternative to the Medicare proposals, the AMA eventually developed its own proposal for helping the medically indigent; it favored a tax credit approach that varied according to a person's income. General tax revenues were proposed as the funding source for the tax credit.

Clearly, government subsidies for the medically needy would increase demand for physician services and result in an increase in physicians' incomes. As long as physicians could charge these subsidized patients the same fees they charged their other patients, their incomes would increase. Thus it was essential to physicians that any legislation enable them to charge what they wanted—what the market would bear. The code name for such a pricing strategy was the physician's "usual and customary fee."

Extending government subsidies to population groups other than the medically indigent, however, would merely substitute government expenditures for the patient's expenditures. There would be little increased demand from this group while the government would become a larger payer of physician services. The AMA was also concerned that the concept of universality would be applied to other population groups in the future. Medicare was viewed by the AMA as a beginning step in the direction of a nationalized health service, similar to what existed in Great Britain at that time. Physician incomes in the United States would be much lower if this occurred.[19]

Subsidies to low-income groups are therefore in the providers' economic interest (as long as the method of payment is according to the providers' preferences). In fact, the demand for government subsidies to pay for medical services for the medically indigent often originates with the providers themselves. For example, the main proponents today for federal subsidies for "uncompensated care," which is the lack of (or inadequate) reimbursement for hospital care by certain population groups, are being led by those hospitals most affected by it.[20]

If the government were to become responsible for the payment of a larger population group, the AMA feared that the government would want to become more involved in determining physicians' fees, and consequently, physicians' incomes. (The AMA's concern has become a reality today.)

Those people who were not poor were then being charged the highest price physicians believed they could bear. If high-income patients were included in a government plan, then the price the government would pay the physician would be similar to its payment for low-income patients.

A government fee that reimbursed the physician one price regardless of the patient's income would be less than the fee the physician charged the higher-income patient. It would be more to the physicians' interest if they could still charge the higher-income patient as they wished, while the government reimbursed them for care to those who currently could not afford physician services or for whom a physician was providing care at a low fee.

Charging the highest price the patient could bear is a profit-maximizing strategy. Such a pricing strategy would also imply that the physician would charge some patients more than others (i.e., the physician would price-discriminate). This does not imply that every physician always does this or even thinks in this way. There were even some physicians, although relatively few, who favored the Medicare legislation. The continuance of a profit-maximizing pricing strategy, however, is a useful assumption for predicting the behavior of the AMA, which represents the economic interests of its physicians.[21]

The AMA defeat occurred over two issues: Medicare covered all aged receiving Social Security, not just the needy aged, which the AMA preferred. Second, the legislation was financed by Social Security taxes, which ensured that all aged who had contributed to Social Security, regardless of their incomes, would be entitled to the programs' benefits. But those were the only issues on which the AMA lost. They were victorious on all others.[22]

First, physicians were to be reimbursed according to their "usual and customary" fees for Medicare patients. Second, they were not required to participate in the program. If the physician participated—accepted assignment—the government *through an intermediary* would pay the physician in the above manner. If the physician decided not to participate, then the physician could bill the aged person directly. The aged person would then have to seek reimbursement from the government, whose payment was less than the physician's fee. In this manner, physicians were free to decide which elderly patients to accept on "assignment" and which to bill directly.

Leaving the decision up to the individual physician whether or not to take assignment on a claim-by-claim basis enabled the physician to price-discriminate; the physician would accept the Medicare payment as payment-in-full for low-income patients, but for patients who had higher incomes, the physician could charge a higher fee. The ability to accept assignment on their own terms allowed physicians to continue charging according to a patient's ability to pay.[23]

Another important economic interest of physicians has always been the concept of "free choice" of provider, which the government also accepted. Free choice means that no physician can be excluded from participating in any method of delivering medical services. Rather than being pro-competitive, free choice in medicine has been used to limit price competition among providers.[24]

An insurance company, for example, could not offer a policy at a lower premium by using a closed panel of physicians who would charge a lower price. Under organized medicine's definition of "free choice," the insurance company would have to permit the patient to go to any physician and pay that physician's usual fee. Physicians would have no incentive to reduce their fees if the insurance company had to pay the usual fee of any physician the patient chose.

Preferred provider organizations (PPOs) and health maintenance organizations (HMOs) violate the AMA's free choice concept, which explains why these organizations have been so opposed by organized medicine. HMOs and PPOs compete for patients on the basis of lower prices (perhaps limited cost sharing) and increased benefits, or both. The patient in return has to limit their use of providers to only those participating in the PPO or HMO. By mandating the AMA's definition of free choice of provider under Medicare and Medicaid, the development of these alternative delivery systems was held back. Price competition between these delivery systems and private physicians and hospitals was precluded.

In 1981, as part of the Omnibus Reconciliation Act, the "free choice" of provider provision was removed from the Medicaid program. As a trade-off to save federal matching dollars, the Reagan administration gave the states greater flexibility to manage their programs. Until 1981, states could not take bids from groups of physicians for the care of the state's Medicaid population, nor were the states permitted to enroll Medicaid patients in HMOs. With the removal of the free choice provision, states, starting with California, took bids from providers for the care of the Medicaid population. California took bids from hospitals; other states negotiated contracts with HMOs. Still other states began to develop innovative delivery systems. Many states currently use some form of case management system for some of their Medicaid population. (Under case management a provider coordinates and selects the patient's use of providers.)

While the free choice provision was removed for Medicaid recipients, it has remained in effect for Medicare beneficiaries. The aged now have the opportunity to join HMOs; however, unlike Medicaid recipients, they cannot be required to join. This difference in choices available to beneficiaries of these two programs is a reflection of society's attitude toward charity. According to opinion polls, "The public is enthusiastic

(66 percent) about requiring low-income people to use less costly clinics or HMOs."[25] Most Americans, however, do not want to be subject to these requirements themselves.

Thus, although physicians opposed Medicare they were able to structure it according to their economic interests. For those aged who were medically indigent, physicians would participate and receive their usual and customary fees through their own physician-controlled intermediary, Blue Shield. There was thus no interference by the government in either the scrutiny or setting of physician fees. When physicians believed elderly patients could pay more than the usual and customary fee, they did not accept assignment and charged those patients a higher fee.

Other Provider Interest Groups

The other provider interest groups that were important participants in the struggle over Medicare were the hospitals, represented by the AHA; Blue Cross organizations, which had been started by and were controlled by hospitals; and the commercial insurance companies.

Hospital utilization rates for the aged were greater than for any other age group. Even if the aged could not pay the hospital—and many of them did not have hospital insurance—it was not possible for community, not-for-profit hospitals to simply turn them away. Hospitals, therefore, could not recover their costs for the care of the aged. Hospitals bore the brunt of the problem of the medically indigent elderly, and many hospitals viewed these bad debts as a threat to the financial survival of the community hospital. For a number of years the AHA formed special committees to explore approaches to alleviating this growing financial problem.[26]

Up until 1962, the AHA had been a strong supporter of the AMA's position. However, as the problem of hospital bad debts for the aged increased, the AHA began to distance itself from the AMA. In 1962 the AHA declared that federal help in resolving this issue was necessary and that the method of financing (Social Security taxes) was secondary to that concern.[27] While the AHA was willing to have a program funded by Social Security taxes, it still favored subsidies only to low-income aged, and it wanted these subsidies funneled through Blue Cross. The AHA was concerned, as was the AMA, that the government not pay hospitals directly.

The AHA was also quite successful in designing hospital payment to their liking under Medicare. Hospitals were to be paid their costs (whatever they were) "plus 2 percent." Hospitals also received an extra differential for nursing care to the Medicare patient. Depreciation rules for hospitals were rewritten so that hospitals were to be reimbursed for assets that were already depreciated and for assets that were donated. Needless to say, like any cost plus arrangement, there were no incentives to keep hospital costs from rising. Not only would hospitals receive their costs, but they would receive an additional 2 percent. In reality the incentive was to increase their costs. The effect of the legislation on hospitals was an embarrassment of riches. Their net income (as a percent of total revenue) and their cash flow were greater than ever.[28]

Before Medicare, Blue Cross found itself in difficulty competing with the commercial insurance companies because of the aged. Blue Cross had been using a "community rating" approach for setting its premiums; all age groups, regardless of their utilization experience, were charged the same premiums. Since the aged had higher use rates than younger populations, the younger groups were subsidizing the aged. As these subsidies increased, younger groups found that commercial insurance companies were designing insurance programs that would pay premiums based on their own group's experience. As younger groups left the Blues, the Blues' rates increased, which led to more young groups leaving. It was an unstable situation for Blue Cross.

The commercial insurance companies and Blue Cross also believed that by becoming the intermediaries between medical providers, hospitals and physicians, and the government, they would have a new source of revenue. The Medicare program would be administered by these third parties. The outcome of the legislation permitted the hospitals and physicians to select the intermediaries. The winners in this phase were again the health interest groups.

The Redistributive Effects of Medicare and Medicaid

The direct beneficiaries of Medicare were the aged, both the poor and the nonpoor (including their families whose financial responsibilities were thereby lessened). Benefiting indirectly were the health providers, physicians, and hospitals. The benefits to the aged were very obvious. The redistribution of wealth to the providers was not. The costs of providing benefits to these two groups were borne (and still are) by the younger, working generations.

The Aged

The aged clearly benefited, although some more so than others. They received increased access to medical services. Physician visits and hospital use by the aged rose. It has also been suggested that life expectancy has increased as a direct result of Medicare.[29]

A universal program that treats persons of different incomes alike will not result in equal use of services. Medicare uses deductibles and copayments. The aged also have to pay a premium to participate in Part B of Medicare. Thus, to the low-income aged, the required out-of-pocket expenditures represent a greater barrier to the use of those services than to the higher-income aged. Medicare data show that after the enactment of Medicare, fewer low-income aged used physician services as compared to the high-income aged. The data also show blacks used more services from hospital outpatient departments than whites, while whites used more services from private physicians. Even after controlling for health status, higher-income aged used more physician services than lower-income aged. In 1969, of those aged whose health was considered "poor," the highest-income aged had 60 percent more physician visits than the lowest-income aged.[30]

Those aged who could not afford the deductibles and copayments of Medicare or who could not pay for services not covered by Medicare, generally chronic and long-term care services, have had to fall back on Medicaid, a means-tested program. States used varying levels of benefits and eligibility rules when they established their Medicaid programs. The federal government pays matching funds, but it is a state-administered and designed program. Initially, some states were very generous in both their benefits and eligibility requirements. However, as the cost of the program began to increase, states became more restrictive. To qualify for Medicaid, an aged person cannot have more than several thousand dollars in assets, excluding a home. The effect of this requirement is that many aged have had to "spend down" to this limit, in effect bankrupting themselves, to qualify for Medicaid.

Many middle-class elderly people, and their children, are shocked to learn that if they or their spouses require long-term care, they must rid themselves of all their hard-earned assets to meet the Medicaid means test. The long and emotional fight over the use of a means-tested vs. a universal program has not prevented the need for many of the elderly from having to rely on a means-tested program.

Physicians and Hospitals

Was it possible to have anticipated the financial consequences of a universal redistributive system designed according to provider preferences? Medicare (without Part B) was estimated to cost less than $2 billion a year. In a statement that could probably match the accuracy of "Peace in Our Time," Robert Myers, the chief actuary for the Social Security Administration, testified that "according to our estimates . . . the financing provided in the bill . . . will be sufficient to finance the proposal for all time to come."[31] Federal expenditures for both Medicare and Medicaid, which was also designed according to provider preferences, exceed $250 billion a year.

The rapid rise in federal expenditures for these programs, the unnecessary services, and the inefficiency and waste of the system, according to one of the major architects of Medicare, Senator Cohen, was unforeseen.[32] The development of new technology could not have been anticipated. However, it is difficult to believe that providing universal coverage for a large population group, reducing their out-of-pocket prices for medical services, and placing limited constraints on the providers would not have had a major effect on the rise in prices and expenditures. If hospitals were to be paid their costs plus 2 percent and physicians their usual and customary fees, and there were to be limited, if any, controls on utilization, costs, or fees, what would constrain utilization and expenditures from rising?[33]

While physicians had the medical responsibility for the patient's care, physicians were not fiscally accountable for that care. In addition to providing needed hospital care, hospitals also served as substitutes for the home and for nursing homes. Since the hospital was well-reimbursed for its services, who objected if a patient preferred to stay a few extra days? If it was difficult to care for the patient at home, the physician would approve a longer stay in the hospital. If the hospital was not fully occupied, this would be in its interest.

During this time period, the late 1960s and 1970s, private health insurance coverage among the working population was also increasing. As the cost of a hospital stay increased, so did the demand for insurance to protect against these high costs. (Less than 10 percent of hospital expenses are paid for by patients directly.) And as more of the hospital bill was reimbursed in full, the constraints limiting hospital cost increases became fewer and fewer.

Physicians and hospitals, and those employed by the hospitals, fared well as a result of Medicare and Medicaid.

The Working Non-Aged

The working non-aged paid for Medicare and Medicaid in two ways: first, through increased Social Security taxes (Part A) and higher income taxes (PartB), and second, through higher medical prices and premiums for their own health insurance. As Medicare stimulated increased prices and expenditures, these were also passed on to the private sector. These increased prices for medical services led to a decrease in demand for health services by the non-aged.[34] The noninsured as well as those with the least comprehensive insurance policies were also those workers with the lowest-paying jobs.

Insurance premiums for medical services in the private sector increased as medical prices and utilization increased. While the burden of these higher premiums affected everyone, their impact was proportionately greater on those with low incomes. Higher-income employees and unions with higher-income members did not bear as large a burden. Employer-purchased insurance is considered a nontaxable fringe benefit to employees. Had the employee received the fringe benefit in cash, for those higher-income employees in higher marginal tax brackets, a greater portion of it would have been taxed away. As the employer paid increased premiums for health insurance to keep up with rising medical care prices, this was not as great a loss to higher-income employees receiving tax-free benefits. Thus higher-income employees did not bear the full cost of increased medical prices.

The method used to directly finance Medicare also placed a greater burden on low-income employees. When Medicare is viewed as a redistributive program based on economic interests rather than charity, the method insisted upon for financing makes more sense. Medicare is financed by a Social Security tax. Both the employees' and employers' Social Security taxes were increased. However, as noted earlier, regardless of whether the tax is placed on the employee or on the employer, the effect is the same—the tax is borne by the employee.[35] The advantage of placing part of the tax on the employer is to disguise its cost to the employee; the tax is not as visible. The employees are unaware that they are also bearing the employer portion of the tax. The working-age population bears the cost of the Medicare program as it does the Social Security program. Thus, a Social Security tax is a clever method of financing a program for which motivation is based on the desire for an intergenerational transfer of wealth rather than charity for the poor. Representing the tax as an entitlement for future retirees, even though the benefit:cost ratio is quite different for future retirees compared to current or near-aged, also tends to blur the burden of this method of financing.

An increase in the Social Security tax to finance Medicare not only has this intergenerational effect but also places the heaviest burden on low-income employees. A fixed dollar amount (the Social Security tax) on a lower income represents a greater percent of that income than if the tax were proportional to income. Hence Social Security is a regressive tax; lower-income employees pay a greater percent than higher-income employees.

Another adverse effect of financing Medicare through an increase in Social Security taxes is that it raises the cost of labor—low-wage labor particularly—to employers. The resultant effect is a decrease in the quantity of low-wage labor demanded.

Thus the method selected for financing Medicare places a proportionately greater burden on the lowest-income employees; they pay a greater percent of their income to finance the program, they have to pay increased prices for medical care, and their insurance coverage is more limited. These consequences are inconsistent with any program whose purpose could be considered charitable.

The Medically Indigent

Paradoxically, the one group also adversely affected by Medicare or any universal redistributive program is the poor. There are two reasons for this. First, the explosion in medical and hospital prices, and consequently in insurance premiums, resulting from the Medicare program has made it more difficult for the poor and near-poor not covered by Medicaid to receive care. At times these groups became medically indigent and qualified for Medicaid. However, not all of these groups sought Medicaid assistance or were eligible. Because Medicaid is administered by each state, there are wide variations in eligibility requirements; in some states, people may lose all of their eligibility if their income rises slightly above the cut-off level. Eligibility is not graduated according to income levels. It has been estimated that approximately one-third to one-half of the population below the poverty level does not receive Medicaid benefits because of differences in eligibility among states.[36]

Perhaps the major impact of Medicare on the medically indigent is the lost opportunity of what might have been done. Federal and state expenditures under Medicare and Medicaid exceed $350 billion a year. Both aged and non-aged poor benefited from the hundreds of billions of dollars spent on Medicare and Medicaid. However, more than 50 percent of government expenditures under Medicare are used by those in the middle-income and high-income groups.[37] A more limited program that did not provide such large subsidies to middle-income and high-income aged could have been redirected toward the poor. A federal program that emphasized the poor would have cost less, would have led to smaller increases in demand, and would not have caused rapid price increases.

Concluding Comments

The purpose of this chapter has been to discuss alternative motivations underlying the passage of Medicare and Medicaid. The charity motivation assumes that the purpose of these redistributive programs was society's desire to help the less fortunate. The Self-Interest Paradigm views Medicaid as the result of charitable intentions by the middle class and producer interests; it is directed solely at the poor. Medicare, however, is consistent with other self-interest legislation. The distribution of benefits and the burden of financing those benefits were based on the amount of political support—money and votes—available from the various groups. The members of Congress, in their desire to maximize their political support, redistributed wealth from those with little political support (namely, low-income workers and future generations) to those with more (the aged, their supporters, and the unions). While there may have been an initial motivation for charity on the part of the middle class to assist the medically indigent, Medicare, as designed by Congress, was not structured for that purpose. Separate legislation, Medicaid, which was a continuation of previous welfare policy, was designed to serve the needs of the poor.

The Medicare beneficiaries were the aged, both the poor and nonpoor (including their families whose financial responsibility was thereby lessened), and health providers, particularly physicians and hospitals. The benefits to the aged were very obvious: care at reduced prices. The redistribution of wealth to the providers was not meant to be obvious, nor was it initially so. These gains to providers were (and are) borne by the younger, working generations who pay increased taxes as well as higher premiums for health insurance.

There are several reasons for attempting to distinguish between alternative motivations describing the passage of Medicare and Medicaid. The first is to increase our understanding of why redistributive legislation occurs and the resulting effects on equity and economic efficiency. Regardless of the stated intent of such legislation, equity and efficiency were not part of the legislature's real intent. Separating the charitable motivation from universal redistributive programs clarifies the debate on how to best improve the problems inherent in Medicare and Medicaid. Are the medically indigent the primary concern of these two programs? Those opposed to the restructuring of Medicare along the lines of a graduated means-tested program have appeared more virtuous than their opponents; they have claimed that the opponents want to remove the aged's "earned right." However the consequences to the poor, the young, and those working, of maintaining the current system have been neglected in this debate.

The second reason for differentiating between alternative theories is to distinguish between the true versus the stated intent of legislation. Understanding the actual intent of legislation provides us with an increased ability to predict legislative change.

The Outlook for Medicare and Medicaid

As part of their campaign to increase their number of seats in the House of Representatives during the 1994 congressional election, Republican congressmen and candidates for the House publicized their "Contract" with America. One of their ten "contract" items was to balance the federal budget by the year 2002. After winning a majority in the House (and the Senate), the Republican House leadership believed they were committed to fulfilling their campaign pledges, otherwise the public would consider them to be no different from the Democrats and vote them out at the next election.

Once the House Republicans started to calculate what they would have to do to balance the budget in seven years, it became obvious they would have to reduce the rate of growth in Medicare and Medicaid spending. It was only because of the House Republicans' belief that they would lose more political support if they did not attempt to fulfill their campaign promises that they were willing to make changes in Medicare.

The House Republicans' proposed changes to Medicaid, while controversial, did not generate the political debate that the Medicare changes did. The House Republicans proposed to reduce the rate of increase in Medicaid spending by $182 billion, or 19 percent, over seven years, from a projected annual rate of increase of 10 percent to 4 percent per year. Further, Medicaid would be changed from an "entitlement" program, whereby spending is tied to specified benefits provided to different categories of eligible beneficiaries, to a block grant program to the states. It would be up to the individual states to decide who is eligible and what health benefits they are to receive.

Many Republican governors favored the block grant approach because it would enable them to limit the amount of state funds spent on Medicaid, unlike an entitlement program, and provide them with greater flexibility in how they spent those funds. They claimed that greater use of managed care and more efficient management of the program, without federal interference, would enable them to save funds without reducing services. Critics claimed that managed care savings would be limited because more than half of Medicaid funds are spent for care in a nursing home. Although 23 million non-aged adults and children make up the majority of the 31 million beneficiaries, they absorb just 27 percent of the money. About 60 percent, or $75 billion, is spent on the elderly and disabled. Critics further complained that if the states reduced nursing home expenditures, the financial and family burden on those aged persons who can no longer remain in a nursing home would be increased.

Since nursing homes were expected to receive less funds, the Republicans included in their Medicaid bill changes that are expected to lower the cost to nursing homes of providing care. Currently, to receive any federal funds the nursing home must meet stringent federal standards. Since Medicaid was to be turned over to the states, provisions of the current law that, for example, prescribe training for nurse aides and require nursing homes to have licensed nurses on duty around the clock, with a registered nurse on duty at least eight hours a day, would be eliminated. Instead of federal standards, the states will be responsible for establishing their own nursing home standards.

Additional proposed changes to Medicaid could have a significant effect on the middle class. Currently, federal law allows the spouse of a Medicaid recipient to keep about $14,000 and other assets. Under the proposed changes, the states could reduce the assets a spouse could keep. Further, states might be able to require the adult children of the aged to pay their parent's nursing home bills. A 1965 law currently prohibits states from doing so. Whether these changes adversely affecting the middle class would be enacted, and, if so, whether the states would implement them, is problematical.

These changes have not received much publicity amid all of the other proposals affecting the aged. The limited public discussion of proposed Medicaid changes has been overshadowed by the larger, much more public, debate over the proposed changes to Medicare.

Each political party attempted to define the terms of the debate over Medicare. The Republicans did not want to use the phrase "cutting Medicare spending to reduce the federal budget deficit" as a reason for their proposed changes. Polls indicated that the public was opposed to this justification for reducing the rate of increase in Medicare spending. Instead, using a routine report issued by the Trustees of Medicare Part A (hospital care) projecting bankrupcy of the Part A Trust Fund in the year 2003, the Republicans claimed their proposals were needed to "save," "protect," and "strengthen" Medicare for future generations without asking any beneficiaries, except for the richest, to pay more.[38] The Republicans claimed that they were merely reducing the rate of increase in Medicare spending from 10 percent a year to 6.5 percent.

The Democrats criticized the Republican plan for "cutting" Medicare by $270 billion (14 percent) over seven years to provide $250 billion in "tax cuts" for the rich. (Tax reductions were another part of the House Republicans' "contract.")

During the August 1995 congressional recess, Republican congressmen returned to their districts to discuss their Medicare proposals with their constituents, particularly with the elderly. Somewhat to their surprise, there was no outcry by the aged. By emphasizing the threatened bankruptcy of the Medicare Trust Fund, the Republicans had, by August

1995, convinced 64 percent of the public that something must be done, a sharp increase from the 33 percent who believed this in April 1995, before the Republican ad campaign started.[39]

Under attack from Republicans that they had no plan of their own to save Medicare, the Democrats finally proposed a plan with a much smaller savings in projected spending ($90 billion compared to the Republican's $270 billion). The Clinton administration and the Democratic congressional leadership each put forth different plans. Forcing the Democrats to come up with their own plan meant that the Republicans had won the battle of the polls. The debate was no longer whether Medicare would be changed, but in what way and by how much.

The political battle of how to change Medicare involved redistributive issues. Depending on how (and by how much) the rate of increase was reduced, the losers could be the aged, healthcare providers, or the non-aged.

Although the biggest beneficiaries of Medicare are the current aged, every attempt was made to impose as little additional cost as possible on this politically powerful group. While the aged would be encouraged to move into managed care plans, the Republican plan emphasized that the aged would still be able to remain in the existing fee-for-service system with no limits on their choice of physician. Further, their monthly premium (for Medicare Part B) would still be heavily subsidized and rise only slightly more than it was expected to rise without any change to Medicare (from a current $46.10 a month to $90 month by the year 2002; under President Clinton's proposal the premium would rise to $83 a month). Only those aged couples with an income of more than $125,000 (an income of more than $75,000 for individuals) would be expected to pay an additional premium. It was estimated that only 3 percent of the aged would be adversely affected by these higher premiums.

The major portion of the savings, under the Republican plan, were to be achieved by reducing payments to hospitals and physicians. By comparison, the Democratic proposal to "save" Medicare would have achieved all of its saving by reducing payments to hospitals and physicians. This plan would have moved the bankruptcy date from 2002 to 2006. The Democratic plan also relied on saving billions by reducing waste and fraud in the payment system; a savings that is painless to any interest group. The Republican plan would have moved the bankruptcy date to 2011, when the first of the baby-boom generation becomes eligible for Medicare.

Surprisingly, the AMA, one of the provider groups targeted to suffer a reduction in physician payments under Medicare, came out in support of the House Republican plan, as did the American Society of Internal Medicine.[40] In return for their support, which the Republicans considered to be very important to public acceptance of their plan, physicians received a number of concessions. For example, the reductions in payments to physicians would be smaller than originally proposed; a limit would be placed on payment of damages ($250,000) to victims of medical malpractice; the aged would be permitted to set up Medical Savings Accounts, which would have no limits on the fees physicians could charge those patients; restrictions on physician self-referral laws to facilities in which they have a financial interest would be loosened; and, perhaps most important, a provision was included to make it easier for physicians to profit from their own managed care plans, known as provider service networks.

Currently, it is virtually impossible for physicians and hospitals to set up their own managed care plans because they would have to establish multimillion dollar reserve funds. But with the expectation that millions of aged will move into private plans, such as HMOs, billions of dollars in new revenues would become available to such plans. By exempting provider networks from the capital requirements that insurers and HMOs are subject to, physicians and hospitals can compete for these funds. If such provider plans go bankrupt, the taxpayer is at risk for the losses. It is for this reason the National Association of Insurance Commissioners opposed this proposal.

Other healthcare groups were also provided with certain benefits to limit their opposition. Hospitals also expect to benefit from the reserve requirement exemption for provider health plans and will receive some relief from the antitrust laws. Teaching hospitals would receive a new "trust fund" to reimburse teaching hospitals for training residents and other education-related costs. Nursing homes will receive changes in the 1987 federal law imposing quality standards on nursing homes. HMOs stand to gain as more of the Medicare population is encouraged to join HMOs. And HMOs, while opposing the competition for Medicare patients from the new (physician and hospital) provider networks, will benefit from a change in the "50-50" rule, which prohibits HMOs from enrolling Medicare patients (particularly in new markets) if the aged represent more than 50 percent of their total enrollment. This requirement has raised the cost to HMOs of enrolling Medicare patients by requiring them to expand their commercial enrollment.

The American Association of Retired Persons (AARP) has been able to soften the effects of the Republican plan on the current aged, to the point where they are minimally affected (only 3 percent of the aged would pay additional premiums). However, by becoming a more vocal opponent of the plan the AARP hopes to reduce the projected savings the Republicans want to achieve by reducing payments to hospitals and physicians. Ultimately, reduced provider payments will reduce access by Medicare patients to fee-for-service providers.

Thus while all agree that changes have to be made to Medicare, the providers and the AARP all prefer that the reductions be as small as possible and made further into the future. If it were not for their pledge to balance the budget by the year 2002, the House Republicans would similarly find it politically popular to delay any serious changes to the Medicare system. Since the Democrats and the Clinton administration are not bound by the Republican's balanced budget pledge, their position has been to minimize the burden of reducing the rate of increase in Medicare spending on any of its current beneficiaries, namely, the current aged and healthcare providers. By attacking the proposed reductions as too large, the Democrats hope to force the Republicans to either renege on their pledge to balance the budget by the year 2002 or to drop their proposed tax cuts.

As of this time, it is uncertain whether Medicare changes will be enacted in 1996. Also uncertain is the size of the proposed changes in Medicare spending. The only things that appear certain are that Medicare will be changed, that the current aged will be only minimally disadvantaged, and that healthcare providers will receive lower payments, but that they will receive additional benefits to soften their burden.

As discussed above, it is unlikely that the restructuring of Medicare and Medicaid will result in greater equity and efficiency. The Self-Interest Paradigm view of government again appears to be a more accurate predictor of legislative change.

The relative political strength of medical and hospital associations has declined as political support for reducing the federal deficit has increased. Regardless of what other changes may be made to Medicare and Medicaid, it is highly likely that the rate of increase in Medicare and Medicaid payments to physicians and hospitals will be reduced.

Proposals to reduce Medicaid expenditures are less controversial than changes in Medicare, even though Medicaid's proposed changes are proportionately greater. Medicaid's payments to physicians and hospitals are already below Medicare's and private insurers. Although many states are moving toward using HMOs and managed care for their Medicaid populations, large savings are unlikely since most Medicaid spending goes to nursing homes for the medically indigent aged and for treatment for the disabled. The likely outcome of a lower rate of federal spending on Medicaid will be fewer benefits for Medicaid beneficiaries, reduced eligibility, and lower payments to providers.

The main reason for the likely difference in outcomes affecting each program's beneficiaries is that Medicaid serves the poor, who are not organized and who depend upon the middle class for their political support, while Medicare serves the aged, who are politically influential.

If the legislative objective were to use an equitable solution for saving the Medicare Trust Fund and to reduce the deficit, then an income-related set of Medicare benefits (and financing) could be instituted, whereby more comprehensive benefits are provided to those aged with the lowest incomes. However, those aged who are not poor and their supporters will oppose attempts to make Medicare a means-tested program.

Benefits to the aged will eventually have to be reduced (before 2011 when the baby boomers begin to retire) as the number of aged increase relative to the working population and as the tax burden placed on the working population for providing medical and retirement benefits to the aged rapidly increases. Future generations will begin to perceive the size of their tax burden for aged programs in relation to the much reduced benefits to which they will be entitled. As this occurs, future generations will have an incentive to try and withdraw from the government's health and retirement system and instead to provide for themselves. The previously diffuse cost of aged health and retirement benefits is becoming a concentrated cost to the working population.

Given the opposing concentrated interests of the aged, the desire by the Congress and administration to reduce the deficit, and the increasing burden on the proportionately smaller working population, a compromise outcome is likely. The most likely form of compromise will be one that does not disadvantage the current aged but instead decreases the availability of benefits to future aged (e.g., moving the eligibility age to 67). Thus the current aged will be protected by their political power.

If the motivation underlying Medicare and Medicaid were based on charity, a greater amount of charity could have been provided to those most in need, of all ages, if the funds for Medicare and Medicaid were combined. A more comprehensive set of benefits could have been provided and a graduated means test could have been used. The working poor could also have been included and a more equitable financing mechanism could have been adopted. The efficiency by which the subsidies were provided could have been improved by greater use of managed care plans, such as HMOs and closed panels of providers. Instead, the rapid growth in Medicare and Medicaid expenditures has decreased the government's financial ability and the middle class's desire to provide more funds for the medically indigent.

There was, and is, insufficient political support for an efficient and equitably financed program for the medically indigent. Programs for the indigent are not designed by malevolent bureaucrats or politicians. Instead, they reflect the preferences of the middle class and the providers of those services.[41] This is the reason true welfare programs (those that serve only the poor) are but a small proportion of all redistributive programs and, unlike universal programs, are less controversial when reductions are proposed.

Study Questions for Chapter 9

1. Contrast Medicaid and Medicare in terms of their intended beneficiaries, the basis of each program's political support, and each program's method of financing.
2. How did the design of Medicare satisfy the two competing economic protagonists, namely, the AFL-CIO unions and the American Medical Association?
3. Describe the "free choice of provider" provision and explain why it was removed from Medicaid but not Medicare. Is this consistent with the public interest theory?
4. Under Medicare, hospitals are paid a fixed price per admission which is increased by a small percentage each year. To stave off bankruptcy of the Medicare Trust fund, this annual percentage increase is expected to increase at a lower rate. This annual update is no longer related to the increasing costs of providing hospital care to Medicare patients. What are the implications of this approach to reducing Medicare hospital expenditures for the aged and for hospitals?
5. Why has Medicare legislation, which used to be very generous to hospitals and physicians, become much less generous?
6. To reduce the federal deficit, the rate of increase in Medicare expenditures is likely to be reduced. Is it likely that current and future Medicare beneficiaries will be equally affected?
7. Using the contrasting theories of government, explain why attempts to reduce the rate of increase in Medicare and Medicaid expenditures will or will not treat both of these programs equally.

Notes

1. Robert Stevens and Rosemary Stevens. 1974. *Welfare Medicine in America: A Case Study of Medicaid*. New York: The Free Press. 26–32.
2. For a legislative history of Medicare, see Eugene Feingold. 1966. *Medicare: Policy and Politics*. San Francisco: Chandler Publishing Co. Also see Richard Harris. 1966. *A Sacred Trust*. Baltimore, MD: Penguin Books; and Theodore R. Marmor. 1973. *The Politics of Medicare*. Chicago: Aldine Publishing Co.
3. The Johnson administration opposed the Long plan on grounds that it violated "the principle of Social Security." Feingold, *Medicare: Policy and Politics* 119, 145–46.
4. Ibid., 136.

5. Peter A. Corning. 1969. *The Evolution of Medicare . . . from idea to law*, Office of Research and Statistics, Social Security Administration Research Report No. 29, Washington, D.C.: U.S. Government Printing Office. 78.

6. Ibid., 83. Other indications of the unions' activity are the following: "The AFL-CIO had made a broad grassroots effort to carry the issue (the Forand bill) to the voters during the 1958 midterm elections" (ibid., 82). "On the other side, organized labor and its allies were equally busy promoting the bill. One project involved mobilization of local pressure in the districts of Ways and Means Committee members. Another involved helping a group of physicians organize in behalf of Medicare" (91).

7. Ibid., 211.

8. After the passage of Medicare, unions promoted comprehensive health insurance proposals based on Social Security financing (taxes) for all persons, for example, Senator Kennedy's proposals and the unions' initiation of the Committee for National Health Insurance.

    Few, if any, of the books detailing the history of Medicare discuss the economic interest of the unions as a reason for their strong support of Medicare and the Social Security method of financing. By omitting the economic interests of the unions, the reader is left with the impression that the unions had no economic interests and were only concerned with the needy aged.

9. Marmor provides another explanation for the design of Medicare. It is based upon society's lack of generosity. Tying eligibility to Social Security contributions suggests that these contributions confer "rights" and that the program would not be viewed as a giveaway (Marmor, *The Politics of Medicare*, 21). Apparently some of the original architects of Medicare also saw this program as an initial step toward a more comprehensive health program which would include more population groups (Marmor, 20, 23, 61). However, unless these preferences were also in the economic interests of powerful interest groups, such a strategy could not have been successful. What made the Medicare strategy successful was that the approach was able to generate great public sympathy while the real fight was between the unions and the AMA over their economic interests.

10. Paul J. Feldstein. 1993. *Health Care Economics*, 4th ed. New York: Delmar Publishing Co. 159–162.

11. Harris, *A Sacred Trust*, 64.

12. Marmor, *The Politics of Medicare*, 112.

13. Corning, *The Evolution of Medicare*, 91.

14. Marmor claims that the reason for opposing the more charitable plan was that Medicare's advocates did not believe that the more generous plan would be implemented by the states (Marmor, *The Politics of Medicare*, 35). It is unlikely that this was the cause of the basic differences between the opposing sides. This explanation neglects the economic interests of the unions and the nonneedy aged. Since the basic conflict was over Social Security financing, it appears that it would have been easier to come to agreement over an implementation system.

15. Harris, *A Sacred Trust*, 138.

16. Ibid., 149.

17. Feingold, *Medicare: Policy and Politics*, 121.

18. Ibid., 122–23.

19. "The reformers' fundamental premise had always been that Medicare was only 'a beginning,' with increments of change set for the future." Marmor, *The Politics of Medicare*, 61.

20. Premium competition between insurance companies has increased in recent years. To keep their premiums competitive, insurance companies are attempting to reduce the amounts they pay for hospital care. Hospitals are therefore becoming price-competitive, which means they cannot subsidize (or ask other private payers to subsidize) the cost of the medically indigent.

    As would be expected, according to the hospital advocates of federal subsidies for uncompensated care, any such subsidies should be given directly to those hospitals providing such care. Such a policy would be more to the economic interest of those hospitals than subsidies that would enable the payer of those services (i.e., the state Medicaid program or the aged person), to purchase all their medical services through an HMO that would provide the same level of services to the medically indigent but use fewer hospital services in doing so.

21. For a discussion of price discrimination as practiced in medicine and organized medicine's attempts to maintain it, see Reuben Kessel. 1958. "Price Discrimination in Medicine," *The Journal of Law and Economics* 1 (October) 20–53.

22. Coverage for nonhospital physician services was not initially included in the Medicare proposals. When it became clear that Medicare was going to pass the House Ways and Means Committee, House Republicans offered a plan (the Byrnes Bill) that included more comprehensive benefits; participation among the elderly was to be voluntary, and the benefits were to be financed by general taxes. Not to be embarrassed by voting for a bill that was more limited, Chairman Mills added a physician component to Medicare (Part B) along the lines of the Republican proposal. Feingold, *Medicare: Policy and Politics*, 142.

    Hospital-based physician specialists, e.g., anesthesiologists, radiologists, and pathologists, were also reimbursed according to the preferences of those physicians (Part B of Medicare) rather than according to administration proposals and hospital preferences (Part A of Medicare). Feingold, *Medicare: Policy and Politics*, 143–45.

23. Lynn Paringer. 1980. "Medicare Assignment Rates of Physicians: Their Responses to Changes in Reimbursement Policy," *Health Care Financing Review* 1 (3) 75–89.

24. Charles D. Weller. 1984. " 'Free Choice' as a Restraint of Trade in American Health Care Delivery and Insurance," *Iowa Law Review* 69 (5) 1351–92.

25. Under Medicare, each physician submitted fees to Blue Shield. The physicians were then able to update their fee profile each year. This was the same procedure used by physicians with privately insured patients participating in the Blue Shield program. As in the case of patients who had private Blue Shield coverage, physicians could participate on a claim-by-claim basis.

26. Corning, *The Evolution of Medicare*, 78–79.

27. Ibid., 92.

28. Paul J. Feldstein and Saul Waldman. 1968. "Financial Position of Hospitals in the Early Medicare Period," *Social Security Bulletin* 31 (October) 18–23. Also see, Karen Davis. 1973. "Hospital Costs and the Medicare Program," *Social Security Bulletin* 36 (August) 18–36.

    As federal reimbursement for Medicare patients became less generous, the AHA proposed (1984) that hospitals be allowed to participate on the same conditions as physicians, namely on a case-by-case basis. Congress refused to go along with this. Such a proposal was opposed by aged organizations since its effect would be an increase in hospital charges to the non-poor aged.

29. Karen Davis. 1985. "What Medicaid and Medicare Did—and Did not—Achieve," *Hospitals* (August 1) 41–42.

30. Karen Davis. "Equal Treatment and Unequal Benefits: The Medicare Program," *Milbank Memorial Fund Quarterly* 53 (4) 457, 468–69. Also, Karen Davis. 1975. *National Health Insurance: Benefits, Costs and Consequences*. Washington, D.C.: The Brookings Institution. 85.

    In more recent years, the difference in visit rates by income category has narrowed. This has been attributed to the effective higher prices being paid by higher-income aged. As physician assignment rates for the higher-income aged declined, the higher-income aged have had to pay the difference between the physician's charge and Medicare reimbursement themselves. Feldstein, *Health Care Economics*, 478–480.

31. Testimony of Robert Myers, *Hearings Before the Committee on Ways and Means on HR 3920*, House of Representatives, 88th Congress Part 1, Washington, D.C.: U.S. Government Printing Office, 1964 58. Also see the insert between 28–29.

32. Wilbur J. Cohen. 1985. "Medicare, Medicaid: 10 Lessons Learned," *Hospitals* (August 1) 44–47.

33. It is possible that certain proponents of a tightly controlled government health system anticipated rapidly rising Medicare expenditures and hoped to use the rapid increase in expenditures as a justification for greater government control over costs and expenditures.

34. John Rafferty. 1975. "Enfranchisement and Rationing Effects of Medicare on Discretionary Use," *Health Services Research* 10 (1).

35. John A. Brittain. 1972. *The Payroll Tax For Social Security*. Washington, D.C.: The Brookings Institution.

36. Karen Davis. 1976. "Achievements and Problems of Medicaid," *Public Health Reports* 91 (4) 316.

37. Gail R. Wilensky. 1976. "Government and the Financing of Health Care," *American Economic Review* 72 (2) 205. If Part B expenditures were included, then more than 52 percent would be used by these income groups.

38. "In Medicare Battle, Republicans Display Skill At Making Words Mean Just What They Choose," *The Wall Street Journal*, September 22, 1995, A14.

39. "GOP Positions Itself as Savior of Medicare," *Los Angeles Times*, September 17, 1995, A44.

40. "House GOP Medicare Bill Wins Over Doctors With Hidden Enticements, Promise of Profits," *The Wall Street Journal*, October 12, 1995, A24

41. "Though polls show public support for the Medicaid program, in practice, eligibility for Medicaid is closely linked to the nation's welfare programs, and in striking contrast to medical care, welfare is an area in which most Americans (71 percent) want no additional spending." Robert J. Blendon and Drew E. Altman. 1984. "Public Attitudes About Health Care Costs," *New England Journal of Medicine* 311 (9) 614.

chapter 10

HEALTHCARE REFORM

The Objectives of National Health Insurance
  Universal Coverage
  Using the Power of Government to Benefit Politically
    Powerful Groups
The Defeat of President Clinton's Healthcare Plan
The Prospects for National Health Insurance

T he election of President Clinton in 1992 and the subsequent control of the Congress by the Republicans in November 1994 led to various attempts at healthcare reform. Problems of healthcare access and rising costs were visible issues leading up to the 1992 election. Although he was elected by only 43 percent of the electorate, President Clinton viewed healthcare reform as an issue for which he received a mandate to enact legislation. With the Democrats having control over both houses of Congress, President Clinton's strategy was to rely primarily upon Democrats in Congress, with little or no Republican support, to enact his healthcare proposals.

Many reasons have been given for the subsequent rejection by the Congress of President Clinton's healthcare program. The plan was developed in secret by a task force believed to have had little understanding of politics. The proposed plan was considered too complicated to be easily explained. The public became concerned that too many drastic changes to the organization and financing of health services were being proposed. And of course, there was opposition by special interest groups, notably the Health Insurance Association of America (HIAA), which aired the famous "Harry and Louise" ads that helped create doubt about the plan in the public's mind.

The Clinton healthcare plan attempted to achieve two conflicting objectives, increased access to care and a decrease in the rapid increase in medical expenditures. These twin objectives go to the heart of the debate over national health insurance. These divergent objectives also illustrate the difference between the Public Interest and Self-Interest theories of government.

The Objectives of National Health Insurance

To understand why this country has not had national health insurance and why the Clinton healthcare plan failed, it is necessary to understand the real objective behind such a visible redistributive goal. By understanding the real versus the stated objective of national health insurance (NHI), it becomes possible to determine what the pressures were that brought NHI to such public visibility. It also becomes possible to then determine the likely structure and financing of NHI, should it ever be enacted.

The public interest and self-interest theories provide competing explanations regarding the objective underlying NHI, the pressures forcing the administration and Congress to enact health reform, and the likely method to finance any redistributive program.

Universal Coverage

According to the public interest theory, the motivation underlying NHI is to increase access to medical care by those with low incomes. The poor either have no health insurance and must fall back on Medicaid if they become ill, or their insurance is less comprehensive than the insurance purchased by (or on behalf) of those with higher incomes. In support of the goal of universal access are the numerous studies that document the size of the uninsured population (approximately 15 percent, or 35 million people) and the problems encountered by those with low incomes seeking medical care.

The financing mechanism consistent with a goal of increasing access to those with low incomes would be an increase in income taxes or a premium that is income-related. The funds to finance universal access would have to come from those with higher incomes. Thus the public interest theory would predict that NHI would be redistributive, with the main beneficiaries being those with low incomes and the costs being financed from higher-income groups.

According to the Self-Interest theory, however, those with low incomes already have NHI; it is Medicaid. But Medicaid is generally acknowledged to be an inadequate program. Since it is administered by the states, eligibility rules vary from state to state, with those states having the lowest per capita incomes also having the lowest percent of their population, as a percent of the federal poverty level, being covered. In aggregate, only about 40 percent of those below the federal poverty level are eligible for Medicaid.

There is also a sharp cutoff from eligibility if a person's income increases. A disincentive exists for a Medicaid-eligible, low-income person to earn additional income because their loss of medical and other benefits would exceed the additional wages earned.

Medicaid also pays providers lower fees than either Medicare or private insurers. Thus many providers refuse to care for Medicaid patients. Consequently, even though a person may be eligible, he or she may have difficulty finding a provider to treat them.

The inadequacy of Medicaid, however, is not the result of some malevolent bureaucrats nor a lack of will on the part of legislators or the administration to improve it. Instead, the funding provided for Medicaid, and its eligibility levels, reflect the preferences of the non-poor, who provide the political support for programs to those with low incomes. The eligibility levels and medical benefits provided to Medicaid recipients reflects how much the non-poor are willing to tax themselves to provide benefits to those who are poor.[1]

If the motivation for NHI were to increase access to care by those with low incomes, Medicaid could be improved. Eligibility could be increased, up to and beyond the federal poverty level, a gradual cut-off of eligibility could be instituted as wages increased, benefits could be enhanced, and more generous payments made to providers to increase their willingness to see Medicaid patients. It would not be necessary to enact a separate NHI program to achieve this.

The middle class, however, is unwilling to fund such an increase in Medicaid eligibility and benefits. *If the middle class are unwilling to improve Medicaid, why would they be willing to support and fund NHI to increase access for those with low incomes?* It must therefore be concluded that the main objective of NHI is not to help those with low incomes by increasing taxes on those who have higher incomes.[2]

Using the Power of Government to Benefit Politically Powerful Groups

An alternative goal of NHI is one that is consistent with the Self-Interest theory, namely, to use the power of government to benefit politically powerful groups. Groups are politically powerful when they are able to provide legislators with political support—votes, money, or volunteer campaign time. Politically powerful groups attempt, through the legislative process, to redistribute wealth by receiving benefits in excess of their costs.

Previous visible redistributive programs, such as Social Security and Medicare, provided the aged with benefits in excess of their contributions to such programs. (With regard to Medicare, other politically important groups also benefited, such as the AFL-CIO unions and physicians.) Regressive taxes, namely payroll taxes, were used to finance these programs, which were borne by the non-aged. The size of the payroll tax was hidden, and made more diffuse, by imposing one-half of the tax on the employer and the other half on the employee. A regressive financing mechanism was necessary if the aged and the AFL-CIO unions were to receive benefits in excess of their costs.

The reason health policies change over time is that groups who have borne a diffuse cost find that the cost has increased to where the group develops a concentrated interest in reducing it. Once a diffuse cost develops into a concentrated interest, the group has an incentive to represent their interests in hopes of reducing that cost.

To understand the pressures for health reform, it becomes necessary to understand the objectives of those groups having a concentrated interest.

Federal Government.   Federal expenditures under Medicare and Medicaid have been rising rapidly. The Medicare Trust fund, which collects payroll taxes to pay for Medicare Part A, is expected to be bankrupt in the year 2002. To forestall bankruptcy of the Trust fund, the government will have to either increase the Medicare portion of the Social Security tax, which is already 2.90 percent on all earned income, pay physicians and hospitals less, and/or reduce Medicare benefits to the aged.

Because it is politically difficult to reduce benefits to the aged, previous impending bankruptcies of the Trust fund were resolved by increasing both the Medicare tax and the wage base and by paying hospitals and physicians less. Both of these choices are becoming more difficult. Although the Medicare payroll tax is now a proportional tax on all earned income, increasing it further raises its visibility and the public is opposed to further tax increases. To continue reducing Medicare physician and hospital payments will result in fewer services being provided to the aged and/or decreased access to care. Thus the government is seeking other approaches to reduce the rise in Medicare Part A payments.

Similarly, Medicaid and Medicare Part B, which pays for nonhospital services, contributes to the federal deficit. Both programs are subsidized from general tax revenues. To control the federal deficit, a goal that has gained a large amount of political support, requires the government to limit expenditure increases in both of these programs. If expenditures under these programs continue their rapid rise, other politically popular programs would have to be sharply reduced or the deficit will be increased even further.

The states have also seen their expenditures under Medicaid rise rapidly. Since the states' portion of Medicaid is funded from general tax revenues and states, unlike the federal government, are required to balance their budgets each year, rising Medicaid expenditures have left the states with the following options. The states could reduce expenditures on other politically popular programs, such as prisons and education; taxes could be increased; Medicaid eligibility could be limited; and payments to providers, hospitals, physicians, and nursing homes could be reduced. To minimize their loss of political support, legislators have limited Medicaid eligibility and reduced provider payments. Continued rapid increases in Medicaid expenditures, however, will force the states to consider the more politically difficult options.

Thus both the federal and state governments have developed a concentrated interest in reducing the rise in Medicare and Medicaid expenditures. Legislators at both the federal and state level would oppose any proposals for healthcare reform that place an even greater financial commitment on the federal and state governments. Instead, health reform is viewed by such legislators as a means of *reducing and/or shifting* government health expenditures.

Employers and Unions.   As health insurance premiums have rapidly increased over time, the cost of healthcare to employers and unions has changed from a diffuse to a concentrated cost. As such, both have attempted to reduce these costs through legislative action.

The recent requirement by the Financial Accounting Standards Board (FASB) that employers must list on their balance sheet and annually expense their retiree medical obligations has caused many large firms, particularly those located in the Midwest and Northeast, to reduce their net worth and earnings per share. General Motors, for example, calculated its unfunded medical liabilities at $20 billion. Any reduction in the rate of increase in medical expenditures would reduce these companies' retiree medical liabilities.

Many large unions, such as the United Auto Workers (UAW), have very generous medical benefits. As the cost of medical care has risen, these unions have had to accept smaller wage increases to maintain their comprehensive medical benefits. These unions' legislative objective has been to maintain their benefits without having to pay the required cost. To achieve this goal, the cost has to be shifted to others, either by paying providers less or by a financing mechanism that requires union members to pay less than their full costs.

Large employers and unions hoped to achieve through NHI a reduction in the rise of their medical expenditures.

Physician and Hospital Associations.   The growth of additional groups having a concentrated interest in healthcare has resulted in a relative decline in the political influence of physician and hospital associations. For example, provider organizations, such as chiropractors, psychologists, and podiatrists, have sought to compete with physicians by becoming eligible for reimbursement by insurance companies and Medicare and Medicaid. HMOs and insurers have opposed medical societies in their attempt to enact restrictive legislation, such as "any willing provider" laws, that would increase HMOs' costs. And the federal government has attempted to lower its Medicare expenditures by placing reimbursement limits on physicians and hospitals.

Also decreasing the American Medical Association's (AMA) and American Hospital Association's (AHA) political influence is that both have a diverse membership. Within the AMA there are many different specialty groups of physicians. Similarly, within the AHA there are separate groups of hospitals, such as the urban, rural, teaching, and state hospital associations, that have a concentrated interest in increasing federal funds to their own constituencies.

When the federal government introduced the new Medicare hospital payment system (diagnosis DRGs) in 1983, it was determined that it would be "budget-neutral," that is, any gains to one group of hospitals would have to be offset by losses to other groups of hospitals. The effect of budget neutrality was to lessen the political influence of the AHA, since the AHA could only favor revenue increases to all hospitals—not to specific groups of hospitals. Each group of hospitals then developed their own lobbying organization to try and receive more federal Medicare funding and to protect themselves against the lobbying efforts of other hospital associations. Hospitals no longer spoke to legislators with one voice.

The new Medicare physician payment system (Resource Based Relative Value Scale, RBRVS) was also based on budget neutrality. One of its objectives was intended to redistribute income away from procedure-oriented specialists toward family physicians. Each medical specialty association engaged in the political process, both to receive higher reimbursement, as well as to protect their own interests. The AMA, even though a majority of its membership is specialists, could not favor one medical group over another for fear of losing the membership of these large medical associations. These medical societies were also very active during the debate over President Clinton's health reform proposal; for example, the American College of Surgeons (52,000 members) and the American College of Physicians (70,000 internists) came out for an overall budget limit and fee controls, which were opposed by the AMA and other medical societies.

Multiple hospital and medical associations, each having its own concentrated interest and representing those interests, have politically weakened their umbrella organizations, the AMA and the AHA.

The AMA and AHA have attempted to represent the interests of all of their members by lobbying for more federal funding and against any further reductions in Medicare payments. While their objective has been to increase their members' revenues, they have been opposed at both the federal and state levels by administrations and legislators who have a concentrated interest in not raising taxes or increasing the deficit.

The AMA and the AHA have therefore favored health reform proposals that increase the demand for medical services in the private sector and have opposed reductions in Medicare and Medicaid.

Health Insurers. Health insurers want to ensure that any health reform program retains the private health insurance industry and, second, that there is an increase in the demand for private insurance.

The health insurance industry is, however, split between large and small insurers. The large insurers would like to see the small insurers exit the industry. The large insurers are in favor of managed care and HMOs because they believe they can develop such organizations and can use their marketing systems to increase their market share. The smaller insurance companies would prefer to sell traditional indemnity and catastrophic insurance, that is, continue to manage risk rather than manage care, as the large insurers are trying to do. (Under the Clinton health plan, smaller insurers believed they would no longer have a role if the large purchasing pools, referred to as "health alliances," chose the insurers and HMOs.) The split between insurers also explains why large insurers favor health insurance reform regulations, such as guaranteed renewability and limits on preexisting exclusions, since large insurers will be more able than small insurers to bear these costs, thereby giving them a competitive advantage over small insurers.

Another important issue health insurers (and HMOs) would like resolved in any NHI plan is which medical treatments are considered experimental and do not have to be covered in their benefit package. Denying their enrollees medical treatments that are considered experimental or that have very low probabilities of success for certain patients leaves the insurer liable for large damage awards. It is also difficult for insurers to calculate a premium if it is unknown which new medical treatments will be part of their enrollees' benefits. Insurers would prefer that the federal government establish technology assessment panels that would undertake cost-effective analyses of new technology and presumably limit access to expensive medical treatments. Opposing insurers on this issue are pharmaceutical companies and technology manufacturers whose revenues and profitability would be decreased.

The Aged. The aged already have NHI for acute care, it is Medicare. The aged would next like to have financial protection against the high out-of-pocket costs of prescription drugs and long-term care. Low-income aged must rely on Medicaid for their out-of-pocket medical expenses and long-term care needs. Middle-income and high-income aged do not want to spend down their assets to qualify for Medicaid if they incur large long-term care expenses. Rather than purchase asset protection (long-term care insurance) through the private market, middle-income and high-income aged would prefer government long-term care insurance so that part of their cost can be shifted to others.

The delay in enacting any long-term care plan for the aged has been its expected large cost. Given the magnitude of such expenditures, the tax required to finance such a benefit to the middle-income and high-income aged is unlikely to be diffuse. Although a regressive tax would likely be used, such as a sales or payroll tax, the size of the tax required would make it visible. Imposing a new tax would also engender political opposition in an era where politicians are reluctant to raise taxes.

The approach by Presidents and legislators to obtain the political support of the aged is to gradually increase the aged's health coverage, such as by including home care as part of Medicare and proposing to include prescription drugs. While these actions and proposals are an expansion of Medicare, they are still for acute care and not for chronic or long-term care. Even these expansions of Medicare (particularly proposals for prescription drugs) are difficult to achieve without a new funding source.

The search by Congress for new funds to finance additional Medicare benefits provides another test of the Self-Interest and Public Interest theories. Prior to the 1988 election, hoping to earn the gratitude (and political support) of the aged, the administration proposed and the Congress enacted (after expanding the administration's proposal) the Medicare Catastrophic Act. This new benefit provided the aged with catastrophic medical coverage, after they had met the deductibles and copayments under Medicare Parts A and B.

Unlike all previous Medicare expansions, the funding for this new benefit was to come entirely from the middle-income and high-income aged themselves. They were to pay higher Part B premiums, which would finance the new benefits for lower-income aged. However, most middle-income and high-income aged had already purchased private "medigap" coverage to limit their financial liabilities under Medicare. (Medicaid remained the catastrophic coverage for low-income aged.) The cost of the new benefits exceeded their value to middle-income and high-income aged. When the aged found out about the costs and benefits of the new legislation, they protested their higher premiums. As shown on TV, the aged chased Chairman of the House Ways and Means Committee Rep. Daniel Rostenkowski down the street to his car. The Congress, realizing their mistake, repealed the legislation the following year. The repeal of the Medicare Catastrophic Act in 1989 made clear to all politicians that the aged expected benefits in excess of their costs.

The political emphasis on deficit reduction (which is made more difficult to achieve by the increase in federal subsidies to pay for Medicare Part B), together with the political reluctance to raise taxes (to forestall the impending bankruptcy of Medicare Part A), has shifted the aged's concerns to ensuring their current Medicare benefits. Whether changes to the Medicare system to forestall its bankruptcy improve equity (including intergenerational equity), in terms of financing and benefits, will be another test of the self-interest and public interest theories. Protection of the excess of benefits over costs received by the current aged, regardless of their incomes, and at the expense of future aged, would be consistent with the Self-Interest theory.

The Middle Class. Visible redistributive issues, such as NHI, require the political support of the middle class. The middle class has a disproportionate amount of political power since political parties cannot form a majority without those in the middle. If an NHI proposal were supported by the middle class, legislators would respond and enact NHI. It therefore becomes important to determine what the middle class's objectives are with regard to NHI and, second, why the middle class was not supportive of the Clinton healthcare plan.

Until recently, the middle class was insulated from the rising costs of medical care. The employer paid the employee's health insurance premium for a traditional indemnity health plan, which permitted the employee and their family to go to any fee-for-service provider. These employer contributions on behalf of the employee are not considered part of the employee's taxable income.

The beneficiaries of employer-paid health insurance are primarily those with higher incomes. When an employer purchases $5,000 worth of health insurance for an employee, that amount is not considered part of the employee's taxable income. If the employee were instead to receive

$5,000 in increased wages, the employee would have to pay federal, state, and Social Security taxes on that $5,000. The employee would be left with approximately $2,725. (Assuming the employee is in a 31 percent federal tax bracket, pays 7 percent state income tax, and 7.5 percent Social Security tax.) The tax savings are greatest for those in the highest income tax bracketts. The higher-income employee can receive almost twice as much medical services when the employer buys comprehensive coverage with before-tax dollars.

Employer-purchased health insurance has been a form of subsidized NHI for middle-income and high-income groups. The cost of medical care did not represent a serious financial risk to the middle class. They were at greater financial risk for the long-term care needs of their parents. The lost federal tax revenue (foregone federal and Social Security taxes) from employer-purchased health insurance was $74 billion in 1994.[3] These lost federal taxes could more than pay for subsidies to cover the uninsured. Yet the Clinton health plan was reluctant to limit these tax subsidies as a means of funding its health plan because the AFL-CIO unions were strongly opposed to a tax cap.

As stated at the beginning of this chapter, President Clinton viewed the 1992 election as a mandate to introduce comprehensive healthcare reform. Although, according to various polls, the middle class expressed a great deal of dissatisfaction with the current healthcare system, the polls did not indicate any consensus on what type of reform the middle class wanted. Middle-income and high-income groups already had subsidized NHI. "Half of the voters . . . said they were willing to pay an additional $20 a month to support a national plan that would provide insurance coverage to all Americans, but only 24% were willing to pay an additional $50 per month."[4]. Willingness to pay higher taxes also varied by the type of tax, with sin taxes being preferred over income taxes. Consequently President Clinton proposed an increase in the cigarette tax.

It was clear that the public was unwilling to tax themselves sufficiently to provide comprehensive health insurance for everyone. The middle class was more concerned with their rising insurance premiums (which meant lower take-home wages), the fear that they would lose their insurance if they became ill or changed jobs, and the greater restrictions being placed on their choice of provider. The middle class basically wanted what they currently had—traditional indemnity insurance with free choice of provider—but at a lower cost. The only way to achieve that goal was to somehow shift the rising cost to others (e.g., pay hospitals and physicians less) and to impose restrictions on insurers to provide the middle class with greater health insurance security.

The United States has had NHI, and spends over $330 billion a year on it, but it is not universal and the subsidies vary according to income and age. Medicaid serves the poor at an estimated $100 billion per year, Medicare is NHI for the aged at about $150 billion per year, and employer-paid health insurance is NHI for middle-income and high-income groups at about $80 billion a year. Although there are large numbers of uninsured, the middle class has been unwilling to tax itself to provide more to those with low incomes.

The Defeat of President Clinton's Healthcare Plan

The Clinton healthcare plan was an attempt to enact a broad, visible, redistributive program. As such, it had to receive the political support of a majority of the middle class. Second, organized groups that would be affected by its design, such as different provider associations, insurers, unions, large businesses, and small business associations, were split on various aspects of the proposed plan. Many legislators in the end believed that they might lose more political support than they would gain if they supported the plan. Thus the design of the Clinton plan failed on both counts. The middle class did not perceive that they would receive net benefits from its enactment, and groups with a concentrated interest were willing to expend political support to change/defeat parts of the proposed legislation.[5]

The objective of the federal and state governments under health reform was to decrease the rate of increase in their expenditures for Medicare and Medicaid. Large employers and unions similarly wanted to decrease the rate of increase in their private health insurance premiums. Hospitals and physicians favored an increase in the demand for their services, but they had been politically weakened by the rise of opposing groups. And the middle class wanted to keep the type of coverage they had, without paying more for it. They were also unwilling to bear much higher taxes to have a comprehensive program that covered everyone.

Given the above concentrated interests, any NHI proposal had to provide benefits (defined above for each group) in excess of costs for most of the above groups, particularly the middle class.

President Clinton's healthcare proposal attempted to satisfy all of the above groups *and* achieve universal coverage for everyone. To accomplish these conflicting goals, a very complex plan (over 1,300 pages) was proposed. Only certain basic elements of the plan are briefly discussed here. To be able to state that universal coverage could be achieved without increased income taxes, the Clinton administration proposed several redistributive mechanisms, the most important being an employer mandate, whereby all employees would have to pay a percentage of their income for health insurance. (President Nixon had previously proposed a variant of an employer health insurance mandate in the early 1970s.)

The employer mandate provided certain political advantages. Although it is equivalent to a tax, an employer mandate is not part of the federal budget. And, since it is imposed primarily on the employer (80 percent), its visibility is decreased. Requiring employers to purchase health insurance for their low-income employees reduces the number of uninsureds, and decreases federal and state government expenditures for Medicaid, which is what the uninsureds would otherwise have relied upon. Large employers and their unions favored it for two reasons. First, large firms and unions, such as the auto industry, were paying between 15 percent to 18 percent of wages for health benefits. Under the Clinton proposal, no firm would have to pay more than 12 percent of wages, effectively rewarding union members with a 3 percent to 5 percent wage increase. Second, an employer mandate would primarily affect low-wage firms whose employees did not have health insurance. This would increase the cost of low-wage labor, thereby making them less competitive against higher-paid union labor.

The health insurance association favored an employer mandate because it would increase the demand for private health insurance. Hospital and physician associations also favored this approach because it would provide coverage for the uninsured and shift low-wage employees and their families away from Medicaid to private insurance, which paid providers higher fees.

According to various polls, the middle class also favored an employer mandate, believing the employer would bear the cost of the program. In this way the middle class could believe that they would not have to tax themselves to provide coverage to those with low incomes. Presumably the burden would be borne by the employer. It was to enforce this deception that the employer was obligated to pay 80 percent of the premium and the employee would pay the remaining 20 percent. The visibility of the burden fell on the employer, even though, in reality, most of the cost would be shifted to the employee in the form of lower wages. (Polls also showed that the middle class was less supportive of an employer mandate if it meant the higher cost of labor would lead to a large loss of jobs. It was for this reason that both opponents and proponents of an employer mandate produced studies on job loss to support their viewpoint.)

Another redistributive mechanism within the employer mandate was to rely on "community rating," whereby employer and employee contributions for health insurance were *not* related to health risk factors. Older workers did not have to pay higher premiums than younger workers. The amount to be contributed on behalf of younger employees, who are less likely to vote, was expected to exceed their expected medical costs, thereby providing older employees with a subsidy.

The major group opposed to an employer mandate was the National Federation of Independent (small) Business. They were concerned that an employer mandate would increase their labor cost; employers would not be able to pass all their costs onto the employees, particularly for those at or near the minimum wage; they would have to lay off employees; and their profits would decrease. Small businesses, located in all congressional districts, proved to be very effective lobbyists opposed to the employer mandate.

Mandated employer health insurance, however, would not meet any of the objectives held by the middle class, nor by those desiring a less rapid increase in medical expenditures. In fact, by itself, an employer mandate would cause a more rapid increase in medical expenditures because it would increase the demand for medical services. President Clinton's employer mandate therefore had to be combined with additional elements to meet the objectives of these other groups.

The Clinton health plan consequently proposed regulatory limits on how rapidly medical expenditures could increase. Several national boards and regional "Alliances" (purchasing pools) were to be established, whose role, in large part, was to assist in controlling both the introduction of new medical technology and premium increases. The Clinton administration proposed that premium increases be limited to the rate of inflation and population growth; a rate of increase much lower than has been occurring and also lower than any industrial country has been able to achieve on a sustained basis.

The Clinton administration also proposed a very comprehensive set of benefits for everyone. Why would the public be willing to pay higher taxes for more comprehensive benefits if they are not willing to buy those same benefits in the private market? They would only favor more comprehensive benefits if they believed they could receive them at a price below their actual cost.

To finance these additional benefits and cover the working uninsured, and provide subsidies to those not employed (to achieve universal coverage), the Clinton health plan relied on an employer mandate, a cigarette tax (that was subsequently reduced to secure the vote of a legislator from a tobacco district), very tight expenditure limits, and the claim that huge savings would occur as a result of the elimination of "waste" in medical services. With an employer mandate, increased benefits, and controls on expenditure increases, demand for medical services would exceed supply and shortages would quickly develop. Elimination of "waste" was to enable supply to be increased without additional expenditures.

To receive the political support of certain organized groups, the administration also included specific benefits for those groups. For example, to assist those companies with large unfunded retiree medical liabilities, the government proposed to pay 80 percent of those costs. Over the opposition of HMOs who claimed it would limit their ability to control costs, the AMA was rewarded with an "any willing provider" amendment, which would enable physicians unaligned with closed-panel plans to have access to patients in closed panels. (Kaiser Health Plan, the nation's largest HMO, was, however, able to exempt itself from this provision, thereby angering other HMOs.) The AMA was also promised exemptions from the antitrust laws, which would have allowed physicians to negotiate collectively with HMOs, as well as obtain relief from large malpractice awards. Chiropractors, who as a group gave $1.9 million to the Democrats in 1993, received permission under the Clinton health plan to receive payment for performing x-rays, previously denied to them under Medicare. To secure the support of nurses, a provision was included that would remove barriers that currently limit the role of advanced practice nurses. And the aged were promised new benefits, including a prescription drug benefit.

As the Clinton administration and the Democratic leadership tried to raise the necessary votes for reporting out a health bill from the various committees, legislators sold their votes for specific constituent benefits. For example, Sen. Daniel Moynihan, whose state of New York includes a number of academic medical centers, inserted an amendment that would have provided all academic health centers with the funds generated by a 1.75 percent tax on all health insurance premiums; this benefit was valued at $75 billion over five years. Chairman Rostenkowski of the House Ways and Means Committee included an amendment that provided for a 3 percent interest rate subsidy to Northwestern Memorial hospital (in his home state) for its $650 million construction program. The oil industry also received special tax breaks to ensure the votes of Sen. John B. Breaux and Sen. J. Bennett Johnston, who are from oil-producing states.

Thus the Clinton health plan promised universal health insurance, with a very comprehensive set of medical benefits and no decrease in access to care or in the quality of care, without having to raise income taxes or place a large financial burden on the public. It sounded too good to be true.

As more information about the health plan became available, public skepticism increased and political support declined. The administration acknowledged at one point that in fact 40 percent of the middle class would have to pay more than they did currently. Middle-income families, particularly two wage-earner families, would pay much larger premiums than previously. Redistribution began to be seen as hurting rather than helping middle-income groups. The complexity of the health plan—national boards to control new technology and the role of the Alliances—concerned those who were fearful of government intrusion in their healthcare. There was a concern, reinforced by TV ads paid for by the HIAA, that with coverage of everyone, more comprehensive benefits, and limits on medical expenditure increases, "rationing" would occur. The middle class started to believe that the drastic overhaul of the health system proposed by President Clinton was not necessary to alleviate their concerns.

In response, President Clinton accused "special interests" of opposing his health plan. In fact, some special interests were for and others were against the plan. Many producer groups, such as companies with unfunded medical retiree liabilities, unions with high medical premiums relative to their wages, physicians opposed to managed care, and nurses who wanted more independent practice, were major beneficiaries of the proposed legislation. The real reason for its failure was the lack of public support. The middle-income and high-income groups wanted something for nothing—traditional indemnity insurance, good benefits, the security of not losing their insurance—all without any additional payment. President Clinton reinforced their view by letting them believe that something for nothing is possible through the elimination of waste. But then the public began to believe that the Clinton health plan was not credible, that it could not deliver all that was promised. Ultimately they believed they would then be worse off than previously.

The difficulty in enacting NHI in this country is not with the special interests as much as it is with the middle class. To achieve change requires making a trade-off. To receive a lower rate of premium increases, the public must be willing to give up choice of provider, access to care, and/or access to new medical technology. It is difficult for politicians to rationally discuss these choices with the public because it means that they cannot then provide the public with benefits in excess of their costs.

The Prospects for National Health Insurance

National health insurance is unlikely to be enacted in the foreseeable future. The middle class is unwilling to tax themselves to provide the necessary funds to expand coverage to the uninsured or to enhance Medicaid. Any expansion of assistance to those with low incomes will have to come from small changes in the tax code that encourage those without insurance to purchase their own health insurance.

The pressures forcing Congress to consider health reform are concerns by the middle class, who provide the political support for such visible redistributive legislation. The middle class is concerned about rising out-of-pocket costs, increasing health insurance premiums, loss of their choice of physician, and fear of losing their health insurance.

Legislators can still gain political support from the middle class by enacting health legislation that provides the middle class with benefits in excess of their costs. Health insurance reform, namely, guaranteed renewability of insurance coverage (within standard rates), limits on preexisting exclusion clauses, and perhaps even portability of their insurance when they change jobs, would alleviate concerns the middle class has with the security of their health insurance. These benefits can be provided without imposing any visible cost. Insurance companies and HMOs would simply be required to provide them. Although the costs of these regulations would seemingly be borne by the insurers and HMOs, in reality those (diffuse) costs would be shifted toward purchasers in the form of higher insurance premiums.

Healthcare market competition is forcing the public to make the trade-offs that politicians are reluctant to propose. The increase in HMO enrollment reflects the public's willingness to choose lower premiums in return for restrictions on their choice of provider. Market competition is also resulting in lower increases in medical expenditures. The federal government has difficulty in replicating these improvements in the Medicare and Medicaid programs. As in other markets, the competitive healthcare market offers different tiers of medical care for those who are willing to pay different amounts. Many politicians have been reluctant to publicly promote multiple tiers of medical care, even though they exist between public and private medical programs and even within the private sector.

To understand the debate about healthcare reform, it is necessary to realize what is the real, as compared to its stated objective. The public interest theory is less able to explain and predict the outcome of healthcare reform than is a theory based on how those who are politically powerful attempt to shift their costs onto those who are less politically powerful. The outcome has little to do with improved equity or efficiency, since those were never the real objectives underlying NHI.

Study Questions for Chapter 10

1. What are the objectives of national health insurance according to the public interest and economic theory?
2. What are the objectives of those groups having a concentrated interest in health reform?
3. The Medicare Catastrophic Act was enacted in 1988 and repealed in 1989. Use the competing theories of government to provide an explanation for these two events.

4. What were the benefits and costs to the middle class of the Clinton health reform plan?
5. Use the competing theories of government to describe the prospects for universal coverage based on an equitable financing mechanism.

Notes

1. The federal government establishes certain minimum eligibility levels and benefits under Medicaid. It is up to the individual states to determine whether those minimums are increased.

2. It is interesting to note that during 1995, Congressional proposals for Medicaid reform involve reducing the rate of increase in federal Medicaid matching funds and allowing the states greater flexibility in how they spend those funds. The GOP budget proposal calls for Medicare spending growth to be held to 6.4 percent per year while Medicaid spending would be limited to 4.8 percent per year.

3. Congressional Budget Office. 1994. *The Tax Treatment of Employment-Based Health Insurance.* Washington, D.C. 48.

4. Robert Blendon, et al. 1992. "The Implications of the 1992 Presidential Election for Healthcare Reform," *Journal of the American Medical Association* 268 (23) 3371–3375.

5. Much has been written by others on the reasons for the defeat of President Clinton's health reform plan. See for example, Daniel Yankelovich. 1995. "The Debate That Wasn't: The Public and the Clinton Plan," *Health Affairs* 14 (1) 7–23. Also see in that same issue the "Perspectives" of several others, 24–36.

11

THE SELF-INTEREST PARADIGM AND THE POLITICS OF HEALTH LEGISLATION

Producer Regulation
Legislation Providing for Medical Research, Protection
   Against Epidemics, and a Clean Environment
Redistributive Legislation
The Legislative Outlook

T he purpose of this book has been to use a Self-Interest Paradigm to explain legislative outcomes in healthcare. The usefulness of this approach should be judged by its predictive ability. While it is unlikely that any one theory will be able to explain all or even a very high percentage of all legislation, a theory is necessary for trying to understand why certain types of legislation were passed and why others were not—unless one believes that legislation is ad hoc. It is natural to try to organize what we observe in some meaningful manner. The criteria for selecting one theory over another should be based upon pragmatic grounds: which approach is better at explaining events under a broad range of circumstances? To reject a theory it is necessary to have a better theory.

The lack of coordination among the different types of health policies in this country has led many observers to decry the lack of rationality in the financing and provision of healthcare. Those who have high incomes and those employed in large companies generally have adequate health coverage. The unemployed and those with low incomes do not. There is apparently little or no coordination of policies and programs to care for the poor, the working poor, children, low-income aged, and so on. The federal and state governments have failed to fill the gaps in insurance coverage to those least able to afford care. Many different agencies within the government provide medical services to the same people. For example, the elderly receive benefits from the Departments of Housing and Urban Development, the Department of Transportation, the Department of Veteran Affairs, the Social Security Administration, Medicare, Medicaid, and so on. This fragmentation and the gaps in coverage have led to inefficiencies in the provision of these services and inequities in how they are financed.

Yet the financing and delivery of health services in this country, in both the private and government sectors, are the result of a rational system. While the outcome may not appear rational, the process was. To understand the outcome it is necessary to have an approach by which the process can be understood. The resulting health legislation was rational from the perspective of those who demand and supply legislation. Both the demanders and suppliers of legislative benefits presumably knew what it was they wanted. The resulting outcome was determined by those able to provide the most political support. The outcome had little to do with what was an efficient use of scarce resources or what was best for the nation's health.

The Self-Interest Paradigm assumes that human behavior is no different in political than in private markets. Individuals, groups, firms, and legislators seek to enhance their self-interests. They are assumed to be rational in assessing the benefits and the costs to themselves of their actions. This behavioral assumption enables us to predict that firms in private markets will try to produce their products and services as efficiently as possible to keep their costs down and that they will set their prices so as to make as much profit as possible. They will be motivated to enter markets where the profit potential is greatest and, similarly, to leave markets where the profit potential is low.

It is merely an extension of the above discussion to include political markets. Individuals and firms use the power of the state to further their own interests. Firms try to gain competitive advantages in private markets by investing in technology and advertising. Why shouldn't firms also make political investments to be able to use the powers of government to increase or maintain profit?

The actions of organizations of individuals are no different from those of firms. Many people would like to use the power of the state to assist them in what they cannot otherwise achieve. For some, this may mean using the state to help them impose their religious or social preferences on others. Still other groups would like to use the state to provide them with monetary benefits that they could not earn in the market and that others would not voluntarily provide to them, such as low-cost education for their children, pension payments in excess of their contributions, and subsidized medical benefits.

It is usually with regard to our public "servants" that the assumption of acting in one's self-interest becomes difficult to accept. After all, why would a person run for office if not to serve the public interest? However, to be successful in the electoral process requires legislators to behave in a manner that enhances their reelection prospects. Political support, votes, and contributions are the bases for reelection. Legislators must therefore be able to understand the sources of such support and the requirements for receiving it. A hungry man quickly realizes that if money buys food then he must have money to eat. Legislators act no differently than others.

Political markets have several characteristics that differentiate them from economic markets. These differences make it possible for organized interests to benefit at the expense of majorities. First, individuals are not as informed about political issues as they are about the goods and services on which they spend their own funds. In private markets individuals have an incentive to become informed when they make large purchases. In political markets many of the issues have such a minor impact on their economic well-being that it does not "pay" for them to do anything about it, let alone become informed on the issue.

Second, in private markets individuals make separate decisions on each item they purchase. They do not have to choose between sets of purchases, such as between one package that may include a particular brand of car, a certain size house in a particular neighborhood, several suits, and a certain quantity of food. Yet in political markets their choices are between two sets of votes by competing legislators on a wide variety of issues. While individual voters may agree or disagree on parts of the package, they cannot register a vote on each issue, as they do in economic markets.

Third, voting participation rates differ by age group. The young and future generations do not vote, and yet policies are enacted that impose costs on them. Future generations depend on current generations and voters to protect their interests. However, as has been the case many times, such as with respect to the federal deficit, Social Security, and Medicare, their interests have been sacrificed to current voters.

Fourth, legislators use different decision criteria from those used in the private sector. A firm or an individual making an investment considers both the benefits and the costs of that investment. Even though a project may offer very large benefits, profitability cannot be established unless its costs are also considered. Legislators, however, have a different time horizon, which not only affects the emphasis they place on costs and benefits but also on when each is incurred. Since members of the House of Representatives run for reelection every two years, they are likely to favor programs that provide immediate benefits (presumably just before the election) while delaying the costs until after the election or years later.

Further, from the legislator's perspective, the program does not even have to meet the criterion that the benefits exceed its costs, only that the immediate benefits exceed any immediate costs. Future legislators can worry about future costs.

It is for these reasons that organized groups are able to receive legislative benefits while imposing the costs of those benefits on the remainder of the population. For those bearing the costs of legislative benefits that others receive, it may be perfectly rational not to oppose such legislation. As long as the cost of changing political outcomes exceeds the lost wealth imposed by legislation, it is rational for voters to lose some wealth rather than to organize and bear the cost of changing the legislative outcome.

At times self-interest legislation may be in the "public interest." When this occurs, however, it is because it is a by-product of the outcome rather than its intended effect.

Those groups able to provide political support to legislators are those who have a concentrated interest in an issue and who are organized to represent their interests. These groups are often a minority of the population. A typical example of such a group are the producers (and the union) of a particular product who perceive gains from legislation. In the health field the organized interests using the political process are likely to be members of a particular health profession, such as physicians and dentists. While all health providers have an interest in legislation that provides them with economic benefits, only those who are able to organize themselves and overcome the free rider problem are likely to be successful in the legislative market.

This discussion does not imply that all organized interest groups will receive legislative benefits. Organized groups will, however, represent their members' interests. Whether or not these groups are successful in that process is another matter.

Politics may be viewed as an exchange relationship just like an economic market. And, as with any economic market, the resulting output depends upon the relative market power of the various participants. When there is monopoly power on the demand side of a market, the monopolist is able to secure a better price than if there were more competitors, each with the same degree of market power. The same analogy occurs with respect to the demand for legislation; when there are no competitors for legislative benefits or when there is only limited opposition to its demands, an interest group demanding legislative benefits would not have to pay as high a price for those benefits (i.e., political support) and would be more likely to receive their benefits. Similarly, when there is competition among the suppliers of a good or service, the demanders are likely to be charged a lower price than if they were purchasing that service from a monopolist supplier. The same is likely to occur in political markets. Legislators who are assured of reelection are in less need of political support than those facing a strong challenge; monopolist legislators, therefore, can afford to exhibit greater independence and can "charge" demanders of legislative benefits a higher price for their services.

Just as in competitive economic markets, competition among demanders of legislative benefits and suppliers of those benefits is likely to result in a more efficient legislative outcome than when a monopoly exists on either the demand or supply side of the market. The greater the number of demanders, the less likely it is that any one will be able to receive large benefits (or all their demands) at the expense of others. Similarly with respect to the supply side, the greater the competition among legislators for reelection, the less likely they will be to ignore some groups' demands, and their receptivity to those offering political support will be increased.

Unless it is likely to be a successful demander of legislative benefits, a group's situation would be improved if its interests were more easily represented on the demand side. Policies that lower the costs of representation, such as increased information on the consequences of proposed legislation, would be one approach. Approaches that enhance legislators' competition for reelection, such as changes in the campaign finance laws, would make it easier, that is, less costly, for those bearing the costs of legislation to have an impact on legislative outcomes.

It has been generally assumed throughout that demanders of legislative benefits in healthcare have had some monopoly power. Similarly, it has been assumed that legislator suppliers have believed themselves to be competitors with regard to their reelection prospects. These assumptions lead to the legislative outcomes hypothesized.

The different types of health legislation may be distinguished according to the visibility of the legislation, their beneficiaries, the groups bearing the cost of those legislative benefits, and the method of financing.

Producer Regulation

One form of health legislation relates to what will benefit providers. Legislative benefits to health providers are generally not obvious. Legislation has been enacted that allows some health professionals to perform certain tasks thereby creating benefits for some practitioners at the expense of others. The legislative competition over tasks occurs at the state rather than at the more visible federal level. The justification set forth for restrictive provider legislation, whether it is on tasks, entry into the profession, or on which providers should be reimbursed under public programs, is protection of the public. However, the only quality measures proposed by the health professions are those that enhance their incomes. Quality measures that have an adverse effect on the professions' incomes, such as reexamination and relicensure, are opposed by the profession.

The public bears the burden of producer regulation in two ways: the prices of medical services are higher than they would otherwise be and, second, the public is not as well protected from incompetent and unethical professionals as they are led to believe.

Health provider regulation is thus financed by a hidden tax on the public. Those who use medical services pay higher prices. The government does not have to propose an explicit tax, which would make the cost of provider regulation more obvious. Instead, a regressive hidden tax is used. The higher prices are the same to all users, regardless of income level.

Although the current movement toward market competition in healthcare is opposed by physicians, hospitals, and dentists, its emergence is, however, consistent with the Self-Interest Paradigm. Business and government (including the administration), the two major payers of medical services, developed a concentrated interest in holding down the rise in medical expenditures and began to seek changes in the medical marketplace. As the cost of medical services to these large payers increased, their incentive to do something about it became stronger. The concern by business with their employees' insurance premiums and increased capacity among physicians and hospitals set the stage for market competition. The applicability of the antitrust laws was a necessary condition for competition to survive. It was no longer permissible for health professionals to engage in anticompetitive behavior.

The administration must limit the rise in hospital and physician payments under Medicare. Continued rapid rises in hospital payments for the aged, which are funded by a separate Social Security trust fund, would necessitate another increase in Social Security taxes. Medicare physician payments, 75 percent of which are funded from general tax revenues, contribute increasingly to the federal budget deficit, which is a festering political problem. An administration that has to keep proposing increased Social Security taxes or is unable to resolve an increasing budget deficit loses political support; less political support would be lost by the administration if it paid providers less.

The medical profession has become fragmented. The increased supply of physicians and excess capacity among those physicians has led to conflict within the profession. The American Medical Association (AMA) finds it increasingly difficult to represent the common interests of physicians. An increasing number of physicians are part of managed care organizations and are not interested in maintaining traditional forms of medical practice or payment methods. Specialty societies are increasingly in conflict with one another, as different specialties seek to restrict other physicians from performing tasks that are within their specialty. As the medical profession begins to split apart according to separate economic interests, physicians are looking toward their own specialty societies for legislative representation. The role of the medical profession in determining health legislation is being diminished.

The rise of competing interest groups, namely government and business, suggests that health providers are unlikely to be able to dominate the policy process as they have done in the past.

Legislation Providing for Medical Research, Protection Against Epidemics, and a Clean Environment

Political support for legislation on health issues comes from both the public and from producers. When a crisis occurs, as when a flu epidemic appears imminent, a drug causes the death or illness of a number of people, or a particular pollution event causes illness among the population, the public demands leadership from its elected representatives to resolve the problem. Crises are obviously very visible. Failure by the legislature or by the administration to respond to these public concerns would result in a loss of political support. Political opponents would take the initiative and receive the political credit.

Unfortunately, as the crisis passes, public support begins to wane. The media turn to other issues. And legislators lose their interest in the subject as its visibility declines and public support diminishes. In their haste to respond to the public, legislators are likely to pass symbolic legislation, which is unlikely to antagonize organized interests that would be adversely affected.

If, over time, the public and the media demand more stringent legislation to deal with the issue, as in the case of pollution, then legislation will be passed affecting new firms in the industry. Existing firms and unions are unlikely to be affected, since they represent an organized constituency able to provide political support. Instead, new firms are likely to bear the burden of new, more stringent legislation. Existing firms are thereby able to use the new legislation to gain a competitive advantage. An example of this approach was seen in the mandate for the use of scrubbers by electric utilities to reduce air pollution.

The other approach used by the legislature to reduce pollution is to allocate federal funds to the states for local building projects. An example of this approach is federal funding for waste treatment facilities. The advantage of this approach is that all legislators can point with pride to the projects they have brought to their areas. For example, the Hill-Burton program, which provided federal funds for hospital construction, was considered immensely successful. Hospitals received free capital, and the funds were allocated according to a formula that ensured that all congressional districts were rewarded. While such an approach is politically popular, it is also wasteful because funds are allocated regardless of need.

The above examples are illustrative of the legislature's response to geographic requests for subsidies. For legislation to be enacted, all legislators must receive a benefit for their districts. While some areas are most in need of funds, other areas must also be subsidized. This approach obviously raises the cost of the program. Further, it is not clear that federal funds are the answer. For some types of projects, for which benefits are local only, taxpayers in those specific states or regions should bear the cost. Further, rather than imposing costs on those causing pollution, e.g., municipalities and businesses, and thereby incurring opposition and losing political support, the polluter's costs are imposed on the general public through the provision of subsidies to the polluter.

The beneficiaries of legislation with spill-over effects are possibly the public (when legislation is truly meaningful and not merely symbolic), producers receiving a competitive advantage, and local governments able to substitute federal funds for their own in solving their waste treatment problems. Those bearing the burden are typically new firms that are less able to offer political support, and the general public, which has to pay for these programs and still not have its health concerns alleviated. (In those cases where legislation may be effective in reducing pollution, it will be achieved at a particularly high cost.)

Legislators' responses to public concerns over the environment and health crises are based on being able to receive public support for their actions. Thus, unless there is sufficient public support for an important issue, legislators will not respond. Further, monitoring both the health hazards and the compliance with health standards by violators is a continuous process. However, if the public's interest declines along with the visibility of the issue, legislators will no longer attach as much attention to the issue as it deserves.

Redistributive Legislation

While all types of legislation result in redistribution of wealth, redistributive legislation is meant to be most explicit in its effects. There are two types of redistributive legislation. The first is based upon a charitable motivation, the desire by the public to help the less fortunate. The second is universal redistribution where the motivation of the voting public is primarily to help themselves at the expense of other taxpayers. What differentiates the two types of redistributive programs is whether a means test is involved.

The beneficiaries of charitable redistribution, such as Medicaid, are those with low incomes. Health providers also benefit because they are relieved of their bad debts and receive an increase in demand by those least able to pay for their services. Welfare-type programs are financed from general tax revenues.

Universal programs, such as Medicare, do not have a means test, and therefore everyone is eligible. The proponents of these types of redistributive programs often justify them by saying that unless groups other than the poor are included as beneficiaries there would not be sufficient political support to enact the program. The methods used to finance universal programs, however, are less equitable than for charitable programs. Usually an excise tax, such as an increase in Social Security taxes, is used. These taxes are regressive in that all people must pay, regardless of income.

The most important medical redistributive program has been Medicare. By using the Social Security system, all of the aged, regardless of income, are eligible. In this manner higher-income aged qualified. If general tax revenues were used as the financing mechanism, it is likely that not all aged would have been eligible; Medicare would have become a welfare program. The basis for eligibility was debated for many years before Medicare was enacted in 1965. Once Social Security was accepted as the financing mechanism for Part A of Medicare, then physician benefits (Part B) were financed out of general tax revenues. There was no opposition to this by the proponents of Social Security financing. The reason for this apparent contradiction is that eligibility for physician benefits was based on the initial eligibility for hospital benefits. The unions were willing to accept a more equitable method of financing Part B as long as all of their members were made eligible through the Social Security system.

Health providers, in addition to the aged, were important beneficiaries of Medicare. Providers were paid according to their own preferences; their prices rose rapidly, as did their incomes.

For groups to benefit from the legislative process, the benefits they receive must exceed any costs they incur from financing the program, even though the total costs of the program may exceed its benefits. The method by which this is accomplished is to finance the program by imposing a small cost on each person. In the case of provider benefits, this cost is often hidden; for example, when restrictions are placed on entry into the profession or on the tasks that other professionals can perform. The price of that profession's services are increased, but it is not obvious that the restrictions caused the increase. When benefits are provided to specific population groups, then the costs are more obvious to those bearing them. However, to minimize opposition, the costs are kept small on a per person basis (by spreading them over a large population base) and they are made to appear to be smaller than they really are. Underestimating future program costs and stating that the employer must pay part of those costs (as in the case of Social Security taxes) are two approaches for lessening the visibility of the program's cost.

Funding for Medicare was provided by the working population through increased Social Security taxes. The general public also bore the burden of this program through payment of higher prices for their medical services. The aged (and the near-aged) received Medicare benefits that were, in aggregate, in excess of their Social Security payments for that program, with the result that the major cost of Medicare is being borne by young workers and future generations. There are few people who would claim that Medicare is as equitable as it could be. Instead, Medicare benefits and payments are closely related to the political support each age group is able to provide.

Political support, not consideration for equity, is the basis of another large medical redistributive program. The purchase of health insurance by employers for their employees is a nontaxable fringe benefit. The major beneficiaries of this government policy are those in the middle-income and upper-income groups, by virtue of their being in higher tax brackets. It has been estimated that in 1994 the government would have collected approximately $74 billion a year in additional income and payroll taxes if health insurance premiums were taxed at the employee's tax rate. Middle-income and upper-income groups receive most of this tax benefit.[1]

Providers of health services, such as dental, physician, vision, and mental services are also important beneficiaries of the tax subsidy for the purchase of health insurance. If employees had to pay for health insurance with after-tax income, they would purchase less comprehensive medical services with a consequent decreased demand for the services of such providers. Health insurance companies also benefit in that the demand for health insurance is greater than it would be otherwise. It is difficult to reconcile the continuation of the tax subsidy for the purchase of health insurance with anything other than the Self-Interest Paradigm.

The Legislative Outlook

The issues that appear to be the driving force of legislative change in the years ahead are likely to be those that deal with the explicit redistribution of medical services. The reason that these issues will come to the forefront of the legislative agenda has little to do with legislators' concerns with the less fortunate members of our society; rather, important organized interests are demanding changes consistent with their own self-interest.

The poor and working poor have inadequate health insurance coverage. The aged want to maintain their Medicare coverage and choice of provider, as well as reduce their risk of impoverishment if they require care in a nursing home for an extended illness. The middle class do not want to lose their health insurance if they become ill or if they change jobs; they also don't want to keep paying an increasing percentage of their income for their health insurance. These population groups, the poor, the aged, and the middle class, are able to offer different levels of political support, hence legislators' responses to their concerns are also likely to differ.

In a price-competitive system, providers cannot subsidize the care of the poor by raising prices to the non-poor. Competitive pressures are the stimulus forcing providers to demand explicit government subsidies to care for the poor. Those providers who are unable to decrease their services to the poor are the major political constituency behind subsidies for the poor and uninsured.

The difference in this scenario from that of 1965 is that the federal government finds it increasingly difficult to provide additional funds for the poor. Any expansion of Medicaid would increase the budget deficit, require increased taxes, and/or switch funding away from other programs with their own constituencies. After 30 years of Medicare and Medicaid and the expenditure of hundreds of billions of dollars, there is still no adequate system to care for the medically indigent.

For the government to ensure that providers are paid for serving the poor without increasing its own financial commitment, would require the government to shift the costs to other groups. One approach that would have achieved this is employer-mandated health insurance. Employer-mandated health insurance would not require the federal or state governments to raise or spend additional funds; hospitals currently providing uncompensated care to the working poor would receive payment from the employee's insurance and such a program would lessen Medicaid (and consequently federal) expenditures that would have been spent on behalf of this population group.

Not all businesses would be opposed to employer-mandated health insurance. Large businesses and their unions would favor it because, first, they would not be affected, since the health benefits currently provided to their employees exceed proposed government minimum mandated benefits. And, second, because small businesses, many of whom have lower-wage employees, would be most affected by an employer mandate. Larger businesses (and their unions) view small businesses as competitors, in which case they would favor legislation that increases their competitors' costs.

Shifting the costs of the working poor onto low-income employees and small businesses is reminiscent of the national health insurance proposals of Presidents Nixon and Carter. Both Presidents proposed that business provide their employees with a minimum level of health insurance benefits. Although the effect of such an approach would be similar to an increase in the Social Security tax, shifting the cost onto employers is not an obvious cost to employees. President Clinton proposed the same approach. The political support for this approach comes from health providers, who would be reimbursed; the federal government, who would be able to reduce its expenditures under Medicaid; and large businesses and unions, who would be unaffected, but who would receive a competitive advantage. Employer-mandated health insurance has a number of political advantages, but it also faces the political opposition of an important group with a concentrated interest, namely, small business.

The failure of President Clinton's healthcare plan means an employer mandate is not likely to be proposed in the near term. However, it will surely come up again when talk of national health insurance is revived and a method is needed for financing it.

The middle class determines the amount of taxes they are willing to pay for care of the medically indigent. Since the middle class is unwilling, according to numerous polls, to raise their taxes to cover the poor and working uninsured, it is unlikely that this country will have any form of universal coverage any time soon.

To disguise an uncomfortably low level of altruism among middle-class voters, opponents of a competitive system place the blame for inadequate care for the poor on market competition, since it eliminates cross-subsidies. The amount of care provided to the poor, however, is the responsibility of society and not health providers. Health providers are willing to provide the amount of care that society is willing to fund.

What is likely to be enacted in the foreseeable future is health insurance reform, namely, limiting the time period of preexisting conditions, guaranteed renewability, and perhaps portability of insurance across jobs. These are middle-class concerns and the government would bear no additional financing costs. The costs would be imposed on the insurers, who would then pass it on to the insured. In fact, such reforms would reduce the government's obligation to those who lose their insurance and must fall back on Medicaid. Large insurers also favor these reforms, since such regulations impose a greater cost on smaller insurers, who might then be driven out of the market.

The other important redistributive issue in coming years is Medicare reform. The impending bankruptcy of the Medicare Trust Fund and the rising costs of Medicare Part B (physician and nonhospital services), which contributes to the federal deficit, will require legislative action. The Public Interest and the self-interest theories lead to differing predictions as to the outcome of Medicare reform. The public interest theory would suggest that making the program more income-related would be a more equitable approach. Either higher-income aged would pay more for their benefits or they would receive fewer benefits than lower-income aged. Greater economic efficiency would also be achieved if the aged had a financial incentive to choose less costly health plans, rather than remaining in the current, higher-cost, fee-for-service system.

Predictions based on the Self-Interest Paradigm would not be based on attempts to achieve greater equity or economic efficiency. Instead, calculations of forthcoming political support would determine the legislative outcome. The group most affected by any change would be the current aged, particularly the middle-income and high-income aged, who have a concentrated interest in retaining as much of the status quo as possible. Under this scenario, any changes in the Medicare program would be phased in so that the current aged are able to retain their benefits. The future aged would face benefit reductions, decreased choice of provider, and/or income-related financing and benefits. One way such a phase-in could work would be to use an income-related financing approach, but to only require those aged making more than $100,000–$150,000 to pay higher premiums. This change would be acceptable to the current aged since very few aged (about 97 percent) would be adversely affected. However, by not indexing these income levels for inflation, a greater portion of future aged would be affected by this provision. Similarly, to limit expenditure increases under Medicare, the eligibility age for Medicare can be increased, as it was for Social Security. Raising the eligibility age from 65 to 67 would not affect the current aged, but would decrease benefits to future aged.

Any change in the Medicare program would also have to be acceptable to various groups of health providers. Merely reducing payments to hospitals and physicians to achieve savings in Medicare would be opposed by these provider groups. Congress will have to provide hospitals and physicians, along with the HMO industry, an opportunity to receive some benefits. One such possibility is to provide the aged with an incentive to move into HMOs, while permitting hospitals and physicians, who are not part of an HMO, to participate in such programs without being required to join an HMO.

One other legislative proposal that concerns the aged is long-term care. The size of the federal deficit and the reluctance of politicians to favor increased taxes has diminished the chances for a new long-term care benefit for all the aged. The increasing number of "old" aged raises the concern over the growing needs for long-term care. Those elderly requiring long-term care must use their own assets. Before they can qualify for Medicaid, they must spend down most of those assets. Many middle-class elderly are at risk of losing their hard-earned savings in this situation. These elderly and their children have an economic interest in having the government provide broader long-term care coverage. In addition to the elderly themselves, there are the economic interests of their children, who would like to be relieved of the financial responsibility of providing for their parents' long-term care needs, as well as to be able to inherit their parents' assets.

Several approaches have been proposed for resolving the long-term care needs of the elderly. All of these proposals, private and governmental, however, are more appropriate for middle-income and upper-income aged rather than low-income aged. Government proposals and private insurance assume that the elderly can afford to pay large deductibles up to the point where a catastrophic insurance program becomes effective.

Proposals to finance the long-term care needs of the elderly implicitly assume that there will continue to be two types of programs. One will be a universal program, which will be more suitable to those able to pay premiums and the initial medical costs of a catastrophic illness. Then there will have to be a means-tested program for those elderly with limited resources. Since the low-income aged currently (and will continue to) fall back on Medicaid, any new federal program is likely to be of primary assistance to the middle-income and high-income aged. It is unlikely that legislators will provide the aged with benefits, such as long-term care, for which the aged will have to pay the full costs. (Otherwise why wouldn't the aged buy it on their own?)[2] It is also unlikely that the aged themselves would bear the full cost of a new program by having the high-income aged subsidize low-income and middle-income aged. It would not be rational for the high-income aged to participate in a program that required them to pay their actual costs plus a large subsidy to cover the costs of other aged.

For the current middle-income and high-income aged to receive a net benefit, part of the cost of a new program must be shifted to other groups.

The most equitable method of providing a new long-term care benefit would be to make it income-related and to finance it from general tax revenues. However, to receive the support of the aged, a new redistributive benefit would have to be a universal program. Until the federal deficit issue is resolved, however, there is a great reluctance to finance a new universal benefit for the aged from general tax revenues.

The traditional approach for financing increased benefits to all the elderly is to increase taxes on both the working population and on future generations. The attractiveness of this approach is that the elderly and their children have high voting participation rates; young working-age populations and future generations are not able to provide equivalent political support. The disadvantage of this approach is that increasing Social Security taxes raises the cost of labor to business at a time when it is trying to become more competitive with foreign producers. Further, shifting another cost (in addition to Social Security and Medicare taxes) to the working population and future generations increases their incentive to eventually organize to decrease those costs.

Redistributive programs are gradually changing; they are slowly becoming more equitable (i.e., benefits inversely related to income). One-half of the aged's Social Security benefits are subject to taxation and the Medicare portion of the Social Security tax is now on all earned income, making it more of a proportional tax. To solve the bankruptcy of the Medicare trust fund and reduce the federal deficit for Medicare Part B, younger generations will have to wait a longer period (to age 67) before they become eligible for decreased benefits. This will eventually decrease the intergenerational inequity that occurs. And it is likely that premiums for Medicare-related programs (Part B) will be income-related. This trend to a more equitable method of financing health and other redistributive programs is the result of self-interest. As the costs of providing benefits become too great to those bearing the cost, changes will occur in the method of financing those costs. The process of achieving increased equity, however, occurs very gradually. Large costs cannot be immediately imposed on a group nor can their benefits be quickly reduced, otherwise it would make it worthwhile for these groups to offer political opposition.

A second trend that appears to be emerging, albeit very slowly, is that greater economic efficiency is being introduced in the delivery of health services. This trend is not the result of a conscious decision on the part of legislators but is again the result of self-interest. As the cost of healthcare became too large, business and government pressed for innovative changes in methods of paying for and delivering health services.

Incentives were provided for increased efficiency. Delivery systems, such as HMOs, and other health professionals are competing with physicians and hospitals. The result is likely to be increased efficiency and innovation in the delivery of services.

The Self-Interest Paradigm does not imply that equity and efficiency will continually worsen. Instead, there is a self-correcting mechanism. As the costs to others of inequity and inefficiency increase, those bearing the burden have an increased incentive to organize and reduce those costs. While self-interest is the initial motivating force for redistributing wealth, it is also self-interest that prevents the resulting inequities and inefficiencies from becoming too great.

Study Questions for Chapter 11

1. How do political markets differ from economic markets?
2. Would competition or monopoly among demanders and suppliers of legislation be preferable in political markets?
3. Why are regressive costs or taxes usually used to finance legislative benefits, according to the economic theory?
4. Contrast the predictions of the two theories of legislation with regard to prospects for government subsidies for long-term care. Consider which groups are likely to be the major beneficiaries, the design or type of benefits provided, and the method used to finance the program.
5. Broad redistributive programs, such as Social Security and Medicare, have provided all aged with large net benefits. Using the concepts of "concentrated" and "diffuse" interests, explain why the aged have been able to receive such large net benefits and, second, why benefits to future aged will be much lower than those received by previous groups.

Notes

1. Congressional Budge Office. 1994. *The Tax Treatment of Employment-Based Health Insurance.* Washington, D.C., March, Table 10, 48.
2. Only in a situation of market failure would there be a net benefit to the aged from having the government provide them with a benefit for which they would pay the full costs. While lack of information, adverse selection, moral hazard, and economies of scale in administration of any long-term care insurance all serve to make this market less than perfect, it is unlikely that any legislated long-term-care benefit will be based on grounds of market failure.

INDEX

ABOUT THE AUTHOR

Paul J. Feldstein is Professor and Robert Gumbiner Chair in Healthcare Management at the Graduate School of Management, University of California at Irvine. In addition to writing numerous articles on health economics, he is the author of six books. His book, *Health Care Economics,* 4th edition, 1993, is one of the most widely used texts on health economics. His most recent book, *Health Policy Issues: An Economic Perspective on Health Reform,* was published by the Health Administration Press in September 1994.

Dr. Feldstein received his B.A. degree in economics from the City College of New York and his M.B.A. and Ph.D. from the University of Chicago. He was Director of the Division of Research at the American Hospital Association from 1961 to 1964, where he was responsible for all data collection activities of the association. During that period he initiated the Hospital Panel Survey. From 1964 to 1987, Dr. Feldstein was on the faculty at the University of Michigan as Professor in both the Department of Health Services Management and Policy, School of Public Health, and the Department of Economics.

During periods away from the university, Dr. Feldstein worked at the Office of Management and Budget and the Social Security Administration in Washington, D.C. and at the World Health Organization in Geneva, Switzerland.

Dr. Feldstein has served as a consultant to numerous federal and state government agencies as well as to nonprofit health organizations. He has also participated as an expert witness in healthcare antitrust cases. Since 1988 Dr. Feldstein has served as a member of the Board of Directors of Sutter Health, a large, not-for-profit, integrated delivery system serving northern California.